PAPER TIGRESS

Rachel Cartland graduated from Oxford University in 1972 and joined the Hong Kong Civil Service. During her time with the government she served in a variety of senior posts and gained wide exposure to policy formulation processes, management and the Hong Kong political scene.

As deputy secretary for recreation and culture, she oversaw the introduction of cable and satellite TV and the setting up of the Arts Development Council. As assistant director of social welfare she had responsibility for an annual budget of HK$25 billion and about 2,000 staff, and for delivering a service of high political sensitivity, impacting all sectors of grassroots Hong Kong.

Since her retirement in 2006, Rachel now undertakes public sector consulting. Her voluntary activities include membership of Vision 2047, the Government Hill Concern Group and the board of the Women's Foundation. She is a co-host on Radio Television Hong Kong's 'Backchat' programme.

PAPER TIGRESS

by

Rachel Cartland

BLACKSMITH BOOKS

PAPER TIGRESS

ISBN 978-988-19003-8-8 (paperback)
© 2014 Rachel Cartland
Some of the photographs on pages 81–96 are reproduced with the kind
permission of Formasia Books Ltd.

Published by Blacksmith Books
5th Floor, 24 Hollywood Road, Central, Hong Kong
www.blacksmithbooks.com

Typeset in Adobe Garamond by Alan Sargent
Printed in Hong Kong

First printing January 2014
Second printing February 2015

Contents

For Michael, in gratitude for the suggestion for the title of this book, for letting me steal some of his stories and for much else besides.
And for the people of Hong Kong without whom my life would have been much less interesting.

ACKNOWLEDGMENTS

I composed this book essentially on the basis of my own memory. As far as I could I cross-checked facts and also sent sections of the draft to people involved for their comments. I received a great deal of help in this process and would particularly like to thank Elizabeth Bosher, Alicia Denny, Robert Footman, Richard Hoare, Esther Morris, Gavin Ure and Lord Wilson of Tillyorn. Any errors that remain are my own and I would be glad to hear any suggestions for improvement.

CHAPTER ONE

Prelude to Hong Kong

'MUMMY, WHAT WAS IT LIKE when you were a little girl? Were there cars and telephones then?' I suppose that every parent of a five-year-old has been asked that question or one like it. It's easy enough to answer a simple factual question but more years of growing up would have to pass before one could try to give a child an idea of the social changes that have taken place in just the thirty or so years that separate you from him or her.

I was born in England in 1950 (a tiger year in the Chinese calendar's cycle of twelve years), left for Hong Kong in September 1972 and never returned permanently to the UK. I went in order to join the administrative grade of the Hong Kong government and this became my lifelong career but it was hardly the result of careful planning. Earlier in 1972 I was about to graduate from Oxford University with a degree in politics, philosophy and economics and scrabbling around for something to do that would earn money, be interesting and would make me feel that I was doing something worthwhile. I was lucky enough to find exactly that.

The fact that I was at Oxford University was also a great piece of luck but I happened to be an adolescent during a period which was probably the apogee of social mobility in the UK, or at least the kind of social mobility determined by success in academic examinations. My parents, John and Mary Howard, had both been quite financially comfortable but that was not the case by the time my sister, Alicia, and I were born. We moved around a lot, chasing my father's dream of restoring the family fortunes while also living in some exotic place. They came from rural Buckinghamshire, both from farming families although my paternal grandfather had made a tidy fortune through his brickmaking business, taking advantage of the clay of the region and the demand for new houses as London extended into suburbia, thanks to the new railway lines being built. After my grandfather's death, things deteriorated and there were quarrels and estrangements so we saw nothing of one side of the family and very little of the other. My father was adventurous, but it was an adventurousness that was set in the context of his times and was always subject to the limits of my mother's tolerance. My mother was passionately loyal but she craved, if possible, to slip no further down the social scale and that her children should ascend again.

The British government after the Second World War had decided to decant population from the crowded slums and bombed-out areas of London to purpose-built new towns which would represent the best in modern architecture and town planning. My father responded enthusiastically and it seemed that using our scanty capital to open a small shop in Crawley New Town selling toys, sweets, cigarettes and knick-knacks would surely be as good as selling shovels in San Francisco during the Gold Rush. This proved, by and large, not to be the case so my father next decided on the ambitious step of emigration to Africa, in point of fact to Rhodesia (now known as Zimbabwe but then a British white-ruled dominion). He was a skilled brickmaker and had managed his family's brickworks, so it seemed that there should be a good chance of employment. There would be a pause while we packed up and made all the necessary arrangements and what better idea could there be than to rent a bungalow near Brighton? Until early middle age my parents' world had been the inland one more or less bounded by the surrounding counties of Bedfordshire, Hertfordshire and Oxfordshire, but in the years between the wars the south coast had been seen as impossibly glamorous. My father's younger sister, Violet, was married to a wealthy garage owner and they had had a holiday home in Bognor Regis. For us to live in Brighton at least for a short while would be just as good, if not better.

One of my mother's strongest principles was that her children should not have to attend a 'council school' but her wish to have us privately educated ran up against the rock of the reality of our financial circumstances. In the village of Rottingdean near our temporary home there were publicly funded schools. They were run by the Church of England and that was considered select enough to meet her criteria and so my sister and I, aged respectively six and eight, spent a term there. There would be no need for us to go back after the holiday as we would be leaving England so soon. Except that we didn't. The weeks slipped by until we had spent almost three months at home. I was reading more books than ever from the children's section of the public library and sometimes the stories featured School Attendance Officers, characters who came to look for young truants and of whom I lived in perpetual dread. No such frightening person actually did come up our garden path although it soon became clear that we were not going to go to Rhodesia after all. Both my parents had turned against the idea after reading the literature for prospective immigrants put out by Rhodesia House in London. They were politically conservative but essentially egalitarian and they felt deeply uneasy about the advice they were given on how to treat black employees in our prospective new home. They didn't like the suggestions on how much food per head to dole out and the message they perceived in it of racial superiority.

Australia was considered but ruled out by my mother's fear of bushfires so my father turned to the study of one of his favourite publications, *Dalton's Weekly*, crammed with small ads for small businesses. And thus it was that, not long afterwards, we found ourselves in a bed and breakfast in London as he negotiated the purchase of a grocer's shop down the Caledonian Road behind King's Cross Railway Station. We children did not go back to school but spent our time ticking off the sights of London in an 'I Spy' book, visiting museums and using the great resource of the Lewis Carroll Children's Library. Our mother was looking for a suitable school but was rather concerned that the only place nearby that passed her test of not being an 'ordinary' school was a Catholic convent, as she had grown up in a community decidedly in favour of the plainer forms of Anglicanism and a new vicar who placed candles on the altar was an object of concern, as if he might be leading the whole village towards Rome. One of her first employers, a photographer, had been a Catholic 'and a convert too' she said, as if that made it much worse. 'The thing about Catholics is that they can do whatever they like during the week, go to confession, get forgiven for it and start all over again,' she said, rather suggesting that from Monday to Saturday this gentleman had run some equivalent of Sweeney Todd's where the customers were turned into pies rather than into nicely hand-coloured photographs showing them off in their most flattering pose. Her misgivings about the London convent school were reinforced when she paid an exploratory visit and found that she had to enter through a door, set in a high wall with a grille in it, and that this door was opened by a nun in a head-to-toe black habit.

Anyway, the negotiations over the purchase of the shop didn't go well and somehow it came to seem that it was not just the nuns and the convent but this entire London district that was not quite right for us. There was recourse to *Dalton's Weekly* again and a synthesis of previous strategies: now we would look for a shop in a seaside town.

There just happened to be a shop in Portsmouth on offer in that particular paper. It was a gentlemen's tailor's but the fittings could be converted to be used instead for toys, confectionery, cigarettes and kits to make model planes and ships. I am not sure why this shop was to emphasise toys and plastic kits more than the previous one in Crawley but somewhere in there seemed to be the thought that it would be nice for us children to live over a toyshop. The shop was on a main road though not the most important one in Portsmouth and there were parallel residential roads running off it. To the left of our shop the roads comprised terraced houses which did not enjoy the status symbol of a bay window; these began in the streets to the right, where some of the houses were even semi-detached. In one of those residential roads off to the right and about ten minutes' walk away from our home there was a private school whose fees were within our parents' means so both my sister and I were enrolled there.

The proprietors of Victoria College were two elderly spinster sisters and the school was accommodated in a pair of private houses that had been run together so that a slightly enlarged garden provided the school playground. School inspectors visited from time to time and the school continued in business so presumably it must have been found fit for purpose. Indeed, there was no cruelty or harsh punishment régime to be detected: the classes were small and the pervading atmosphere was one of gentleness. The curriculum was, however, decidedly odd since it seemed designed to prepare us for a life as shopgirls in the kind of department store that had existed some forty years previously. Thus, we spent many lessons on a subject called 'Tots', which was simply the adding up of long columns of figures. We also had copybooks in which to practise Copperplate handwriting and would carefully pencil out in curlicues such axioms as 'Punctuality is the politeness of princes'. It is hard to imagine that these copybooks were still being produced in 1960 so perhaps the school had amassed a good supply of them in years when they were more current. Although I felt, and some-times said, that Binsteed Road Junior School, which was in one of the neighbouring streets with no bay windows but had an asphalt playground and posters and plants in the classrooms, seemed more like my idea of what a school should be, the atmosphere in our school was soothingly unruffled and we obediently filled our days with the tasks we were given, though it is hard to say that there was a commensurate long-term effect on my penmanship or timekeep-ing. Another of the Copperplate royalty-connected aphorisms, 'A cat can look at a king', was perhaps closer to the life philosophy that I ended up adopting but since that was also one of my father's favourite sayings, that might have happened anyway. The mental arithmetic was useful but we could probably have better learnt some other things as well in the time devoted to it.

As during our time in London, the public library was the greatest resource, the only slight drawback being the rule that books could not be changed within the same day that they were borrowed. It was, all the same, not too difficult to read one's way round the entire children's section, both fiction and non-fiction and to go around with a head full of dreams and information about the world beyond the half-dozen streets or so around our home.

The England in which we were growing up practised a fiercely selective school system at the junction between primary and secondary school. Unless your parents were in the small minority who paid school fees so that you stayed in a private school, the 'eleven-plus' examinations would determine whether you went to a grammar school where the education was academic and there was a chance of progressing to university or to a secondary modern school where the curriculum was intended to be vocational and, realistically, the chances of university were minimal. There was also a kind of hybrid between state and private schools called a 'direct grant' school. We happened to be living close enough to one of these, Portsmouth High School for Girls, to make a place there a practical possibility – if only I could pass the exams.

Portsmouth High School was, in fact, located in Southsea, the resort town that blurred into Portsmouth and was administered as one entity with it, though all we who lived in the area could say with certainty whether an address belonged to Portsmouth or Southsea. It was Southsea that had originally lured my parents into giving up their dream of London and moving down to the south coast. It had its bracing gusts of sea air and the walk along the sea front from Clarence Pier (Billy Manning's Funfair) to South Parade Pier (Floral Clock, Illuminated Rock Gardens and Canoe Lake with pedal boats for hire). Portsmouth was the gritty naval town full of associations with Admiral Lord Nelson and his victories in the Napoleonic Wars. The Naval Dockyard was still an important employer and an apprenticeship there a highly regarded opportunity even though the great flood of workers who bicycled out of the gates after the hooter sounded to mark the end of the day gave a misleading impression since cuts and rearrangements in Britain's defences were undermining Portsmouth's traditional economy. Likewise, the trippers and holidaymakers were about to desert Southsea for the sunnier shores of the Mediterranean.

Anyway, Portsmouth High School was certainly academically the best girls' school for miles around. Its junior school was in a cosy Victorian building called Dovercourt and all the girls there had parents who paid the fees each term. Every one of those girls would also normally pass into the senior school where they would, though, make up only half of an intake of just over sixty, with the remainder coming from those who had passed the high school's entrance exam, and who, thanks to a complex combination of grants to the school and means testing of families, would normally pay no fees at all.

By the early 1970s when my school and university education had been completed, the eleven-plus and the direct-grant schools were both on the way out. It was considered that they were too divisive, with the eleven-plus failures condemned at the age of ten or eleven to an unjust sense of stigma and diminished life chances. The direct grant schools were forced to choose whether to become totally fee paying (as Portsmouth High School did) or to be absorbed into the state system, the rationale being that taxpayers should avoid subsidising fee-paying parents. I was thus very fortunate to have the chance of benefiting from the last few years of the life of the direct-grant schools. It saddens me that young British girls in my circumstances do not now have a similar opportunity. Both data and anecdote suggest that social mobility has lessened. I well recall how indeed those children who had not passed the eleven-plus exam did seem to feel that in some senses their lives had ended when hardly begun but, on the other hand, it seems only reasonable to give children with an aptitude for academic study the education that best suits them so that they can compete on equal terms for university places. The best strategy would surely have been to devote adequate and generous resources to technical and craft schools for those more suited to that path. Experience seems to have shown that university entrance chances cannot be evened out if there have been no interventions at the secondary school stage.

When I took the eleven-plus and the high school entrance examination I had no complaints about the fairness of the tests, which comprised straightforward papers in English and maths and intelligence tests, with composition writing in addition for the high school. It did not seem to me that you needed to have had a specially privileged education or background to be able to do well in them. As it turned out, I was offered places at the local grammar school and at Portsmouth High School and my parents eagerly accepted the one at the high school. After all the processes had been completed, not only was I judged eligible to pay no school fees at all but also to receive a free season ticket for the bus ride to school and free lunches while I was there. Secondhand uniform and school equipment was available as well but my parents were having none of that and my mother and I went to one of the grandest department stores in Southsea, the school's 'official supplier', and bought mountains of stuff: a lacrosse stick, grey sports shorts, off-white sports sweater, a maroon webbing belt, a soft grey felt hat and a hat badge engraved with the head of Minerva encircled by the inscription 'Knowledge is Now No More a Fountain Sealed' as well as a lot of more ordinary things. To this day, I have no idea how she managed to pay for it all.

The school was all that might have been expected of it. There were laboratories for different kinds of science: physics, chemistry and biology. There were libraries divided up by age group. The teachers taught subjects that they had studied at university, and these included Spanish, Greek and Latin. The school resonated with purposefulness and an almost palpable conviction that there was still something to be done in the battle to ensure that girls and their education were taken seriously. Even if it was almost a hundred years since some members of the medical profession were sure that higher education would render girls infertile by overtaxing their brains there was still a rather prevalent feeling that females were irretrievably more stupid than men. Teacher, librarian and nurse were, by and large, the only jobs that well educated women were expected to take. I remember as a teenager watching a television programme in which an older male dentist, ranged against a younger female one in a serious studio discussion, asserted that she was biologically incapable of entering his profession.

By the time I was sixteen or so, my father was almost sixty, in poor health and with next to nothing in the way of financial resources. None of this, though, was to deter him from trying out a strikingly new idea, dreamed up with his friend who owned The Wishing Well, the shop next to ours which sold greetings cards and 'fancy goods' (gifts and saucy postcards for the holidaymakers in Southsea who had somehow strayed into our part of town, as well as such miscellanea as the little cardboard boxes to send rectangles of wedding cake to friends and family who hadn't been able to make the ceremony). First in partnership and then just by my father on his own they opened and ran a betting shop in vacant premises almost opposite their own two shops. In fact, the move was not as improbable as it might have first seemed. In the rakish days before my sister and I were born, my parents had loved horseracing and my father had been a keen though not excessive gambler. He would still sometimes take us children to the Portsmouth Dog Racing Track where under the floodlights the greyhounds raced after the electric hare that they could never catch and provided an adrenaline thrill even though it was widely held that there was little point in betting on the outcome as 'dog racing is always fixed'. Opening a betting shop offered the attraction of novelty, a new way to make a fortune. In 1961, the law had been changed so that people could legally bet on horseracing away from the racecourses and there was a whole set of rules introduced to govern the betting shops where this kind of gambling could take place. However, there was not yet one of these establishments in our part of town and this seemed to offer an opportunity too good to be missed.

There was clearly much ambivalence in the legalising of betting shops. The message of the regulation of their operations was 'Yes but no but. . . .' Betting shops could exist but their existence must be played down as much as possible with opaque paint covering the windows so high that no one could look in and see what was going on and no one under the age of eighteen could enter during opening hours. Once I had passed that birthday I used to help out when I wasn't at my normal Saturday job selling fruit and pick'n'mix sweets at Woolworths. The operation of a betting shop is a satisfy-ingly self-contained way to make money. We would go in not long before racing hours started, taking with us *The Sporting Life,* the racing newspaper, and pin up the sheets with details of the day's fixtures on the cork boards in the front part of the shop, which was the punters' portion. Then we would pass through to the other side of the counter that ran across the shop and marked out our domain where we worked out the winnings and losses – our own and our customers'. In the mid-sixties, smoking was broadly considered to be an unhealthy habit for the smoker but there was no concern about secondhand smoke and no laws against smoking anywhere, so there was a mighty fug once racing hours had begun and people had settled themselves in for the afternoon. The 'blower' that was a vital part of the shop's fittings was not for ventilation but was the loudspeaker that relayed the racecourse commentary for which we paid a subscription. All the time, Dad would be counting up the bets as they came in on each race, considering whether there was so much money out against him and the risk was so great that he needed to 'lay it off' by phoning through his own bet to William Hill, the big bookmaker's in London, so as to limit his losses if the favoured horse won. These were tricky calculations especially if they involved the final stages of more complicated bets like accumulators, roll-ups or Heinz 57s but Dad had a real facility for this. A lot of the bets were pretty simple, just wins, places and each ways and it was easy for me to learn at least how to pay out accurately. No calculators, of course! By the end of the day we would know whether or not we had come out on the winning side and to what amount.

Among our most faithful customers were the staff of the 'Great Mountain' Chinese restaurant a few doors down the road, where we sometimes used to go for dinner on a Saturday night. Until I went to Hong Kong, these were the only Chinese people with whom I'd ever had any contact and communication was limited by their poor English and our non-existent Chinese. From this acquaintance though I did draw two conclusions: first, that Chinese people love to gamble, which turned out to be right and, second, that banana fritters were an integral part of their native cuisine which, a little disappointingly, proved to be incorrect.

The men of the Great Mountain were pleasant enough but the same could not be said for everyone who came through our doors. We discovered that one of the problems of the bookmaking profession is that you have to mix with some people who are not really very nice. The area in which our betting shop was located was not a crime-ridden one and walking the streets late at night was not a risky activity, yet a business like ours couldn't help but be a honeypot to criminals and ex-convicts. They were not on drugs but they drank a bit and became garrulous and difficult and there was always a low level of threats and intimidation to contend with as well as the odd burglary now and again. All the same, it was probably the most lucrative thing that we ever engaged in at any time during my childhood.

Dad had previously been outraged by the bank manager, who had tried to call in his overdraft with the insulting words, 'Well, you're only a small shopkeeper, you know.' In fact, it led to his taking his business from Lloyds Bank to the National Westminster. Then came the news that Ladbrokes, the big betting-shop chain, wanted to open up close to us, which would surely be a disaster. This time, however, the great cat's cradle of government rules came to our aid as they specified that betting shops had to be some distance apart from each other, presumably in the belief that this would make it more difficult for someone to lose all his savings on a sure thing at Kempton Park or Fairyhouse racecourses. Dad studied the legislation, lodged an objection and went to the magistrates' court where he gave a fine speech on the rights of the entrepreneur and the iniquities of Ladbrokes' proposal. The bench succumbed to his oratory and ruled in his favour which meant that later on Ladbrokes had to buy him out so that they could open their shop. Even this stroke of luck did not make us rich; it just ensured that for a while we did not worry quite as much about the costs of a modest day-to-day living.

None of this was too much of a distraction from my studies for my Advanced Level exams in English, history, French and Latin. Not every year but quite often, Portsmouth High School succeeded in getting a few pupils into Oxford or Cambridge University and my year turned out to be one of those. The school suggested that I could be one of the girls to stay on for an extra term after A-levels for intensive preparation for the Oxbridge exams which took place just before Christmas. Although I could leave school immediately after that, the date of going to university would be not until the following autumn so that the entire educational process would in effect be lengthened by a year. This could not have been an altogether welcome prospect for my parents as it would mean a further delay until I was fully self-supporting but they agreed to the plan. A few years earlier I had been part of the school team that competed quite successfully in a television quiz show called *Top of the Form* and this had led to an invitation to tea with the lord mayor of Portsmouth in his rooms at the Guildhall where he entertained us adorned in his mayoral chain, even though worn over his day-to-day suit. This had all been glorious enough but a place at Oxford would certainly be a much more substantial achievement.

Miss Marion Thorn was the headmistress at the high school and we were all, quite rightly, in awe of her. She was short and stocky and wore tweed skirt suits that were somehow quite mannish, as were her heavily framed glasses behind which were eyes of a startling, piercing blue above a heavy jaw and framed by very white hair. When she spoke her voice sounded like the queen's but deeper and more authoritative. She remembered every girl who had ever been at the school during her long tenure, which had included supervising its evacuation during the Second World War. She was kind and had a sense of humour but her presence was too over-whelming for us easily to recognise that. She was decisive and disposed of matters quickly. She told me that girls from the high school who went to Oxford chose Lady Margaret Hall as their college and added that although I might take the entrance examina-tion in English, considered one of my best school subjects, I might find that I would prefer to study politics, philosophy and eco-nomics. And so it came to pass.

At that time, it was about five times more difficult for a girl than a boy to go to Oxford or Cambridge as the colleges that made up the universities were sex segregated and there were about that many more places in the men's colleges. The entrance examinations were a more intense version of A-levels in one's chosen subject plus a general paper which aimed to search out a capacity for original thought followed by a series of interviews at the college one had applied for. There were always stories at the men's colleges of applicants who had breezed up without going through any of the proper procedures but had managed to convince the dons that they would be an adornment to the college, or of students whose only claim was prowess at rowing or rugby or being the heir to a dukedom or a throne. Places at the women's colleges were too precious to be handed out for such frivolous reasons. It would have been hard to imagine having a chance to get in without the expert coaching that the high school provided, apart from the general paper where I enjoyed answering questions on speculating what it would be like to be an anthropologist stumbling on a tribe with no future tense in their language, inventing a short story that included all of a given number of disconnected words and trying to tease out the issue of how far it is possible to form truly original judgments on the merits of works of art. Later on, our philosophy tutor Mrs Sybil Wolfram (who would scarily begin the dissection of your attempt at an essay with 'Well, I quite liked the first sentence') in a more mellow mood asked us whether we realised that the most crucial part of our entry process had been our brief and seemingly rather bland conversations with the principal, Dame Lucy Sutherland. 'Yes, it all depended on whether she liked the cut of your jib,' before adding hastily, 'the cut of your intellectual jib, of course,' just in case we might nourish any illusion that Dame Lucy, who was rather reminiscent of Miss Thorn though smaller and slighter, could ever permit any less exalted standards of judgment.

There was fairness too in the financial arrangements where means testing once again came into play. As it happened, I was awarded a scholarship for my performance in the entrance examinations but this was for a token amount of fifty pounds. What really mattered was being assessed on the basis of my parents' income as eligible to pay no tuition fees and to receive the maximum level of maintenance grant, which was quite enough to live in a perfectly reasonable fashion and without embarrassment among one's peers, though obviously not matching the wealthier ones. There was not a penny ever to be paid back and, indeed, no obligations of any kind. It was all part and parcel of what was intended to be an equitable education policy and it did not last. In the years ahead, the number of places in British universities was greatly expanded with an accompanying increase in costs until it was noticed that graduates could normally expect to earn more over a lifetime than non-graduates and could therefore be expected to take the costs of their university education in the form of a loan or advance, to be repaid once they were earning.

It was as well the financial arrangements were so reasonable as the family coffers were not bulging. The betting shop and toyshop had both been sold and we were now running an 'open all hours' grocer's down near the greyhound stadium. The burden was falling more and more on my mother as my father's health worsened and he was beginning to spend more time at home. He fixed on the idea that I should have something appropriate in which to take my possessions to Oxford. I could have seen to this myself as I had savings from various temporary and part-time jobs that I had had but he was determined to do it. He came across a competition in which the prize was a million Green Shield stamps, popular trading tokens that could be exchanged for household goods. It was a word game requiring contestants to make as many words as possible out of a collection of letters. To the best of my knowledge, Dad never read a book but he loved crosswords and anagrams and I brought home a big dictionary from Portsmouth Central Library where I was working until I went to university. He devoted himself to this task day after day and sent in sheets of paper covered in columns of words which yielded enough stamps to get not just a suitcase but also a tea tray to take with me. Cups and glasses I bought for myself as he was adamant that I was not to develop a habit of drinking sherry from mugs, and he also counselled that in pubs I must not ask for a port and lemon, well known as being a prostitute's drink.

Oxford is the oldest university in the English-speaking world, formally established in 1249 and informally some three hundred years before that. Lady Margaret Hall, invariably known as LMH, was the first college of the university for women and its first students were admitted in 1879. The intervening six hundred years meant that the most central sites to build a college had already been bagged and the women's colleges were located more or less on the fringes of the town. LMH was to the north in archetypal Victorian suburbia but with the compensation of twelve acres of gardens running down to the River Cherwell. It began with only nine students which was just as well as the first principal, Dame Elizabeth Wordsworth, contrived to lose all the fees collected somewhere in a London railway station and had to ask them to stump up all over again, which they readily did, presumably a tribute to her forceful personality. By the time I arrived there in 1969 the student numbers were around four hundred and the college was housed in a pleasing collection of diverse but harmonious buildings, for some of which my grandfather's company, Samuel Howard and Sons, had supplied the bricks, made of red Buckinghamshire clay in his Prestwood Brickworks; this dated from the 1930s when my father was still working there.

The university was like a big pudding that had been stewing for a millennium. Its flavour was so intense and so variegated that it was impossible to sample it all, especially since a three-year undergraduate course comprised just nine terms of eight weeks each. For me, the most stunning thing was the physical beauty of the place, strengthened and deepened by a wealth of literary and historical associations. Its spirit seemed to have survived intact since the time of Chaucer's 'Clerk of Oxenford' of whom it was said 'gladly would he learn and gladly teach'. The dominant ethos was still a search for truth, whatever the cost. In those days, tourists and visitors were not so much in evidence so the university felt as if it really belonged to us and there were many discoveries to make. There were cuts and alleys and the traditional design of the colleges was the quadrangle, surely one of the friendliest forms of building ever devised. The old colleges had hidden away behind a flat façade a series of courtyards, made lovely by grass and trees and flowers, that rang with the casual camaraderie of the students whose rooms encircled them. The open windows would let everyone share whatever record was playing. Music like Simon and Garfunkel's *Bridge Over Troubled Water* album was a common soundtrack to our lives. There were memorable theatrical experiences too of more traditional music. The first time that I saw *Marriage of Figaro,* Mozart's thrilling drama of reconciliation and wisdom painfully won, was in a student production staged in an intimate hall that dated from the seventeenth century and I enjoyed the sunny optimism of *Salad Days* in Brasenose College's walled garden and an original play about the Pre-Raphaelites in Keble College Chapel under the gaze of *The Light of the World,* Holman Hunt's great painting of the period.

It was a wonderful time to be young, and in England. As well as the pop, rock and folk that seemed to belong to us only, having sprung fresh-minted from the Beatles or Bob Dylan who were just a bit older than us, there were beautiful new clothes for us to wear.

When we came to Oxford we were told that it was not considered acceptable for girls to wear trousers when meeting our tutors, but we could wear them at other times of course. We could be practical and alluring in miniskirts and sweaters teamed with knee-high boots or we could be true to Oxford traditions and adopt a more romantic style: long dresses in flower-filled prints, shirts with ballooning sleeves like troubadours', scarves or kaftans from India and Afghanistan, fringed and embroidered with mirrors inset in geometric patterns. I loved them all but particularly the fashions that made me feel as if every day was dressing up to take part in some pageant of a life that was not everyday, but poised between the Oxford of ghosts and shadows and a future that might be utterly, extraordinarily different, thanks to the new ideas that were emerging everywhere.

The Americans at Oxford joined in all those things too but they were always a little more serious and melancholy, as the shadow of Vietnam and the question of whether they or their boyfriends would or should be compelled to fight there hung over them. Bill Clinton, who would in just over twenty years' time become the forty-second president of the United States, was a contemporary, in Oxford on a Rhodes Scholarship, one of those awarded to exceptionally talented men from the US and the British Commonwealth (none given to women until 1977). I knew several Rhodes Scholars but I would just be inventing things if I pretended that I ever consciously met Clinton although from his own accounts of his time at Oxford he seems in the reactions that he had and the way he lived to have been much like the people that I did know. It was surely no coincidence that the only British student of my acquaintance who had the same troubled air was at Oxford on an army scholarship and dreaded going to Northern Ireland, the violence of which he understood better that we did. For the rest of us, the issues that would divide and pain Britain, the miners' strike, the 'troubles' in Northern Ireland, were a few years in the future. Spurred on by the ferment spilling over from the French students and the *événements* of 1968, every British university had its greater or smaller dose of protests, sit-ins and demonstrations, but the political activism, even though sincerely meant, had something of the theatrical about it: a sort of drama that would not spill over into real tragedy. Angela Davis and Che Guevara made good subjects for posters to decorate our rooms as a change from the works of Mucha and Toulouse-Lautrec. We were liberal and humane enough but in an untested way. We were against colour prejudice and shocked by apartheid in South Africa and the civil rights abuses in the southern states of the US but the fact was that our own acquaintance was really quite limited. My American friend Susan Lightbody (the most exotic person I had ever met) squealed when she saw the hockey team photo my sister had sent me. 'Rachel,' she said, 'they all have such WASP names!' And so it was: our schools and neighbourhoods and the circles in which we spent our leisure time were racially homogeneous.

My own political views were the vaguely left of centre stuff that probably represented the average student view at the time. An exception to this was a girl called Ann Widdecombe, who was one of the group of six PPE students at LMH. She was a little older than the rest of us, having already done a degree in classics. Her defining ambition, however, was to be a Conservative member of parliament which was not a very usual thing for a young woman in the late 1960s to want to do. She had concluded that the most likely way for a career in Conservative politics to begin was with a degree in PPE and being active in the Union, the historic university debating society. She had thus begun her careful pursuit of her dream, which culminated in her becoming a cabinet minister, a novelist and a television celebrity.

Some of the other girls asked me if I would stand for election as president of the college's Junior Common Room, which meant organising student activities and negotiating on their behalf with the authorities. I had to ask my tutor's permission for this. 'You shouldn't do things just because people ask you to,' said Mrs Wolfram. 'I agreed to translate a book by Claude Lévi Strauss just because someone asked me to and I'm finding it a frightful chore.' Her advice was doubtless sound but I did not listen to it, stood and was duly elected, in a rather easy process in which much in the way of canvassing votes did not seem to be expected.

As JCR president, I was approached by the television company, Granada, who wanted the college to put up a team for the 1972 *University Challenge* television quiz. It was all set up rather casually; the producer, Douglas Terry, a charming man, delivered some question papers to assist us in the selection process. Not that many people were interested in trying them but we gave them out under exam conditions. I saw no reason why I shouldn't do it myself as it could be arranged so I could not get a favoured look at the answers. We were equally nonchalant in our approach to team formation. We just took the four who had scored best in this preliminary test and I was one of these and became captain. Apart from me, studying philosophy and politics, we had one historian, one lawyer and one reading English, so we were bound to be a bit handicapped when it came to science questions. In fact, we did quite well and got knocked out around the semi-final stage. It was an enjoyable experience, involving paid-for trips to Manchester and a filming process that was quite straightforward. We ended up with each team member being given a copy of the *Shorter Oxford English Dictionary*, which was a massive volume, and a fairly small sum of money for the college, which was used to buy a set of engravings by Victor Pasmore, a then-fashionable artist.

The quizmaster was Bamber Gascoigne, a really pleasant person with no TV star airs and graces. His aim was to set contestants at ease and to run his show as efficiently as possible. He was unflappable even when we came up against a team from the London School of Economics – then a hotbed of student radicalism – who decided to make some sort of statement against bourgeois capitalism by basically goofing around throughout the filming. We got lots of fan mail afterwards on the lines of 'How nice to see you sensibly dressed, well-spoken girls showing up those nasty oafs from the LSE.' In fact, if the letter writers had known us beyond the image presented in a half-hour programme they would have found out that we were not such heroines of the Counter Revolution as they supposed. At that particular time, though, we were more interested in winning the match which, as it happened, we did. It was also true that my own favoured political cause and area of activism was comparatively sedate.

As president of the LMH Junior Common Room and hence representing its undergraduates I was involved in negotiating with the authorities to relax rules like the one that said that no man could be in the college overnight and in the university as a whole arguing in favour of colleges becoming co-educational. The process was quite civilised with probably a tacit recognition on the 'grown-ups" side that our victory was inevitable. During this period, Dame Lucy Sutherland retired as principal of LMH and when I spoke at her farewell dinner, I was suddenly gripped by doubts and wondered whether her predecessors would have approved of what we were doing. They had had to be such courageous pioneers to get even a foothold for women in the university, and now we were working to transform their legacy into 'just another college'? Too bad, one has to be pragmatic and make compromises and this was the only feasible way to secure an equitable number of Oxford places for women. Soon after I had graduated, the wheels began turning fast and there are now no single-sex colleges and no advantage in being a man when it comes to Oxford University entry.

Indeed, the grown-up world was beginning to loom larger as graduation neared. The Oxford system for my degree course meant that we were undisturbed by examinations for more than two years between the second term after our arrival and the final term so for many of us that meant a certain amount of blowing the dust off the books and lecture notes towards the end together with decisions on 'what next'. Some wanted to prolong the fairytale existence and thought that post-graduate study at something or other, travelling to Nepal or India by the cheapest means possible or a suitably unconventional occupation like running a puppet theatre might be a good way to do it. I liked the idea of travelling myself but I knew that it was imperative that I was fully self-supporting. Conversely, I was also attracted by the idea of some career that was not stereotypically female. I began by applying for graduate traineeships in old, established industrial companies, of which there were still quite a number in the UK. The personnel manager of one such told me pleasantly, 'Well, we've never employed a woman before and we don't think we're going to start doing so now but we thought we'd have you along to have a look at you.' This led to no outburst of rage on my part; I found it irritating but hardly unexpected and since there was no anti-discrimination legislation in force, there was absolutely nothing to be done about it.

I became a frequent visitor to the University Appointments Board and always saw the same endlessly optimistic staff member: in appearance, a brown-eyed cherub although perhaps Raphael or Leonardo might have painted out his all too human bald patch. One day when I reported back disconsolately from yet another unsuccessful job hunting expedition, Mr Cherub turned to the very bottom of the very bottom drawer of his filing cabinet. 'Now,' he said hopefully, 'how about this?' In those days before laser printers and word processors, our expectations for printed documents were lower but this really was remarkably scruffy: a single sheet of mimeographed poor-quality paper with the kind of uneven typing that helped detectives, in fiction at any rate, to find clues and track down murderers. It was recruiting for the administrative grade of the Hong Kong government. Hong Kong, on the southern coast of China, was Britain's last remaining sizeable colony and the job on offer seemed to boil down to 'running Hong Kong'. There was an upfront explanation that similarly qualified women would be paid less than their male counterparts as equal pay for women was still being introduced in phases. All the same, when Mr Cherub and I did the exchange rate calculation even the pay for women seemed to be well over a thousand pounds a year – pretty generous compared with what was on offer for graduates in contemporary Britain. Mr Cherub had turned into Mr Magician: out of his filing cabinet he had produced a substantial job possibility which also satisfied the wanderlust!

It was a rather general wish to travel rather than any special interest in China that led me to apply for the position. I was lamentably ignorant of that great country but I was not alone in this. In politics we studied Britain's constitutional history and its sociology, the same for the USA, a little dash of Europe and communism in the context of the USSR; other areas tended to be covered only if they fitted in with some Western-centric theme like 'imperialism'. Chairman Mao's China had been more or less cut off from the Western world since the Communist Revolution of 1949 and from the mid-1960s this isolation had been deepened by the Cultural Revolution. No one wanted to recreate the notorious folly of Sidney and Beatrice Webb in the 1930s who had let themselves be duped into uncritical praise of Stalinist Russia but we had allowed to creep into the vacuum of our ignorance a hopeful belief that Mao had created a fairer society and tackled problems of mass poverty. Later on, as we learnt more about what had actually taken place in China since the Second World War, a more complex, and generally less creditable, truth emerged. In 1971, the Chinese suddenly invited the Americans to send a table tennis team to China and in the following year President Nixon's historic visit took place. This lifting of the curtain seemed to make things more strange rather than less so. It seemed so odd to try and conduct international relations through the vehicle of a fairly minor sporting event and the pictures from the Nixon visit with the drably dressed Chinese leaders and the performances of revolutionary operas by young men and women who apparently never had a non-conformist thought in their lives showed a place that looked as alien as another planet.

It was possible to learn much more about Hong Kong but I am afraid that I did not make any great effort to do so before I entered the recruitment process to become part of its government. I was aware, more or less as a piece of general knowledge, that a significant part of the colony was held by Britain on a lease from China and that was due to be handed back in 1997, but that was twenty-five years away, longer than I had already been alive and therefore, emotionally, really a very long way off indeed. At that time, too, 'Hong Kong-made' was a by-word for the cheap and shoddy: metal and plastic toys and household goods that fell apart almost as soon as you had bought them. I knew nothing in detail either of how Hong Kong was run. I knew that it was a British colony and I had a general belief that colonialism was 'wrong' and a 'bad thing' yet on the other hand I had a rather optimistic view of history as being on some sort of positive and progressive trajectory as well as an assumption that British people could generally be expected to try and behave in a fair and decent manner; and thus was ready to consider a career as a latter-day imperialist in an open-minded kind of way. On the basis of such haphazard preparation, I found myself soon afterwards in King Charles Street, Whitehall for an interview. At that time, the upper echelons of the Hong Kong civil service were mainly, though not entirely, made up of British men who had either made an entire career in the government or had moved there from some other colony that had gained independence. Although many things that the Hong Kong government did were passed to the Foreign Office for approval, this was often automatic and Hong Kong actually enjoyed a large degree of autonomy in most of its internal administration, including deciding who to take on. The first three young civil servants, known as cadets, had gone out to Hong Kong in September 1862, as part of a systematic effort to improve the administration of a British colony where, among other misfortunes, the registrar general, one of its most senior figures, had had to be dismissed because of his 'long and intimate connexion with the pirate, Machow Wong'.

The room in which I was interviewed probably dated from around that period; it was large but low-ceilinged, panelled in wood but also decorated with flamboyant paintings from the high imperial era and on the other side of the table at the far end was a small group of conventionally dressed men of the British middle and professional classes. At least they did not begin by telling me that there was no point in my being there as I would never be taken on. Their manner was, if anything, rather hesitant, certainly not overbearing and one seemed much like another so it made little difference which one was actually speaking at any one time. 'H'mm, e'rrm, Miss Howard, Hong Kong is awfully crowded, you know. How do you think that you would e'rrm cope with that?' 'Well,' I replied, 'I've lived in south east England all my life and that's rather crowded, by British standards, at any rate and I certainly don't mind trying somewhere more crowded.'

And this proved to be the pattern of the interview. These amiable gentlemen would describe some facet of life in Hong Kong, and ask if I thought I could 'cope' with it, a question to which obviously I would invariably answer 'yes', although at the same time having to admit that I could call upon no directly relevant experience to justify my confidence. In this way, we went through the weather ('very hot and humid, Miss Howard, but improving by mid-September which is when we would expect the young cadets to arrive') and areas of cultural differences, including a diversion into Singapore and a broad agreement that if they wanted to run their government in a way different from what we would do, well, perhaps they were entitled to and we should respect their different approach to things. I boxed slightly clever when asked what I thought about a career in a place on which the lease was due to expire in 1997. 'Well,' I said grandly, 'I would only be forty-seven then so that would be a good time to start something new.' (This was not at all an accurate reflection of how I felt. I could not really imagine what it would be like to be thirty, let alone forty-seven). Despite the apparent goodwill on both sides of this interview, the model the board had decided to adopt made it rather difficult to spin things out and we were soon nearing the end: 'If we were, er um, to take you on, Miss Howard, you would, erm, be the only female expatriate member of the administrative grade.' 'That,' I said firmly, 'would be just fine as far as I'm concerned.'

I was soon back in King Charles Street, wondering whether I had not just emerged from some sort of time-travelling rabbit hole but one which also blurred fiction and real life, for surely what I had just experienced belonged in the pages of a novel that Evelyn Waugh had somehow omitted to write. So I continued to think for many years and so I described it when asked to contribute my experience of the recruitment process for Steve Tsang's book *Governing Hong Kong*, which was published in 2007. However, when I read it in that context, I began to understand that my interview was not quite as unfocused as it had seemed. Those who were setting the recruitment policies were quoted as explaining that they were looking for 'a chap who could move easily amongst his peers in that sort of way, a chap who had already shown some interest outside the academic world, that he had some other activities going, some other interests going; preferably someone who'd had something involving work with the community at large, so he knew what it was to look after a community.' Presumably the same qualities were also sought in chap-esses, as we females found ourselves described. It is certainly true that my life to that date had blessed me with quite a degree of tolerance towards 'all sorts and conditions of men' and a willingness not to be too surprised by anything. Perhaps this came across somehow or other as I was shortly informed that as long as I managed to achieve a Second Class degree (fortunately, at that time, Oxford did not yet divide Seconds into Upper and Lower Classes) I might, if I wished, join the administrative grade of the Hong Kong government.

And did I say 'Yes'? Of course I did. After all, if you don't embark on an adventure when you're a twenty-two-year-old with no commitments, when will you?

CHAPTER TWO

Early Days in Hong Kong

WHEN I LEFT FOR HONG KONG on 18 September 1972, it was the third time I had been outside England. I had never been to Scotland, Ireland or Wales but I had been once to visit my school pen-friend in France and in my last long vacation I had been to Spain with two university friends. The trip to Spain had involved going on an aeroplane and I carefully observed the details of checking in, luggage, etc., so that I would be well prepared for the forthcoming journey to Hong Kong. It was a flight of about twenty hours with several stops along the way since in those days it was not possible to get all the way without refuelling. The airline was the British Overseas Airways Corporation, later integrated into British Airways, and with Virgin Atlantic not existing at all and Cathay Pacific not yet licensed to fly this route, it was the only way to go. It seemed quite all right to a neophyte like me and not deserving of its nickname of 'Better on a Camel'.

As it turned out, I had company on the flight. The brother of an Oxford acquaintance was a BOAC pilot, on that flight as a passenger. David Pedder told me that their family believed that they were descended from William Pedder, Hong Kong's first harbour-master, appointed in 1841, having arrived as first lieutenant of her Britannic Majesty's armed steamer HMS *Nemesis*.

We landed at Kai Tak, Hong Kong's airport for commercial airliners, which was replaced by Chek Lap Kok Airport on Lantau Island in 1998. The final approach to Kai Tak was famous through-out the aviation fraternity. It involved flying over the crowded tenements of Kowloon City with the plane going so low that it really seemed as if you were suspended at the level of people's homes and that the washing would be knocked off the laundry poles that hung out of the windows. At what felt like the last possible moment before colliding with a red and white checkerboard which looked as if it was just positioned at the end of a city street, the pilot would make an abrupt turn to the right and come to a juddering halt on the runway. More often than not, as soon as the plane landed, the air would be filled with a really staggeringly filthy stench. This was the Kai Tak Nullah. Hong Kong's imperial legacy included some words, mostly of Indian origin that were more or less unique to the colony and 'nullah' with its meaning of a concrete-lined storm drain was one of these. In fact, they were pretty much open ditches but they could take up a lane of a main road. All the nullahs smelt bad because waste of all kinds found its way into them but the Kai Tak Nullah with its proximity to the unregulated and insanitary Kowloon Walled City, very crowded even by Hong Kong standards, smelt worst of all. A little strangely, after enough time had passed and one had made enough flights back into Kai Tak, the smell seemed more homely than revolting. That reaction was perhaps the true test of citizenship, the sign that one had become a real adopted son or daughter of Hong Kong. This was of course, some way off for me as I pushed my luggage trolley into the surprisingly small and unimpressive arrivals hall.

I was met by Mr Albert Lam, the principal assistant secretary in the Establishment Branch of the Colonial Secretariat. In other words, he worked in personnel management or human resources, although rather a senior sort of person to be sent out late at night to meet a girl of twenty-two who was yet to do anything useful. I was to come to understand that I was one of an unusually sizeable batch of young graduates recruited to the administrative grade and we were accordingly being carefully looked out for. He carried no board and I wasn't wearing any special badge, but with my distinctive red hair I must have been easy enough to spot. Chinese tend to look for different things from Westerners as marks of differentiation: face shape and skin tones rather than shades of hair colour but mine was unusual enough to stand out and in the early years I would sometimes be aware of people staring at my head with some interest.

We were on the Kowloon Peninsula which, apart from some areas of grand houses quite close to the airport in Kowloon Tong, was mainly an area of factories, government housing estates, tenements and squatter huts. To the north were the largely rural New Territories, so called because they had been leased to Britain after the ceding of Hong Kong Island and Kowloon; it was the expiry of the lease on 1 July 1997 that cast a shadow over the future of the whole colony, which was not viable without this hinterland. Albert and I needed to get to Hong Kong Island, the location of the headquarters of government and all the major businesses. There was an official government car waiting for us and if we had taken the Cross Harbour Tunnel between Hung Hom and Causeway Bay we could have been on Hong Kong Island within minutes. However, the tunnel had only been open for just over a month and its use was not yet thoroughly accepted as part of daily life and the toll was an expensive HK$5. A general circular had been issued within the government to coincide with the opening of the tunnel, adjuring civil servants to pay due regard to economy when using it for official business and taking the most junior member of the administrative grade to her quarters could hardly have been considered justifiable. Accordingly, we drove through Kowloon to Jordan Road and took the vehicular ferry, which was $2 less, to its pier on Hong Kong Island, at the westward end of the Central District, close to the Macau Ferry pier and the 'Poor Man's Night Club', a large open area where in the evenings street entertainers as well as hawkers of snacks, cooked food, cheap toys and novelties plied their trade, under loops of casually strung up, blazing bright kerosene lamps.

Once we were on Hong Kong Island, it was a short journey to 'The Hermitage', at the junction of Kennedy and MacDonnell Roads, which was to be my home for the next few years. Rarely was a building so inappropriately named since it was a block of government quarters mainly for single people, either young or experienced bachelors. British colonies, unlike, say, the French, operated on the theory that expatriate staff would not settle and live there indefinitely but would eventually return to the UK. From that proposition flowed the justification for providing a temporary home for them. When my sister visited later, she described the

Hermitage as 'bedsitter heaven'. The furniture and fittings were perhaps a tad too heavy and old fashioned for that but I could see what she meant, as we were provided with not just a one-bedroom flat but also cleaning and laundry services carried out by elderly Chinese ladies who came in every day, and there was a basic but tolerable restaurant on the premises.

It was rather like being in a student hostel but with no rules to speak of and some of the men saw this as an opportunity for a prolonged adolescence, one that was fuelled by healthy salaries that allowed access to the girlie bars of Wan Chai and then, as often as not, an eventual visit to the venereal diseases clinic. In those days, there were many single expatriate civil servants, particularly police officers, but also engineers, lawyers and all sorts of technicians. The women were mainly teachers at the government schools for English-speaking children.

Relationships between the sexes were in an odd state of flux. In the West, we females were trying to carve out equal opportunities for ourselves in jobs and education but we still had to work out strategies to avoid or even fight off attempts at 'date rape'. The sexual revolution of the '60s had not hit Hong Kong at all and sex before marriage was an unacceptable idea. Conversely, some people assumed that all Western women were totally promiscuous though, equally, they were judged frighteningly unattractive due to their large, clumsy shape and size. Western music had hit Hong Kong, and the Beatles were screamingly popular, although mostly the soppier items in their oeuvre, as well as anything from the more melodic ends of the folk and pop charts. Acts like the Platters and Patti Page were respectfully listened to long after they'd been dismissed as old hat in the West. Psychedelia and dropping out had no appeal at all for aspiring youngsters who wanted to make their way from squatter huts or resettlement estates to a precious place in one of Hong Kong's two universities and a job that would enable them to make a substantial contribution to the family finances. The strength of family bonds and the discipline this imposed was undoubtedly a major reason for this conservatism, although I think that the 1967 anti-government riots were also relevant since at that time the overwhelming majority had decided to support the British establishment, at least passively, as the radical alternative seemed so much worse. There had been exceptions: students and school-children who came from loyal communist backgrounds and who might even be interned or imprisoned, but as dedicated socialists these young people tended to be puritanical too.

As part and parcel of the arrangements for the transfer of sovereignty, or 'handover', the Hermitage was eventually demol-ished and on the site an imposing glass building was erected for the use of China's Ministry of Foreign Affairs as its Hong Kong headquarters. And a natural consequence of the handover and the passing of time, was that some of those young people who had been imprisoned during the riots found important positions in the new establishment.

That first evening, Albert (we were encouraged from the begin-ning to be friendly and call our colleagues by first names) pointed out the Colonial Secretariat building down in Lower Albert Road, at walking distance from my new home and asked me to come to his office there the following day. The topography of Hong Kong facilitates standing at windows and pointing downwards, since buildings cascade from the top of the Peak down to the harbour, and indeed on the next day I was again standing at a window with Albert Lam while he indicated two adjacent buildings on Queen's Road below us. 'You must go to the Hongkong Bank and open an account there. Don't make a mistake and go into the other one: that's the Bank of China.' This warning was a mild joke but also meant half seriously. The Bank of China was one of the Hong Kong faces of the Chinese government and it was only five years since it had played a prominent part in the 1967 riots: plastered with posters denouncing the colonial government and with loudspeakers on the roof blaring out communist music and slogans. The Hong Kong government had retaliated with its own loudspeakers on the roof of Beaconsfield House located on the opposite side of Queen's Road, home of the Government Information Services, playing Cantonese opera. Now, in 2013, Beaconsfield House, recalling a small Buckinghamshire town, has been replaced by the Cheung Kong Centre, named after China's mighty Yangtze River and owned by Mr Li Ka-shing, the richest man in Asia; while the Bank of China is one of Hong Kong's note-issuing banks, with a network of branches and its shares quoted on the local stock exchange.

I suppose that if I had gone into the wrong bank I would just have been quickly hustled out since at that time there was a strict division between left-wing entities and the rest of Hong Kong and they wanted interlopers as little as we wished to step into their territory. I have a poor sense of direction but it was in fact almost impossible to avoid going into the correct bank. This was not, of course, the Norman Foster–designed building, which was opened in 1985 but like all the best modern architecture still looking contemporary today although also, frankly, like the back of a giant refrigerator. Its predecessor, which I was entering, had been there since 1935 and was very splendid in its own way. The dominating feature of the interior was a great barrel vault decorated with a spectacular gold mosaic with allegorical figures depicting trade between the East and West. The perfect Temple of Mammon! Indeed the mosaics used the same techniques as in St Mark's, Venice and at the opening ceremony its general architectural magnificence (it was the tallest building between Cairo and San Francisco) had been compared to Durham Cathedral. It proved much more transient, however. While I was handing over the advance of salary available to new recruits who needed something to help them through their first month, payday normally being at the end (the mighty volume of Establishment Regulations that dealt with per-sonnel matters had an answer for all of life's little contingencies), the executioner's axe was hovering over a building that was already considered too small and the process of replacing it began within seven years. By and large, Hong Kong was a deeply practical and pragmatic place and there could be no reprieve on the grounds of a handsome mosaic ceiling.

I walked out of the bank and into the shock of heat and humidity. I turned right into Pedder Street, named after the puta-tive ancestor of my companion on the flight to Hong Kong. He certainly would not have recognised it from the days when he kept sheep around his house-cum-office on Wyndham Street just above and when the harbour waters lapped right up to the bottom of 'his' street. Reclamation, the other Hong Kong predilection on a par with demolishing and replacing buildings considered 'too small', had put paid to that. In 1972, though, there were a couple of low-rise buildings left which within less than fifteen years would be replaced. One was the charming pale blue wedding cake of a Victorian building that housed the Hong Kong Club, while the other was the Edwardian General Post Office, not quite so charming in its harsh red-brick exterior but all the same a nice break in the skyline and with an interior worthy of the setting for the opening of a Kipling short story with its gilded Biblical motto 'As cold waters to a thirsty soul so is good news from a far country'. Lieutenant William Pedder might have had further to walk to the harbour in 1972 and he would not have recognised much of the shipping apart from the junks; Hong Kong waters were full of real working junks with faded, patched grey and brown sails, still rigged as they had been since the Sung dynasty, contemporary with Europe's Middle Ages, and the engines that helped them along in the twentieth century were not apparent at first sight. On the other hand, a time traveller from 2013 would have been surprised by the casual way in which private cars were able to park anywhere in Central and by the enormous expanse of prime land on the seaward side of the Hongkong Bank taken up by a cricket ground, which was only accessible to the members of the exclusive Hong Kong Cricket Club. The cricket ground was replaced even sooner than the Hong Kong Club and the GPO although this time not by a skyscraper but by a park where office workers could sit in shade during their lunch breaks.

That day was a solitary one for me but I was not the only recruit to the administrative grade that year; there were ten of us altogether of whom six were single expatriates living in the Hermitage. I had had special permission to delay my arrival by a couple of weeks so that I could be bridesmaid at my best friend's wedding. This meant that my name would come at the bottom of all lists as we were arranged strictly 'in order of seniority'. As it turned out, this had no ill effects on me though it might have done as sometimes, in the way bureaucracies work, a line would be arbitrarily drawn across the roll and only those above it considered for some treat or advancement. I met my fellow Hermitage-dwellers that evening and was shocked to discover that one of them was a . . . GIRL.

While I had been at Oxford, Liz King (later Bosher) had been at Cambridge and we both felt that we had been bamboozled by the recruitment board. 'They told *me* that I was going to be the only one,' we said more or less simultaneously. However, as time went by, we got over our disappointment at having to share our pioneer status and began to see the advantage in having two women together so that we could compare notes on the often slightly isolated situation in which we found ourselves. Liz and I became good friends. The only drawback to this double recruitment was that as our lives and careers unfolded in rather similar ways we found that people often mixed us up.

It was the first time for many years that the Hong Kong government had gone specifically to British universities to look for young people to become administrators. The 1967 riots had made it seem, for a short while, not quite certain that Hong Kong would even remain a British colony but might get absorbed willy-nilly back into China before the contracted date of 1 July 1997. Then it was thought that the service could function by recruiting from local universities topped up with a sprinkling of 'retreads', people who had had a career in some other colony which had become independent, so making them available to Hong Kong. This was feasible since processes and nomenclature were quite similar in British territories all around the world. However, Hong Kong's economy and consequently government activity were expanding so fast that there was more demand for administrators than could be met by these means. And so we came to fill the gap.

We had the backgrounds typical of Colonial Service recruitment almost from the beginning: Oxford and Cambridge Universities plus one from London, and all having studied arts or languages (one Chinese and one Arabic). That year only two young locals were recruited: Canice Mak and Shelley Lee. We became especially friendly with Shelley who was very hospitable and invited us to her home over the Chinese New Year holiday. It was a quite typical Hong Kong family of the time with numerous siblings all studying hard, eventually to do well in professions in both Hong Kong and overseas.

It could hardly be commended that in an era of increased localisation only two recruits had been managed to be found. It may be that the recruitment board was setting the wrong type of standard, being too keen to find locals whose English was at the same level as the expatriates, who normally could manage only limited Chinese. The following year Murray MacLehose instructed the recruitment board to find more Hong Kongers, and when they protested that they would not be up to scratch he instituted the year-long 'Oxford Course', which was tailor-made for the Hong Kong government by Oxford University and gave the Hong Kong civil servants who were sent on it not only academic programmes but also travel in Europe and elective subjects like art appreciation. Almost everyone who went on it found it an excellent, mind-broadening experience but as the transfer of sovereignty neared there were fears that the course might be considered an attempt at indoctrination of Hong Kong's ruling elite and it was ended.

No one could accuse the Hong Kong government of not having given careful thought as to how we young expatriates should be prepared for our roles in the administrative grade, even if we were not able to enjoy the two years of language training in Canton that had been the practice in pre-war days. Some senior people had apparently favoured longer language training while others thought that we would be needed at our desks more quickly and so a compromise was reached. We were going to be taught Cantonese in Hong Kong, for six months full-time and then six months part-time. Before the language classes began we would have a two-week attachment to a government department and the part-time training would be accompanied by time spent in some other office. At the end of that year, we would be given our first proper postings.

I was paired up with Tony Miller, one of the other newly arrived expatriates, and later director of housing and then secretary for financial services, to spend a fortnight getting to understand the work of the Urban Services Department. It would almost be simpler to list what this department didn't do rather than what it did as there was such an amazing range of activities. It was responsible for disposal of every kind of waste and rubbish, cleansing and sanitary facilities, markets, hawkers and abattoirs, restaurant licensing, burials and cremations as well as theatres, museums, libraries, beaches, parks and gardens. I suppose that the rationale for its remit was by taking reference to the kind of services that a British municipal council would provide. The staff were a mixture of generalist administrators, office support staff and professionals such as librarians and health inspectors. We were not at all ungrateful but we were young and I don't suppose that we gave much thought to the disruption caused to their own schedules by the requirement to take us out, guide us around, give us lunch and so on.

Before I came to Hong Kong I had been worried about the limitations of my wardrobe when it came to fulfilling my new role, which I had vaguely envisaged as being smartly dressed with other smart people, wrinkling our brows over complex policy issues. I had bought a fake suede emerald green trouser suit in a sub-Yves Saint Laurent-style and a chic long black raincoat with white press studs all the way down the front and white trim. The trouser suit was too heavy for a Hong Kong September and the raincoat turned out to be total madness since when Hong Kong was wet it was also very hot and its cool season was notable for its dry weather. I had not considered the possible need for clothes suitable to wear in a sweltering humid climate for trips to live poultry markets or for following through the journey of Hong Kong's household refuse from collection in lorries to compression by giant compactors to standing on the great landfills at Junk Bay and Gin Drinkers Bay or for an on-site briefing on Chinese burial customs (exhumation after seven years so that a filial son could scrub the bones which would then be placed in a niche or bone pot) and how these burial customs impacted on government policy, which was desperately keen to encourage cremation in view of the shortage of land.

Our visit to the abattoir was preceded by lunch at the Carlton Hotel, which had an excellent position in North Kowloon, quite rural and with an impressive view from the terrace across to Hong Kong. The set menu was tongue with salad which was, perhaps, a touch unfortunate as properly cooked tongue is in appearance, so very, well, tongue-like. Mr Lau Pai-ping, the senior health inspector who was looking after us that day, was already obviously quite nervous about how the afternoon was going to go and clearly felt that a young lady might not be robust enough to withstand it, asking me anxiously over and over again whether I thought I was going to be 'all right'. It's sometimes quite a good tactic to get so keyed up in advance that if the reality is anything less than appalling it will seem like quite a relief. And this was one of those cases because although the abattoir was noisy and hectic it was also clean and efficient and to my inexpert eye the pigs and cattle seemed to be slaughtered as humanely as possible. The main thing that a visitor needed to be aware of was to stand clear so as not to be knocked over by a swinging carcass on the dressing line. On the other hand, given the quantity and sharpness of the knives on the premises, it was easy to understand why, according to Mr Lau, staff relations had to be handled with particular tact and sensitivity. He was a kind and caring man altogether; it grieved him that the workers left the feverish atmosphere of the abattoir for cramped homes in crowded housing estates with the consequence that they never enjoyed much real respite.

By this time, we couldn't help looking forward to seeing something of the department's more fragrant side. We were proudly shown round the City Hall on Hong Kong Island's seafront which had been opened ten years previously and was the colony's only government-provided cultural facility, housing a theatre, concert hall, the central library and a tiny museum and art gallery, as well as a *dim sum* restaurant where we would make our first attempts at eating with chopsticks. The day was grey, rainy and cloudy and we had to make a diversion to pick up Rei Oblitas, Hong Kong's cultural supremo, who was still living in the same area as Hong Kong University, from which he had been recruited. The drive towards the harbour and the view across to Kowloon was an artistic experience in itself. The hills with ribbons of mist cutting across them were a revelation. Suddenly, you could see that those watery Chinese ink painting landscapes were not fanciful at all but rather an accurate depiction of a unique landscape.

The Urban Services Department's empire was far too big for us to be shown more than a sample, but on another occasion we were taken to Shek O Beach on the south eastern side of Hong Kong Island facing the South China Sea and, since it was a weekday, this beautiful inlet was completely deserted. The weather was clear and bright. Back then, Hong Kong had no air pollution to speak of and battalions of Black-eared Kites wheeled in the pale blue sky, riding the air currents and completing an idyllic scene. We sat outside a simple cafe, eating noodles and drinking Coke. However, the health inspector who was our designated 'minder' to take us to and from the beach, show us the lifeguarding and other facilities, looked a bit distant and aloof, even somewhat disdainful. When it was time to go, he suggested that we stop off on our way back to the Hermitage as he wanted to show us Aldrich Bay on the eastern tip of the island.

Aldrich Bay still exists as a name on the map but it has long since been reclaimed and it is now an area of middle-class housing and shopping malls. It was a real bay then, an area of grey stinking mudflats. In the twilight, we walked out along a rather rickety boardwalk and came to one of the many wooden squatter huts that people had built there. Sitting outside was a woman who might have been young and might have been middle aged, it really wasn't possible to tell. Her clothing was a shapeless black tunic and her hair was yellow-green, discoloured by chemicals, not deliberately dyed. A scrawny little boy with waxy pale skin leant against her knees. They were both working mechanically on assembling plastic toys from a box of components at her feet. This sort of piecework was one of the reasons why Hong Kong was already the second-most prosperous economy in Asia after Japan. We retraced our steps with our guide, who offered no comment. We got back into the car, identified by its number plate beginning with 'AM' as part of the government fleet. We drove back to Bedsitter Heaven.

Not all our time in the Urban Services Department was spent on outdoor visits. Sometimes we were in their offices, which were practical and served the purpose, though not in any way grand or ornate. The activity there was a bit more like what I had imagined I would be coming to before I arrived in Hong Kong. It was especially impressive to see demure Chinese secretaries taking down English language dictation in Pitman's Shorthand. Later on, I learnt how to give good dictation myself, mentally seeing the draft scroll before my eyes and carefully including all the punctuation to try and minimise the need to make corrections later while at the same time keeping an eye open for a frown that meant it would be better to spell out the word concerned. Since the secretaries were not native speakers they could often cope with something quite technical but would be baffled by apparently simpler constructions like 'but since'. As time went by and most work was being done directly onto computers the dictation-taking secretary became a rarer and rarer breed and asking if it could be done was a pretty certain way of inducing panic.

More senior expatriate colleagues tried to give us helpful briefings about working in Hong Kong. Relations between Chinese and British staff were at something of a transition stage. It was policy, and widely accepted, that posts should as far as possible be localised and preference not given to expatriates. It would have been unacceptable to have been rude to, or bullied a Chinese, on racial grounds; I never heard a civil servant use 'Chink' or any similar term. Conversely, we all tolerated the ubiquitous Cantonese term *gwailo* for a Caucasian, though I sometimes wondered whether it was really so pleasant to be described as a 'devil', 'evil spirit' or 'ghost', depending on one's translation, however inoffensively the speaker intended it. There was undoubtedly some pointless stereotyping and too often sentences that began 'Well, Chinese always. . . .'

Expatriates who had been in Hong Kong for a long time were proud to call themselves Old China Hands and to give us solemn lectures on cultural dos and don'ts, particularly on the matter of 'face', which you must never allow a Chinese to lose. I thought that this was a bit over-done: after all, no one in the whole wide world likes to be made to look foolish and will probably resent the person who has been the cause of it. As time went by, however, I began to understand the importance of being sensitive to cultural differences. Traditional British reserve and Chinese diffidence were quite a good natural match so it was not too difficult to learn how to calibrate and, in particular, to avoid causing offence by outright confrontation, but instead to find some intermediary through whom to express one's displeasure. Getting things wrong could have awful consequences in an office setting. There would be no overt recriminations but suddenly everything from getting a new supply of pencils to agreement to one's policy proposals would become inexplicably difficult.

It was quite a miracle that I had enough time to learn all this stuff since by the end of that first fortnight I had decided definitely and definitively that I had bitten off more than I could chew and I was going to leave Hong Kong forever and for good. It wasn't the visit to Aldrich Bay and the other manifestations of poverty that put me off; in fact they were quite an incentive to stay as a combination of youthful idealism and the many good things that I could see in the government's operations made me believe that there was scope to improve things enormously. As I analysed my emotions, I concluded that the overwhelming issue was the heat and the humidity, which made everything so difficult and made me feel that I couldn't function effectively at all. A small but grating problem was that of my hair, to which I was used to paying minimal attention. In England it stuck on my head without any effort on my part and I brushed and combed it every day, washed it once a week, and got a certain amount chopped off when it seemed to be getting too long. In Hong Kong, though, this didn't seem to work; after about fifteen minutes outside I felt reduced to a pool of sweat and the same applied to my hair which became totally flattened and almost invisible, an effect which did not disappear. Eventually, I learnt that I simply had to wash my hair every day, even though this ran counter to traditional Chinese health lore which foretold awful consequences (such as rheumatism in the head) from washing one's hair too frequently or improperly.

What worried me the most though was that I remembered that I had been told at my recruitment interview that the weather would be getting cooler in September. If this was 'getting cooler' how could I possibly cope as it got hotter? My informants had not been wrong, of course, but they had been slightly misleading. September was indeed cooler and less humid but only by a small amount: thirty degrees and seventy-nine per cent humidity rather than the thirty-one degrees and eighty-two per cent humidity of August. It was really in the middle of October that the temperature and humidity began dropping significantly towards the lovely winter weather. Having no similar experiences to call on, I didn't understand how adaptable the human frame can be nor did I fully appreciate how much more comfortable life in Hong Kong would become as air conditioning replaced electric fans.

It was all the same hard to contemplate a return to England and the accompanying sense of failure. My parents would be disappointed and we would face quite a dilemma: how was I to live if there was to be a long period of job hunting, with no student grant to rely on? I decided to make one last effort before I threw in the towel. I had been given the names, addresses and telephone numbers of two people in Hong Kong and I decided to find out if there was anything that they might say or do which would make me reconsider my decision.

The first was Mr KC (Casey) Liu of the Casey Company. The brother-in-law of one of my closest friends at Oxford worked in his family's firm of Cecil Gee, which sold trendy menswear to the aspiring young professionals of the 1960s. Casey ran an import/export agency and one of his customers was Cecil Gee, for whom he had sourced some shirting. My contacts, Rowley and Liz, had said that they would let Casey know that I was going to turn up in Hong Kong although, as it happened, they hadn't yet got round to doing so. I had only his name and office address and no telephone number but I resolved to go and pay him an impromptu visit that Saturday. For civil servants and businesspeople alike in Hong Kong office hours normally included Saturday mornings but we had been given the day off; we were in a sort of limbo between being students and working people. Quite possibly, the Urban Services Department thought they deserved a break from taking us to look at public lavatories and so on.

I accordingly went to Number 1914, Prince's Building in Central. Later on, I learnt that nothing about Casey was a matter of chance: either he had devised it himself or had thought through its implications. ('Beginning of the First World War, see. So no one ever forgets where my office is.') I had set out from the Hermitage with a feeling of bravado and indeed some irritability masking my sense of personal failure. I told myself that I was disappointed in Hong Kong and everything in it. These emotions began to change to trepidation as I saw that I had arrived at a smart office in perhaps the smartest building in the Central District and, even more so, when having asked for Mr Liu, I was shown a door marked 'Managing Director'. I knocked and entered on hearing a slightly abrupt 'Yes' from inside. A portly middle-aged man raised his eyes from the heap of papers on the desk that he stood behind and looked at me over his reading glasses with his bright shrewd eyes. 'Yes,' he repeated in the same rather gruff tone. 'Who are you?' 'I'm a friend of Rowland Gee,' I said. 'Ah,' he expansively replied, 'Friend of Rowland Gee, friend of mine. What are you doing for dinner tonight?' 'Nothing,' I said sulkily. 'OK. Come to Hilton Hotel at seven o'clock.'

I fished out the bridesmaid's dress that I had first worn a month or so previously and that had been chosen with the express aim of also being able to be worn for evening functions later on and, as instructed, got myself to the Dragon Boat Bar of the Hilton Hotel. Casey was there as was his wife, Lena, who was what Chinese people call a *kwan yin,* a beautiful, cool, elegant woman. As I discovered later, she had a principle against the flaunting of wealth and disdained designer labels (at that time things covered with Dior monograms were fashionable but, as she said, you might as well just pin your bank statement to your back if showing off was your motivation) preferring instead the classically simple combination of a tailor-made *cheongsam* with a jacket over it.

Casey told me just a little bit of his life story: he had been a marine engineer with Butterfield & Swire before striking out on his own. He also mentioned that he celebrated two birthdays, the second commemorating the day on which his mother had sneaked out of the house and got him back from the Hong Kong hillside where his grandmother had left him, as was the custom in those days in cases of sickly babies who were not expected to survive. He had, of course, not just survived but thrived. There was a period of frailty before his long life ended in 2007 but until then he was always full of optimism, enthusiastic about exploring new things. He decided that diamonds would be a good business to get into and in late middle age became a qualified gemologist and opened up a diamond cutting factory in Aberdeen on Hong Kong Island. He spent the last part of his life in Canada where he did a lot of boating (having always been annoyed that the Royal Hong Kong Yacht Club had advised him that he was too old to take up such a hobby) and, with no previous musical experience, became a pretty competent violinist when already in his seventies so as to enrich his new hobby of collecting antique instruments. That evening back in 1972 in the Dragon Boat Bar, he put his hand in his pocket, brought out something and said animatedly, 'Look, look at this.' It was a digital wristwatch, the first I had ever seen and indeed I had never even heard of such a thing. It seemed magically revolutionary and super-efficient to have the minutes flashed up as they clicked by. For the first twenty-two years of my life, there had been little in the way of technological change that had an immediate impact on our daily lives. All that was about to change with a wealth of new electrical and electronic inventions many of which, like that watch, would be manufactured in Hong Kong.

However, we were not due to have a quiet family dinner. Running your own company meant not just long hours in the office but also entertaining clients in the evenings and at week-ends and that was what we were going to do that Saturday. We were driven the short distance to Wan Chai and the Asiania Restaurant and Nightclub, at that time one of Hong Kong's more fashionable places. We were shown to a very large round table and the reason for that became clear when about a dozen German gentlemen arrived, to all of whom Casey hoped to sell some textiles. I had never been to a formal Chinese dinner before and did not know much about it, being ignorant of such things as the fact that the soup would be served towards the end of the meal rather than the beginning and that there would be some nine courses served one after another. This had a particular impact because as the Asiania was a nightclub there was a band playing and the courteous Germans felt it incumbent to dance, which basically meant that Lena and I, as the only women at our table, would be taken onto the dancefloor between every course, to be watched politely by the other ten and returned with a click of the heels and a slight bow after a short twirl. What amazed me about this process was that on each return there would be something new to eat nicely presented in a bowl or on a plate beside my chopsticks. I wondered how long this would last but the number of partners more or less balanced out the number of the courses and I went back to the Hermitage feeling that I had had a much more interesting and amusing day than I could ever have expected. Casey and Lena were very special people but they also represented something quite characteristic of Hong Kong at that time: an enormous energy and enthusiasm and a willingness to tackle life and its challenges head on.

Emboldened by this success, I decided to approach the other person whose contact details I had, the Reverend Joyce Bennett, a distant relative of mine. My family roots lay in Buckinghamshire and I was a descendant of long-established clans of farmers, butchers, dairymen and clayworkers. Because of complex webs of marriages between large families, I was related to some people through both my father's and my mother's side. There had however been a great fracture which had taken place just before I was born and had led to my parents moving away and leaving that way of life for ever. The reasons for it had the ingredients common to these sorts of family rifts: love affairs, elopements, divorce, second families, disputed wills and a business that faltered once the founding patriarch died. One of the results was that my sister and I grew up having little contact with our extended family. My mother, however, could not resist giving us a bowdlerised version of our history and we heard many stories of life on our maternal grandparents' farm, in which Joyce was a supporting character. She was described as a cousin though the relationship was more complex than that and she was probably a sort of second cousin, by blood on my mother's side of the family and by marriage on my father's side. Brought up in London, where her father owned a butcher's shop located just off Oxford Street, Joyce, who was some seven years younger than my mother, often came to the farm on holidays (although, poor girl, she was famous for being made sick by the shortest journey in the pony and trap that was their main means of transport) and during the Depression of the 1930s when my mother was working in London, she would go to Joyce's family home on her day off on Sunday. Soon after the Second World War, Joyce had been the cause of much sensation within the extended family because she had decided to join the Church Missionary Society, which sent her to Hong Kong. Her training in the UK had been as a teacher and she worked in education in Hong Kong, but in parallel she was pursuing her vocation within the Anglican Church which culminated, in 1971, in her becoming the first English woman to be ordained a priest. This was possible more than twenty years before such a thing took place in England because the Hong Kong Diocese was allowed to take this decision independent of other dioceses. There was relevant history, too; a Hong Kong born woman, Florence Li Tim Oi, had been ordained an Anglican priest by Bishop Ronald Hall in 1944 in China as a means to allow the community in Macau to continue to be served despite the chaotic wartime conditions. Miss Li temporarily surrendered her priest's licence in 1946 as her ordination had proved very controversial within the church but it meant that in Hong Kong the idea of a female priest was not as alien as it might otherwise have been.

As a consequence of my parents' estrangement from the rest of the family, I had never had any communication with Joyce and her presence in Hong Kong had had absolutely no effect on my decision to go there. However, my mother somehow or other had Joyce's address and telephone number and she gave these to me before I left England. This time I telephoned first and if Joyce was at all surprised, she did not display it. I suppose she was used to dealing with human waifs and strays and she invited me to dinner at her home. She was by then principal of St Catharine's School for Girls, Kwun Tong on the eastern side of the Kowloon Peninsula and lived in a flat on the school premises.

Nowadays, Kwun Tong is quite a mixed sort of area with some poor-quality older tenement housing but also modern public and private housing estates and middle-class shopping malls. Then, it was a place of great poverty, inhabited mainly by the refugees who had been arriving in waves from China ever since the establishment of the People's Republic in 1949 and who provided the bulk of the workforce for the factories that were the backbone of Hong Kong's burgeoning prosperity. In the beginning, it had been expected that, as in the past, these refugees would return to China when the situation had stabilised but this did not occur and instead squatter huts, flimsy wooden constructions that relied on illegally tapped electricity, and wells or public standpipes for water, sprang up all over the colony, which at that time had relatively large areas of undeveloped land, particularly on hillsides. A fire on Christmas Day in 1953 in Shek Kip Mei which rendered some 50,000 squatters homeless forced the government to begin a rehousing programme. It began building what were termed Resettlement Estates, which although they were fire and weather proof were provided only with communal toilets, kitchens and washing facilities. The accommodation was also extremely cramped; legend had it that some administrator had decided to base the space allocation on British Navy standards for hammock space and, whatever the origin, it was just twenty-four square feet per person. By 1968, some forty per cent of the population of almost four million was in government housing of one sort or another and the standards in the newer blocks were better than in the Mark One Resettlement Estates, although they were still very basic and not at all spacious. Furthermore, the 'squatter problem' had not been solved despite this massive building effort: sometimes it seemed to be like filling a sieve.

In those days, there was no Mass Transit Railway and ferries were a major means of transport, not just to the Outlying Islands but also across and around the harbour. So I got to Joyce's home by a journey first by boat and then by one of the red minibuses ('nine person cars' as they were known in Cantonese) that ran everywhere as useful components of the public transport system, even though they were largely unregulated, often dangerously driven, and widely assumed to be in the grip of triad gangs.

It is quite interesting to meet a blood relative for the first time, especially when you are already grown up and have some frame of reference. She reminded me of my mother and of my mother's younger sister, who was always as kind as she could be, despite the family quarrels and had had us to stay in the house she shared with my grandmother, and although Joyce was some twenty-five years older than I, I could see that we were somehow cut from the same genetic cloth too. I later discovered that she and I also shared some personality traits, including a complete inability to sing in tune. Joyce differed from all of us, however, in that her expression was totally imbued with serenity. She was not quiet, retiring or disengaged from everyday life, quite the opposite in fact, but her inner conviction that, in the end, 'all manner of things shall be well' shone through.

Even if her general appearance was what might be expected of a spinster missionary schoolmistress in an all girls' school, it would have been a mistake to believe that the environment in which she operated was a genteel one, or one to whose realities she was blind. The school, and therefore her home was up above Kwun Tong on its own on Crocodile Hill (Ngok Yue Shan), so it had magnificent views of the harbour and Kai Tak Airport and its runways, but it was nevertheless very isolated. She told me that when she first moved in she had had a visit from an inspector from the local police station who had asked, with some concern, whether she lived there on her own. 'Oh no,' she soothingly replied, 'Lau Je lives here too.' Lau Je was her live-in servant of a type then common in Hong Kong but more or less an extinct species now. These ladies wore wide black trousers and a tight-fitting top in sparkling white. They never normally married, providing devoted years of service to their employers but, on the other hand, enjoying complete sovereignty over the kitchen and, often, a mutually supportive relationship that transcended a purely financial transaction. The women in our family were fairly short as a rule and Joyce was no exception but Lau Je was even more so. The Inspector apparently looked at these two small ladies and then gulped and gave his considered advice: 'I think you should get a dog ... a large dog.' Joyce was a careful and reasonable person and she did get a dog, who was alleged to be a German Shepherd and, indeed, looked like one but my own observation of Chris, as he was named, suggested that it was very fortunate that he was never put to the test as I think he would have been more likely to offer a gentlemanly paw to an intruder than to bare his teeth and bite.

St Catharine's School for Girls was a haven for many of its pupils, whose lives were marred by poverty, physical abuse and incest, which was a particular problem arising from the cramped and unorthodox living situations of a refugee population. A respectable number were able to go on to university and Joyce was always conscious as well of the importance of the 'frills' of art and music which some believed to be more properly reserved for the elite. The girls had a great record of achievement in the local schools' speech and music festivals and, years later, when I asked the Education Department for a selection of artwork for a government conference room, the ceramics all came from St Catharine's. Joyce had gone by then, having retired and returned to England in 1983, but long afterwards I heard people in the education sector speaking of teachers who had worked in her school and absorbed her ideas as an especially impressive breed.

As I rode the ferry back to Hong Kong Island, I was forced to reflect that I really should give this place another chance. Wouldn't it be foolish to turn my back on a place that contained such interesting, quirky and positive people? 'Yes, yes,' the twinkling lights round the harbour seemed to be saying, 'Stay with us. Your life will have more possibilities than you could ever have imagined.' And so I did.

CHAPTER THREE

Lee Gardens and Kowloon City

OUR LANGUAGE STUDIES WERE TO BEGIN with six months in the Government Training School in Lee Gardens, located in a nondescript and utilitarian office block, a short and inexpensive shared taxi ride from our quarters in the Hermitage. The Lee Gardens area itself was not without interest, though. It was probably best known in the community as the location of the Lee Theatre, an Art Deco building which staged Cantonese Operas as well as showing films, and which was demolished in 1991 to make way for another of the ubiquitous shopping malls. In the 1970s cinemas were popular because they offered air conditioning together with entertainment and so whole families right down to the babies would go into the screenings, taking with them quantities of chicken wings so that they could dine in comfort too.

As often happens, different minority groups clustered together and while the North Point area of Hong Kong Island was favoured by the Shanghainese and the Fukienese, the Lee Gardens area was in those days a centre for the White Russian community, the origins of which lay in flight into China to escape the Bolshevik Revolution before further moves down to Hong Kong. The main impact of this on us was in our favourite lunch place: the Mazy Restaurant which basically offered borscht and beef stroganoff. The Mazy Restaurant had quite a following among local people as a not too expensive nor intimidating place to try out Western cuisine and the arcane art of using knife and fork. The conclusions drawn from the experience were, perhaps, as faulty as the concepts of Chinese food that I had gleaned from the Special Fried Rice of the Great Mountain Restaurant back in my schooldays in England.

We had some courses in basic legal principles, a remnant from the days that had actually ended in 1961 when district officers in the New Territories were required to act as magistrates. The bulk of our time, however, was to be spent learning to speak and understand Cantonese, the Chinese dialect of Hong Kong as well as the neighbouring Guangdong Province, Macau and by much of the Chinese diaspora throughout the world, the origins of much of which lay in Southern China. Sadly, there was much less emphasis on learning to read and write Chinese characters. The accepted wisdom (though, with hindsight, I think it was wrong) was that it was too difficult for Westerners to learn sufficient Cantonese on the basis of the written characters and so 'romanisation', a phonetic approximation of the language in the Latin alphabet, became all important. This was not straightforward on account of the essentially tonal nature of Cantonese so something was also required to indicate whether the word should be pronounced in a high, high-falling, high-rising, level, low-falling, low-rising or low-level tone. There were several competing forms of romanisation but the one that we were taught was 'Sidney Lau', which used a superscript number at the end of each word to show the tone. It was an elegant, user-friendly system but we speakers of 'Sidney Lau' are now a dwindling band since, insofar as any foreigners today learn Cantonese rather than Mandarin, some other romanisation, usually that dreamt up by Yale University, is the norm.

We, however, had not only Mr Sidney Lau's textbooks but Mr Sidney Lau himself, a rather lean and spectral but decidedly human presence haunting our corridors, for Mr Lau was the principal of the Hong Kong Government Language School. The story was that he had previously run a language school in Guangzhou, teaching to foreigners the purest, finest Cantonese and in the wake of the Communist Revolution had brought his school and all his teaching staff down to Hong Kong and somehow managed to find a berth for the entire crew with the Hong Kong government. The teachers were in awe of Mr Lau and, generally, their lives must have been quite trying as their pupils were rather troublesome too. We ourselves became somewhat childish under the influence of a return to the schoolroom, refusing to be too impressed by Mr Lau, saying behind our hands that he looked like a tortoise without its shell and making jokes about the Chinese names that the government had devised for us based on the sounds of our English surnames. 'Howard' became 'Ho Hau Wan' in the standard form of the surname followed by two given names, the English translation of which in my case was 'graceful cloud' but Robert Upton, later deputy secretary for security and then director of planning, soon turned that into 'a blot on the horizon' and, until people began to forget about it, I had to grit my teeth and tolerate the friendly but hardly grown up nicknames of 'Blot' or 'Blotlet'.

We were, nonetheless reasonably biddable compared with the usual student cohort of expatriate police officers, bored and doubtless feeling that daily Cantonese vocabulary tests were not what they had envisaged when they had signed up for a life as gun-toting cops in the land of Suzie Wong. The school would also accept a few fee-paying outsiders to make up the numbers. These were quite often newly arrived missionary schoolteachers, although in our class there was Jenny, a breathtakingly pretty English blonde, who was the wife of a jockey who rode at the nearby Happy Valley racecourse. 'I've done this course a few times,' she confided during our first tea break, 'but so far I've always had to give up at Lesson Five, because it gets difficult then.' Sadly, Lesson Five proved to be yet again an insuperable hurdle and after a few weeks we saw Jenny no more.

Our teachers came from a culture in which schoolmasters did not have to amuse or engage their pupils but could depend upon automatic respect and obedience; the discomfort of the diminutive Wong Chit-ming and the reserved PK Lau was quite obvious as soon as they entered the classroom. One of our instructors though had the measure of us and was unafraid; this was Mrs Moy. She was not tall but must have been stunningly attractive when young. She had an unusually fine *embonpoint*, expressive almond shaped eyes and, altogether, the air of an empress. We were driven through her lessons by the power of her personality. Occasionally, some bold student, perhaps Robert Upton, would try to divert the flow with a question. 'But why, Mrs Moy? Why is it like this?' Mrs Moy would come to a halt, her entire body expressing amazement at the

temerity of such an interruption. Her bosom would heave and her
eyes would flash. 'Why? You are asking "why", Mr Upton? Because
it is *our way.*' This was, indeed, quite a good general pointer as to
how to adapt to an alien environment and, suitably abashed, we
would dutifully lower our heads to our books again.

With Jenny's sad tales in mind, we were all a bit concerned as
Lesson Five of *Elementary Cantonese* loomed on the horizon. After
all, passing our language exams was a necessary condition for
staying in the employment of the Hong Kong government. Lesson
Five dealt with 'classifiers', just about the only tricky grammatical
concept that we would come across. A classifier was a word slipped
in before every noun. It was not so remote from English usage: in
the phrases 'a bottle of beer' or 'a glass of beer', the words 'bottle'
and 'glass' are, in effect, 'classifiers'. The difference in Chinese is
that there is a classifier for every noun, with a whole range of
different classifiers to be paired with its appropriate noun. There is
no translation for many of these as the concept does not exist in
English and so they tend to be given 'piece' as an approximation
and to turn up in the belittling Pidgin English so beloved of certain
writers of Hong Kong fiction in sentences like 'Oh, Missee, one
piece very bad man come to house now.'

In fact, if Mrs Moy had cared to do so, she might have suggested
a reason for the existence of classifiers. This lies in the fact that
monosyllabic Cantonese as compared with, say, English, has many
words of broadly similar sounds but different meanings. The
classifier can help to signal which word the speaker actually intends.
The other means of distinguishing one word from another is the
one that really does give many Westerners much trouble: the tone
in which the word is pronounced. Those who had a good ear for
music could get to grips with this but I was stuck, as I had never
even been able to sing in tune. There were plenty of horror stories
about the embarrassing mistakes that we could soon be making in
public speeches in our careers, since, for example, the words for
'nine', 'dog', and 'penis' were easily confused as were those for
'charitable' and 'insane'. Even in our daily interactions in the local
restaurants, we might believe we were asking for the bill when our
waiter would hear that we were offering to sell him some eggs. Some

of our group, although not I, in time became very adept, able to boast of near-perfect tones. I mainly relied on the goodwill of my listeners and mostly found that an effective strategy. Cantonese could be rather snobbish towards other Chinese people, deriding them for the slightest slips in choice of words or any oddities in pronunciation. They were much more forbearing towards foreigners, being like Dr Johnson when it came to dogs walking on their hind legs and women preaching, so amazed that it should be attempted at all that much could be overlooked in terms of the quality of what was being offered up.

The third component of our language studies, together with grammar and pronunciation, was vocabulary and this had its own idiosyncrasies particular to our course. We had to be introduced to various important concepts through what we studied. Thus we learnt the proverb 'One monk will carry water for drinking, two monks will carry water for drinking but with three monks there is no water to drink.' The metaphorical meaning of this was to do with the concept of buck passing but the linguistic point was that single sentence had three different words for 'carry', depending on the number of people who were doing the carrying and whether the bucket was held on a yoked pole or not. A hint of national pride could come in and so when learning how to form comparisons our sample sentence was 'I know several Westerners who are as industrious as Chinese.' A significant influence was the fact that the bulk of the students were normally trainee expatriate police inspectors and much of the course material was tailored to their needs. We were accordingly taught both formal and colloquial terms for all the many police ranks and the words for such things as 'handcuffs', '.38 calibre revolver', 'bail', 'pleading guilty' and 'same old story', with sentences to be translated including things like 'In that police station there are ten probationary inspectors.'

It was perhaps no bad thing that our lessons reminded us of the gritty Hong Kong of murder, mayhem and violent crime as we were otherwise living in something of a bubble of a rather old-fashioned colonial way of life. It was advisable, in line with protocol, to go and 'sign the book at Government House'. This had been something to be done in all colonies by new arrivals and we were also, one by one, invited to dinner there. The bridesmaid's dress that had taken me through the Lius' dinner at the Asiania Nightclub and Restaurant came out of the wardrobe again. Wedding clothes in those days tended to be rather demure if you were not Mick Jagger's bride in a white trouser suit, and this dress was no exception. It was full length and Empire line with a high neck and short puffed sleeves in a white fabric scattered with little mauve flowers. It probably looked quite odd but naturally no one was bad mannered enough to suggest that.

Everything was very formal but in some ways that made things easier. Married couples were split up but the seating was male and female alternating, with the senior lady guest seated at the governor's right. You would never be stuck for conversation since 'the table was turned' so that you spoke to the person on your right for the first course, to the person on your left for the next course and so on. Everyone knew that there was a duty to keep the talk pleasantly and inoffensively rolling. I sat next to a visiting journalist from *Time* magazine and told him with only slight exaggeration what a godsend his publication was to someone cut off from the UK press. A Chinese friend once asked me whether it was permissible to speak at Western formal dinners. Somewhat surprised at the question I asked her why she thought it might not be. 'Well,' she said, 'in films, when they show one of those events, guests seem to be whispering to the person next to them.' There was certainly a contrast with the raucous jollity of a Cantonese meal where shouting across the round dining table was the norm.

A mildly challenging moment came at the end of our meal when the servant in the smart white Government House uniform with brass buttons and red epaulettes brought round a great platter of fruit for each of the guests to choose from. What would be not too difficult to eat in such august company? The already cut small bunches of grapes were a popular choice while out of the corner of one's eye one could marvel at the governor as he speared an apple on his plate with his fork and dexterously peeled and cut it up with the knife in his right hand.

Led by Lady MacLehose, we females went off to the drawing room while the men stayed behind with port and cigars. I was familiar with this practice from plays and books although it was the first time I had seen it in real life. I was too engaged with keeping up with doing the right thing to wonder whether this division by sex made any sense and whether the ladies were missing out on any important discussions. Twenty years later, though, it came home to me how big a change there had been when I was involved in an impromptu and rather significant meeting held over the washbasins in the ladies' room in a government office building!

After coffee and a decent interval, we were allowed to return, which was the unspoken signal that it was time for all the guests to disperse. The same quiet efficiency that had characterised the event ensured that, for those of us who did not have our own cars with chauffeurs, taxis arrived. They came in past the sentry boxes at the main gate where policemen kept guard, around the immaculately swept semi-circular drive, leaving on the left the governor's tennis court and on the right serried ranks of well disciplined dahlias and came to a halt before the spotless white steps above which loomed the incongruous Japanese tower added to Government House during the Occupation of the Second World War. I sat back and returned to the Hermitage, whose other residents had doubtless spent the evening in very different ways.

The life we were leading could, to some extent, have been depicted by John Betjeman. There were aspects of expatriate society which seemed to be relics of a repressed and proper British middle-class world of the England of some twenty years previously, untouched by the swinging sixties. There was a keenness for tennis and amateur theatricals. We sniggered our way through a performance of *The Desert Song,* kindly taken along by some senior people who might well have thought we were rather appalling. In search of social life beyond the company of our own little group, though, we soon found ourselves signing up for the Hong Kong Stage Club and their readings and rehearsals. I began a modest romance, which did not last, with Adam, a pukka young Englishman working for Gilman's, then a medium sized trading company offering the same kind of import/export intermediary services as the more prominent Jardine Matheson. Adam had a flatmate, and she was the kind of person who reminded me that, despite occasional appearances to the contrary, Hong Kong was not really stuffy or ordinary at all.

Adam and Tim, another young chap from Gilman's, had been allocated a flat in a rather smart new block in Conduit Road, halfway up the Peak both literally and metaphorically. There was a bedroom not being used and Tim decided to sub-let it. Their tenant was Anna Ding, a Chinese lady of about forty, although she looked much younger than that, with a round face, an unwrinkled skin and her short black hair in the sort of cut that the Beatles sported when they first became famous. Anna was the receptionist at the New Zealand Insurance Company and very punctilious about the uniform that she wore for the job: a long-sleeved navy blue dress with white cuffs that she could detach and scrub until they sparkled.

Like most of the Hong Kong residents of that time, Anna had not been born in the colony. Her father had been the head of customs in Guangdong Province, an important official in the tempestuous days between the last emperor and the coming to power of the Communist Party. Polygamy was the norm, especially for the wealthy, and Anna's father had seven wives, although her own mother had died when she was four years old. They lived in traditional style, the wives in small individual houses round a courtyard and the husband in grander quarters of his own, visiting the seven little houses as the fancy took him. On Sunday mornings, the entire troop together with all the children, of whom Anna was the eldest, would take a table in a Guangzhou restaurant to eat *dim sum*. It was always she who had to sit next to her father and chat; he had nothing to say to any of his women. During those years he slept with a pistol under his pillow and this was not a piece of theatre in a period of shifting loyalties and lawlessness. Once it was clear that it really was the communists who had won he decided, not unreasonably, that it was not safe for him to remain, with or without his pistol and he left the country, at a time when it was still fairly easy for a wealthy person to do that. He took none of his family with him and made for Canada. He became a stockbroker in Toronto, married a German lady and had another couple of children.

Back in Guangdong, his wives and children did their best to adapt to a new way of life but it was hard as their property was taken from them and they were denounced as offspring of the landlord class. Anna was in communication with her father and was the only one who was daring enough to want to make an escape, which was indeed a life-threatening exercise. She was athletic and a bit of a tomboy. When it was the hobbies period at her school and the other girls knitted and embroidered, Anna used to go out to dig the vegetable patch. She had also been her age-group provincial champion in discus and javelin. Thus it was that at the age of fifteen, she rode a bicycle down to the border between China and the then-Portuguese colony of Macau, making it look like a day's picnic and consequently with almost nothing in the way of possessions. Her father had arranged a boat that took her to Hong Kong where she became one of the hundreds of thousands striving to make a new life away from the chaos that was engulfing China. She went to Canada, but that was not a success. Although she had attended the famous True Light Middle School in Guangdong, Anna had never had any pretentions to be an intellectual (indeed, she claimed that it was only earnest prayer that had allowed her to get through the primary school examinations so she could go to True Light) and her father was quite disappointed that she could not establish herself in the same sort of prestigious and lucrative career that he was now following. She returned to Hong Kong and took up some less demanding jobs, although when I met her she was still visiting Canada annually, at which times she would be given a present of a wardrobe of new clothes.

Anna had a superb natural eye for putting outfits together so that she looked stylish and, in her later years, even quirky, but never flashy. Her eccentric English and her wry realism were endearing. She also had a record of achievements in her recent past, about which she did not boast but which were doubtless a major contribution to her self-confidence. She had turned out to have a flair for speed and an outstanding talent as a driver. The Macau circuit was already famous for its races and Anna had gone there and, for three successive years, had been the Ladies' Champion in cars, go karts and motorbikes. Anna became a dear friend.

My working life was about to take a different path, far away from the sedate dinners at Government House. Truly, a lot of thought had been given to a good sort of preparation for us young recruits and there was one further six-month stage before we were launched into doing a job in a normal way. We were to combine part-time language learning with an attachment to the sort of department where we could experience the grittier side of life. Our Cantonese lessons were now entrusted to the Kowloon outpost of the New Asia College of the Chinese University. We were a bit more sensible and diligent, gradually trying to transform ourselves into responsible civil servants. The curriculum and the approach to teaching were more conventional than in the Government Language School and that is, perhaps, why I can recall almost nothing of them. It was, however, an outstandingly memorable period for one of our group; shortly afterwards Tony Miller married our beautiful teacher, Miss Wong Nga-ching. For me, though, the next excitement was an attachment to the city district office, Kowloon City, which turned out to be full of interest.

In early 1973 the ten city district offices were at the cutting edge of the government's efforts. It was only some five years since pundits all over the world had been, as often before and since, writing off Hong Kong as a viable, sustainable entity. In this case, the consigning to history's dustbin had been occasioned by the 'Disturbances', a euphemism for violent riots, arson, murders and bombings that had dominated life in Hong Kong for some seven months in 1967. To a large extent, these were a spillover from the Cultural Revolution that was raging in China. Left-wing organisations and sympathisers streamed up to Government House to read from Chairman Mao's *Little Red Book* at its gates and to engage in fierce clashes with the police along the way. The Disturbances were ended by a combination of the Chinese government's reluctance to press its apparent advantage and take back Hong Kong, the energetic and effective tactics of the police and the civil administration and their courage and determination in carrying them out as well as by the great majority of the population demonstrating their preference by stolidly insisting on continuing normal life, even if, say, it meant walking from the far end of Hong Kong Island to the central business district to get to work when there was no public transport. All the same, the government recognised that there were other, more worrying, undertones in the picture. The original flashpoints had been a series of strikes and labour disputes in factories in Kowloon and it had to be admitted that there was too little understanding of what was going on at the grassroots, inadequate care for their difficulties and too little attention paid to simmering social discontent before it got out of hand. It was decided that the urban areas needed what already existed in the rural New Territories: district officers who would act as a sort of conduit in their individual areas, explaining government policies to the people as well as relaying back reactions, responses and concerns that had not yet been registered by the higher echelons. In addition, they would, as far as possible, settle minor disputes and, on a small scale, provide desirable amenities and organise local events and carnivals.

In its early days, at least, the city district officer scheme was amazingly successful, achieving much of what had been hoped for. A major reason for this was that the Establishment Branch, which was responsible for postings, was asked to send to the CDOs the best and the brightest among the young administrative officers. Consequently, the monthly meetings when the CDOs came together to discuss common issues were gatherings of the witty, the intelligent and the good looking. They included Jack So, later head of the Mass Transit Railway Corporation and then the Trade Development Council, Rafael Hui, later chief secretary for administration, and the handsomest one of the lot, my new boss, Tony Neoh. Tony was Chinese but of Singaporean origin, which explained his unusual surname. He was also uncommonly tall, with a charming smile, a wide range of intellectual interests, and completely bilingual in spoken English and Cantonese although he was only just catching up when it came to written Chinese, as he had gone to St Francis Xavier School where he had been able to opt to study French instead. As it turned out, he did not stay in the government for very long but went to England and qualified as a barrister at Gray's Inn, then to California to be admitted to its Bar. He practised back in Hong Kong but developed particular expertise in the financial field, eventually becoming chairman of the Securities and

Futures Commission and a valued adviser to the Chinese government as it entered the unfamiliar territory of setting up and
regulating stock exchanges for itself.

A big group from the office would go out together to eat lunch
each day. It was the normal thing to do and we would go to one of
the many nearby *dim sum* restaurants where trolley loads of little
dishes were pushed around, each server calling out the name of
what he or she had to offer so that the diners could take bamboo
containers of their favourites as they wanted, with a tick on the
sheet of paper on each table so that at the end the total cost could
be arrived at quickly and efficiently. I had been brought up 'not to
be fussy about food' especially if I was in some sense or another a
guest and, anyway, the *dim sum* were delicious even if initially
unfamiliar. I became reasonably adept at eating chickens' feet,
holding them tightly in the chopsticks while chewing off the fairly
modest amount of meat. One day, intrigued by the texture of what
was in my mouth, I asked for the English name. Those next to me
were stumped and had to pass the question to Tony. He roved
through his mental dictionary for a moment or two only. 'I think,'
he grinned, 'that cow's diaphragm would probably be the closest
translation.'

The geographical area for which we were responsible was very
diverse. Our office had a shopfront and was on the ground floor,
right on the pavement, so that it was easy for our 'customers' to
access us. They would come in to look at the big range of pamphlets
and brochures that we had available, to ask about baffling government
forms and procedures, to swear out statutory declarations, which
was a service that we offered, or, if they knew us well enough, simply
to pass the time of day and tell us what the government should be
doing about this or that burning issue. The things we gleaned from
these conversations were to be put into regular reports, to be
collated at headquarters into a document called 'Talking Points'
which was intended to provide a summary of public opinion
throughout the urban area. 'Local leaders in Kowloon City are still
worried about the rate of violent crime and also the dangers posed
by illegal tapping of electricity by squatters. . . .' we might say. If we
were due to hand in something and pickings had been thin we

sometimes resorted to 'Diners in restaurants in the district were heard to express the view that. . . .' while refraining from mentioning that we were simply typing up what we had ourselves been chatting about over lunch. Although we were quite conveniently situated as far as the majority of our clientele were concerned, our location had the definite disadvantage of being right next to Kai Tak Airport. Whenever an aeroplane passed overhead, which was very often, conversation became impossible. We all got used to it although people who phoned us up found it rather unnerving. At the back of our 'shop' we had the normal style of government offices with registries full of filing cabinets. These contained, among other things, the contingency plan to be referred to in the event of a plane crashing somewhere in Kowloon City; discouragingly, there was a considerable emphasis on where enormous quantities of body bags were to be found.

Socially, our district was mixed with pretty much the entire spectrum of wealth and class distinctions. Kowloon Tong was the undoubted posh end of town. It was laid out rather like an English garden suburb and the height restrictions imposed by the proximity of the airport saved it from high-rise development even if the residents had wanted it. Instead, there were fine old houses occupied by just one or two families. Nowadays, a few remain but more have been converted into short stay hotels for assignations or, alternatively, into expensive kindergartens. The former are quite discreet while the latter stridently advertise the benefits of a superior start in life that they will confer on the offspring of those who are able to stump up the fees. The Kowloon City of my day was also known for its educational establishments, but they were the prestigious secondary schools like Maryknoll for girls and La Salle College for boys. Entrance to such schools was by a stringent process that made the UK's eleven-plus look quite effete. The Secondary School Entrance Examination, sat all in one afternoon, with papers in Chinese, English and mathematics was decisive and, although the situation was improving, the norm had been that there were simply insufficient places for all to receive government-funded education after the age of eleven. Nonetheless, many of my colleagues in the government had managed to find a route through this system from humble beginnings to higher education and stable, well-paid work.

There was also the Beacon Hill English Primary School, in those days very much the preserve of the expatriate, with just a few pupils of Eurasian or Asian nationality. Tony Neoh sent me there to explain to the headmaster and the committee of the parent-staff association the government's latest campaigns, rousing the populace to combat litter and also violent crime. 'Lap Sap Chung', the litterbug, a grotesque dinosaur dreamt up by Arthur Hacker, who worked for the Government Information Services, was for a time one of the most recognisable figures in the popular culture of Hong Kong. The shattered dagger of the Fight Violent Crime campaign was not so familiar. My mother back in England was dumbfounded when she heard what I was up to. She considered our city of Portsmouth an essentially peaceable place and believed that violent crime was well beyond the boundaries of my experience. In the thirty-odd years that have elapsed since then, the relative positions on crime statistics seem to have reversed and so it may perhaps be that my anti-crime pep talk did some good. Who knows what life of banditry those parents and teachers might otherwise have been tempted to embark upon?

To Kwa Wan was a rather traditional area, populated by respectable tradespeople and members of the hard-working lower middle classes. It was fairly easy for us to communicate with the residents as they tended to have organised themselves in groupings by neighbourhood (the *kaifong* associations) or by clan, reflecting their places of origin in China. Like most of those that I met during my stint in Kowloon City they were friendly and welcoming towards me. Mr Chan Kwok-leung, the acupuncturist, invited me and my visiting sister to his home and stuck needles into us to demonstrate his craft. His wife was a superb cook and in a kindly gesture had cooked Western food for us though it proved quite a test to eat a large breaded pork cutlet with chopsticks since they did not possess knives and forks and, indeed, never thought of using such outlandish cutlery. A highlight of the Hong Kong social calendar was the garden party held at Government House to celebrate the Queen's Birthday, which was also a public holiday. There were a few places for our clan and *kaifong* leaders which meant them going to Hong Kong Island, something that they would normally almost never do, since everything that they required could be found within a short radius of their homes in Kowloon. Having rather tentatively nibbled at sandwiches and sipped tea on the terraces, this little band of tourists was led off by one of their number whose experience had been more varied for some sightseeing in the metropolis. They went down to the waterfront to marvel at the recently completed Connaught Centre (now Jardine House), then the tallest building in Asia and distinguished by a design concept which basically covered the entire structure in round windows looking like very large portholes. Before catching the ferry home, they also took in the Edwardian General Post Office, the attraction of which was that it resembled the settings of foggy London town that they had seen in the movies.

The most notorious part of our district, however, was an area of six-and-a-half acres that comprised the Walled City, sometimes rather confusingly called simply Kowloon City. Just about every aspect of the Walled City was odd and confusing. It was an enormous historical and political anomaly. There had been a fort on the site for many centuries before the arrival of the British in Hong Kong in the nineteenth century and in 1847 a fine *yamen,* offices for the Chinese imperial military stationed there, had been constructed. The New Territories were leased to the British in 1898 for ninety-nine years, to add to Hong Kong Island and the Kowloon Peninsula which they already held. (It was the ending of this lease in 1997 that triggered the transfer of sovereignty of the entire territory of Hong Kong, since by then Hong Kong and Kowloon were not viable without the hinterland of the New Territories). An agreement in the 1898 negotiations was that the Walled City should remain under Chinese sovereignty. Within a year of the lease being signed, the British at the height of their power and, one might say, with their arrogant disregard for those of other races, expelled from the Walled City the officials and soldiers who represented China, then under the rule of the Qing dynasty. It seemed that the assumption was that the Walled City would somehow naturally be absorbed into the sphere of British administration but instead it remained a source of aggravation and the cause of many disputes between the two governments. Arguments about this small area inflamed passions within China and would often lead to popular demands to grab back the whole of Hong Kong. It therefore seemed more politic to accept that British jurisdiction would not be exercised there and it would be left undisturbed by police and other government officials. The physical walls disappeared during the Japanese occupation of 1941 to 1945 as their stones were used to extend the runway at Kai Tak but this had made no difference to the attitude adopted towards this place.

In our Kowloon City District Office there was a staff member whose only real qualification for employment (but a highly valuable one) was that he was related to Walled City families, knew his way around there and visitors who were accompanied by him would not be attacked or molested. Thus, I could venture into this notorious place. Because there was no building regulation or requirements about foundations the tenements, which contained a mixture of residential flats and rooms, as well as factories, some making things that were legitimate and others that would be illegal outside, leant crazily against each other with narrow, unevenly paved alleys separating one row from another with great tangles of electrical cables hung haphazardly around. The inhabitants were equally careless and would lie on camp beds in the open puffing on long pipes filled with opium. The edges of the Walled City that faced out towards 'normal life' were the preserve of the unlicensed dentists, offering a service at rock-bottom prices but at some risk to their patients' teeth.

There were a few outsiders who went into the Walled City regularly and without any sort of a bodyguard. These included Jackie Pullinger and her friend Mary, two English girls about five years older than I was. They had a base in Lung Kong Road, one of the streets that formed an unofficial boundary to the Walled City, and I used to visit them there. They were of a type that I recognised from my schooldays; confident, kindly, reliable girls from comfortable professional backgrounds. Teachers would ask them to help to organise the choir or the Junior Red Cross and indeed Jackie and Mary were running a youth club in their big whitewashed first-floor room. To call their protégés 'youth' was perhaps rather patronising; these were thugs, heroin addicts, triad members, thoroughly macerated in all the many vices that the Walled City had to offer. I was not only asked to go there myself but also to bring along other colleagues. Michael Cartland (and, yes, I eventually married him) came to chat to them about policy on education and social welfare while Elizabeth King underwent a particularly unnerving experience, taking part in the youth club's blood donation drive, conducted by candlelight following a power cut!

Jackie was a particular sort of Christian. Starting out from the English Home Counties, she had bought a boat ticket for the longest voyage that she could on the basis that she would get off where God told her to do so. The ship's final destination was Japan but Jackie disembarked in Hong Kong and found her way to the Walled City where her principal activity was ridding junkies of their addiction by praying over them. Mary went back to England to marry an army officer. I rather supposed that Jackie would do the same sort of thing but about that I could not have been more wrong and our lives would intersect again from time to time.

There were a few other social service organisations daring to operate within the Walled City. One of these had recently set up a chapel within the *yamen,* as well as a simple school and clinic. There was to be an opening ceremony and Tony Neoh proposed that I should represent the government.

Accordingly, I showed up one Sunday afternoon, clutching the romanised version of the Cantonese speech that I had been practising all week. The *yamen* had an open courtyard and that was where everyone was gathered. Although many of the people who lived in the Walled City were criminals, this was by no means true of all, others were simply poor and needed to find the very cheapest accommodation. They might go outside the Walled City to work or else labour in the factories that were located there, many of which, rather worryingly, given the general hygiene levels and the lack of running water, produced noodles and other foodstuffs. Because of the day of the week, the audience included plenty of children. Later on, when I had a post in the Social Welfare Department, veteran staff who had run the food relief programmes of that period and before told me that they used to call little victims of malnourishment like these 'matchsticks' on account of their skinny bodies topped by a disproportionately large head and a shock of black hair. In the Walled City hardly any sunlight penetrated the closely packed buildings so their skin had a waxy pallor too. Their clothes were simple: shorts and singlets for the boys and a dress and a pair of pants for the girls, flip-flops for the feet of both sexes. Nonetheless, everyone was cheerful and looking forward to this out-of-the-ordinary event. I got through my speech successfully and lined up with the platform party for the formal ribbon cutting. I was then presented with a wrapped parcel, a rather touching surprise. I took off the paper to reveal a picture of a boat made out of painted shells with my Chinese name in white paint on the glass that covered it. Strangely, though, I was quite aware of a suddenly very different mood among the crowd, a sort of tension and uneasiness which, thankfully, seemed to dissipate as the celebratory bottles of soft drink were handed around.

In the office on Monday, Helen Ng, an Executive Officer responsible for running various district programmes and a couple of years older than I, asked how things had gone and I thought she might be able to help me understand the brief jolt that had seemed to have occurred. I gave her an account of the afternoon. 'And then,' I said, 'I was standing there with this gift and I looked as happy as I possibly could and went, "Thank you, thank you ... it's very beautiful."' Helen looked almost as shocked as the people in the courtyard the day before. 'So you opened it in front of the ones who had given it to you. We Chinese people would find that very impolite.' Patriotism tinged with defensiveness surged in my breast. 'Well, we English people would think it was exactly the right thing to do. I was just showing everyone how much I appreciated their kindness even though, to be honest, the picture wasn't really to my taste.' In an unconscious echo of Mrs Moy, Helen responded: 'But that is not our way. We Chinese people believe that we should be modest and not behave as if we expect special things or want to check a present to see if it's good enough. If you are given something like that you must never, never unwrap it but just accept it without making a big deal out of it and put it on one side. When you're at home you can find out what it is.'

She then approached the problem from another angle. 'There is a Chinese saying: "Westerners reading the results of the civil service entrance examination in old China." Because you start reading from the wrong edge of the page, you wouldn't understand the results and would think that the person who was actually bottom had come out top.' Helen sighed gently. 'The meaning of the saying is that Westerners get everything back to front.'

I would gladly have stayed longer in Kowloon City, learning more and having more experiences but our allotted time for this attachment was almost up and just under a year in the government had convinced me that it would be more prudent not to get involved in a battle with the Establishment Branch which looked after our postings and everything else to do with our welfare. Furthermore, the next move would be to a proper job, where I could really do something rather than being an extra for whom little tasks had to be invented, no matter how tactfully that was done.

We understood that we would likely become assistant district officers in the New Territories, which was an exciting prospect. I was therefore disappointed to discover that I was being sent to the New Territories Administration headquarters, which didn't have the same ring of adventurousness as being in the Outlying Islands or Castle Peak. And this feeling was compounded when I was told where my office would be: the North Kowloon Magistracy, a court building that was located in the urban area. How incongruous was that! All the same, the incongruous seemed to be the expected in Hong Kong and sometimes the outcome could be surprisingly good.

CHAPTER FOUR

Falling in Love

JUST AS I HAD SUPPOSED when I had heard about this posting to
the New Territories Administration headquarters, I was to be
working in an office that coordinated and controlled what was
going on in a still largely rural area from a building that was situated
in a crowded part of Kowloon, slightly up on a hill and overlooking
streets of little shops and tenement flats as well as some of the older
type of public housing estate.

Anyway, it was here that I fell in love even if the object of my
affection was rather unlikely. I fell in love with government files.
The New Territories administration had some that were particularly
seductive. One day, I opened an elderly looking one that had been
delivered to my in tray to discover what at first seemed like a
smudge, but on closer inspection to be a dead insect that had been
deliberately taped to a piece of paper at a date soon after the end
of the Second World War. *This is a sample of what is devastating
crops in the North New Territories. Could you please pass this to Father
Ryan and see if he can find out what it is,* said the handwritten note
beneath. 'Father Ryan and the Flying Plague': it could have been a
story from the Golden Age of English detective fiction. In fact,
Father Thomas Ryan was a Jesuit schoolmaster who had taught
English at Wah Yan, one of the Catholic schools that nurtured the
elite of Hong Kong, and he also wrote and broadcast on music and
the arts. Despite this unlikely background and his lack of knowledge of entomology or any of the allied subjects, the colonial
secretary had decided to make Father Ryan director of botany and
forestry as well as giving him responsibility for establishing a
Department of Agriculture. This was apparently because of the

favourable impression that Ryan had created in Chongqing, part of 'Free China' where he had lived during the war, having been allowed by the Japanese to avoid internment and leave Hong Kong because he was an Irishman and therefore considered neutral. It seems to have turned out to be a wise choice, however unconventional, since Ryan proved able to organise people and gather information, presumably also about that little fly that had been preserved for so long for me to find almost thirty years later. He worked hard at planting and pig breeding and setting up a Wholesale Vegetable Marketing Organisation, which helped to prevent exploitation of the otherwise vulnerable small farmers. And after a year or so he handed over to someone more professionally qualified and returned to the Jesuits.

Wonderful stories like this were hidden in so many of our files. A file could be rather like a novel but with some blanks that the reader had to guess at. The twists and turns of some ostensibly tedious policy issue would show how those dealing with it had become passionate about justifying their own opinions to the point of becoming over emotional and eventually losing touch with reason, like the central character in some small scale Shakespearean tragedy. Equally, a patient reading of old papers could tell you how to solve today's problem because buried in that mass of paper it was possible to find the misapprehension or misreading of a set of circumstances or characters that set off a train of mischief that lasted for years. The files were, of course, our sacred texts and if we could find something on the file signed or initialled by someone sufficiently senior that had once authorised something that we wanted to do then we had a precedent, one of the most valuable chess pieces that any civil servant could hold.

The priests and acolytes of the files were the clerks, at that time an important part of the entire team and possessors of relatively well paid and prestigious positions, although that of course has now all gone with the advent of e-mail, the paperless office and a still somewhat chaotic approach to the new age of communication, with less attention paid to record keeping. In those days, we relied on our clerks to open up new files and correctly index all the documents with details neatly written in red ink and carefully underlined with government-issue metal rulers and to string them together with the tags still known in colloquial Cantonese as 'blind man's tags' because a factory for disabled workers was their sole supplier. If you asked to 'see the related correspondence' you were relying on the clerks' intelligence and memory to help you to find the missing clues in one of those administrative mysteries. The clerks also operated the useful 'bring up' system, which allowed the administrator to scrawl in the margin 'Bring up in one week, one month, one year', or as Les Pogue, an impish man who never let things become too serious, wrote 'next muck spreading time'. The file would then disappear from one's desk for the specified amount of time although perhaps Les never saw his files again at all since it would surely have been beyond our cleverest clerks to work out what on earth he meant.

Most of the files were buff or white and open to all. The confidential files were pink and kept in the Confidential Registry, guarded by a heavy metal door and overseen by a British lady. To an outsider, this looked rather thrilling but we knew that most of those pink files were that colour because someone had decided 'better safe than sorry' and the contents usually never lived up to the cover. Like philatelists spotting a Penny Red or birdwatchers with a spoonbill, we cognoscenti were only impressed by the combination of orange and 'Secret' or, rarest of all, 'For UK eyes only'.

And what were we doing with all these files? Were they just to allow us to play some esoteric game of paper shuffling to keep ourselves occupied until we could end the day and then the years of our employment? Of course not; what we wrote and sent out had a real effect on real people's lives. What we were principally doing in those days was building three very large new towns: Tsuen Wan, Sha Tin and Tuen Mun. The first was an extension of an existing factory area, the second constructed in a largely agricultural area while the third was based on a small fishing village. The intention, although not entirely achieved in practice, was that these would be self-contained communities of hundreds of thousands of residents who would be able to work nearby and also find all the facilities that they needed locally. By the late 1970s Hong Kong was the world's leading manufacturer and exporter of garments, toys and games and watches and clocks. It was also highly significant in the production of fabric. Around that time, my husband was working in the Trade Department and a textile magnate once introduced himself with the words: 'My industry is shrinking, dyeing and finishing'. Very soon, that statement was true in other senses, and for other industries too. As Mainland China opened up, Hong Kong manufacturing moved across the northern border. Ownership and control remained in Hong Kong and more wealth than ever before was generated, but the finished products became China's exports and no longer Hong Kong's. In parallel, Hong Kong transformed itself into an economy based on services, particularly financial services and so employment opportunities began to cluster in the central business districts of Hong Kong Island and Tsim Sha Tsui and people who lived in Tsuen Wan, Sha Tin and Tuen Mun became commuters, taking long journeys into shops, restaurants and offices rather than walking to a nearby factory production line.

In the new towns, there were massive new public housing estates which also contained schools, markets and premises for welfare organisations. The flats might be small but the weatherproof self-contained accommodation was a great improvement on the squatter areas where so many were still living. They were also different in concept from the original resettlement estates, which offered only the most basic kind of shelter. These estates were intended to provide true public housing for all who needed it. There was careful planning of libraries, town halls with theatres, hospitals, post offices, police and fire stations and everything else required for daily life, on ratios calculated according to the size of expected population. Sha Tin was a little different from the others because it possessed some 'extras'; it was already the home of the Chinese University and had been chosen as the site of the new racecourse, with a dedicated railway line to serve it. In each of the three incipient new towns, the government's efforts were spearheaded by the district officer, who was an administrator and by the town manager, who was an engineer. Much time and effort was needed not just to build the new but also to negotiate clearance and compensation for what was in existence: farms, fishponds and villages. Considering the magnitude of what had to be done, the achievements were something to be proud of.

The overall feeling, then, was that all that paperwork was far from meaningless, and that by carrying it out conscientiously and with all the intelligence I could muster I was a useful part of a team that wanted to do things that were constructive and made our community better than it had been. This recurred throughout my working life; it was really a privilege to be able to earn a living in such a satisfying way.

Inevitably, things were not all rosy and one of the darkest stains was that of corruption. The Independent Commission Against Corruption was set up in 1974 but before then there was a period of a sort of phoney war in which the subject was getting closer and closer to the surface but had not quite broken through into full view. Although there was gossip about a few notorious names from the past, administrative officers were not corrupt. By now, it was more or less openly accepted that there was a great deal of corruption within the police and a certain amount within the public works departments and other front-line civil servants who were responsible for things like regulating hawkers and markets. There were also many tales circulating of the firemen who would not turn on their hoses until they had been paid and who subsequently required yet another payment to turn them off, and nurses in the public hospitals who expected a tip from the patient or the relatives in return for the most basic kind of care. The corrupt were cunning and would extract bribes from those local people whom they believed to be vulnerable while an expatriate would likely be left alone, which added to the ignorance of what was really going on. Conversely, if a local person could take a powerful looking expatriate along to an interview with an official who was probably just waiting for a bribe, then problems might suddenly melt away and the request that had previously been so difficult could be met. Joyce Bennett had this experience when she accompanied a friend to get immigration documents.

Everything had been brought into focus by the investigation of Chief Superintendent Peter Godber, who had clearly amassed a fortune through corrupt activities. Even though he had gone on the run and it was several years before he was returned to Hong Kong and was imprisoned, a new and more urgent debate had been engendered. Those who, even if not corrupt themselves, had grown used to the old way of doing things, would say, feebly, 'But Godber did such a great job during the '67 riots', rather like the Londoners who defended the East End gangsters on the grounds that they were always kind to their mothers. Similarly, the prevailing belief was that the systemic corruption in police stations was organised in such a way that 'non crimes' like prostitution were protected while 'real crimes' like murder would not be tolerated. All the same, it was deeply unsettling to consider the vulnerability that naïveté might create. In my then line of work, we were always asking for advice on matters connected with things like compensation to be paid to villagers, land values and so on. The answers would sound plausible and we didn't have the expertise to argue but there was so often the doubt at the back of the mind as to whether we were not somehow contributing to some illicit profit somewhere along the line.

An out-of-the-ordinary interlude occurred in 1975. Queen Elizabeth II visited the colony for the first time, and it was not only her first visit but the first by any reigning British monarch. Hong Kong displayed all the energy and enthusiasm that it had directed towards constructing vast amounts of public housing and to planning its underground railway, the building of which was about to begin, to drawing up an exciting and original programme for the queen and her consort, the Duke of Edinburgh. It was decided that one item would be an 'indoor garden party' in the Ocean Terminal on the Kowloon waterfront. This would neatly avoid the risks of the weather, which would certainly be hot and humid and possibly a downright downpour in May, the month of the visit, while also showcasing what was then Hong Kong's only large-scale shopping mall. Positioned among the throng of guests would be a few groups of selected citizens, and it was decided that as a novel touch, these groups would be introduced to the royal visitors by the youngest members of the administrative grade. I was chosen to be one of the introducers; my group was to represent various aspects of the religious life of Hong Kong and was to include the Reverend Joyce Bennett. What could be nicer or more straightforward?

Naturally, several rehearsals were required for this important event. My group, as might be expected, turned up on time and obediently took their positions.

I noticed that Abbot Sik, an imposing figure swathed in orange robes who represented the Buddhists, was also wrapped in a deep silence but I supposed that that simply reflected his contemplative approach to life. The party representing the queen and entourage were approaching; the arrangement was that the royal couple would divide up and each walk through different parts of the venue and we were on Her Majesty's route. As on the day itself, interpreting from Cantonese to English for the queen would be the responsibility of Denis Bray, the secretary for home affairs, a senior member of the administrative grade who although British had been brought up by missionary parents in Southern China and whose spoken Cantonese was as perfect as any native speaker's. Now the Royal party was up with us and rather suddenly the venerable abbot floated forward as if on wheels, adjusted his wooden prayer beads, let a calming smile play across his beatific countenance and spoke at great length. There was some consternation, though, on Denis's face. 'I can't understand a word he's saying. He's speaking Mandarin.'

There was no shame in this admission; in those days there was no official contact with the Chinese government, and indeed there was no intercourse between the two places, apart from the Hong Kong Chinese who would cross the border at festivals to visit relatives in Guangdong Province, which was the native place of the overwhelming majority in Hong Kong. Tourists and other residents of Hong Kong were restricted to going to the Lok Ma Chau Lookout Point in the New Territories and staring, through binoculars or telescope, across a rather uninformative vista of paddy fields and fishponds, its only distinction being that we knew that we were looking at China, otherwise sealed off from the outside world. As far as we were concerned, Chinese language meant the Cantonese of southern China and the traditional full-form characters handed

The Portsmouth High School team in the television quiz show "Top of the Form". I am third from the left.

Our TV performance earned us tea with the Lord Mayor of Portsmouth. I am sitting nearest to him.

Lady Margaret Hall's team in the 1972 season of the "University Challenge" TV quiz. I am sitting above my surname "Howard."

The corner shop in Portsmouth which my parents owned and ran in the late 1960s/1970s. They kept the name "Hawkes" from the previous owner. The dapper gent at the door is Uncle Fred, my father's brother-in-law.

The last of England. In September 1972 I was bridesmaid at my best college friend's wedding, which took place in London. A couple of weeks later, my dress came with me to my new life in Hong Kong.

Central District, Victoria Harbour and the Kowloon peninsula, seen from The Peak.
Photo: Formasia Books Ltd.

Hong Kong Island's Central District, headquarters of government and business. *Photo: Formasia Books Ltd.*

A working junk. A common sight in Victoria Harbour in the 1970s.

1972. Joyce Bennett on the balcony of her flat overlooking the industrial area of Kwun Tong in Kowloon.

1973. Performing the opening ceremony of the social services centre in the Kowloon Walled City.

Inside the Walled City social services centre for the remainder of the ceremony.

View from my balcony in the Hermitage in 1973. The swathe of green identifies Victoria Barracks where British military personnel lived in bungalows amid lush surroundings of trees, birds and butterflies. This area became Hong Kong Park later on. On the seaward side of the open area of car parking is Murray House: I did not realise that within 15 years its stones would be under my custody. The tall white building in the centre is the Furama Hotel. The bulge at the top is the revolving restaurant. Care was needed if you put your handbag on the floor beside you: too far away and it would be a full circuit before you saw it again. To the left of the Furama is Sutherland House, where Cable & Wireless was located, a place of Christmas pilgrimages. In those days when an international 'phone call was difficult and expensive, it was necessary to book beforehand and physically go to the office in order to shout a few seasonal platitudes as loudly and clearly as if they were to be transmitted to England under their own power.

1975. Queen Elizabeth II visits Hong Kong. That's Her Majesty under the round dark hat (honestly, it really is). I am to the left of her as she meets a selection of dignitaries.

July 1976. David Akers-Jones gives me away when I marry Michael Cartland.

Myself, Anna Ding and Michael after the ceremony.

Our wedding reception. The plan had been for a barbecue on the roof of the Excelsior Hotel but the typical July rains forced us inside. Archie Chan, husband of Anson, is on the far left. In the middle are Edith and Li Fook-kow (FK), who was the third local Chinese to be admitted into the Administrative Grade. He served at the highest levels of Government and at that time was Secretary for Social Services. Some twenty years later his son Andrew was appointed the first Chief Justice of the Hong Kong SAR. Anson Chan sits next to FK and next to her is Hamish Macleod, later Financial Secretary. In the group standing behind, Anton Irving is to the left of me and we are facing Lena Liu.

Late 1970s. A young refugee after the hazardous journey across the South China Sea from Vietnam in a leaky river boat. *Photo: Formasia Books Ltd.*

Newly arrived refugee boats from Vietnam were held at a raft in the harbour where they could be supplied with food and water until they had completed the quarantine period for bubonic plague. *Photo: Formasia Books Ltd.*

The front entrance of Dunrose, the house provided for the District Officer, Yuen Long.

Mainland sailing junks or river boats could often be seen moored off the Western praya of Hong Kong Island in the early 1970s. *Photo: Formasia Books Ltd.*

1975. Liz King sits in the stern of the *Bull 'n' Bear* as we return from a day's hiking on Lamma. An outing like that was as relaxing as a whole week's holiday.

Liz chats to Haminah Wahab and and me at Liz and Colin Bosher's Hong Kong wedding reception in 1978. In the foreground, Michael is chatting to Lau Wong-fat, already prominent in Tuen Mun and later to become chairman of the Heung Yee Kuk.

Left: Liz on Repulse Bay Beach. Right: Alan Beith (later Lord Beith), a visiting Member of Parliament being briefed by Government architect Trevor Holmes on the traditional craftsmanship being used to restore the Tai Fu Tai mansion in the New Territories.

1979. Anna and Arthur Starling at the party we gave at Dunrose in honour of their wedding. We set out tables on our wide verandah for our guests.

Christmas Day 1977 on the front steps of Dunrose. Denis and Cecilia Shackleton are standing at the back, below them Anton Irving behind Anna Ding and to the right Michael behind me.

London, 1985. Party after our daughter Caroline's christening. From left: me, Caroline, Rev. Joyce Bennett.

A corner of the front garden of Dunrose. Pippa our dog and I at the foot of the official flagpole. Pippa came from the SPCA and was a real mixture. When we moved house we felt that flat would not suit her and gave her to the Gurkha Engineers Officers' Mess next door. They looked after her devotedly but sadly could not prevent her running onto the road, perhaps to look for us, where she was killed by a car. The naval cannon must surely have had an interesting history but for us its purpose was decorative only.

At the party following the christening of our daughter Caroline in London. From left: my mother, Joyce Bennett, Auntie Edith (my mother's sister).

1992. Girl Power rules in broadcasting. From left: Elle Shum, Commissioner for Television and Entertainment Licensing, myself, at that time Deputy Secretary for Recreation and Culture with responsibility for broadcasting policy and Cheung Man-yee, the famously charismatic Director of RTHK.

The 1994 Chinese New Year celebrations at RTHK. In the middle of the line-up for the toasts is Sir Run Run Shaw, patriarch of TVB and Shaw Studios as well as a major philanthropist. He stands out in his traditional Chinese attire, with a white cuffed jacket. To his right is Stephen Ng of Wharf Cable and to his left Hamish Macleod, the Financial Secretary, Sir Roger Lobo of the Broadcasting Authority, Cheung Man-yee of RTHK, Gary Davy of STAR TV and myself.

1995. Party to celebrate the full re-opening of Ocean Park. To my right is John Corcoran, the then newly arrived Chief Executive of the Park. I don't know the identity of the gentleman to my left but he was a lot of fun.

1995. Each year the Governor would give his Policy Address setting out proposals for the legislative year ahead and there would be follow-up press conferences by senior civil servants. When I was Acting Secretary for Recreation and Culture I decided to hold our event at the Academy for Performing Arts, giving that estimable institution some positive publicity, I hoped, and with their School of Chinese dance ensuring attractive photos.

30 June 1997. Shelley Lee's handover-cum-birthday party. From left: Henry Ching, me, Shelley, Michael, Jack So.

Ladies lunch at Liz Bosher's house. Standing behind me are Cheung Man-yee, Shelley Lee, Liz and Lily Yam. We worked together closely in the late 1980s and early 1990s.

down through the centuries, not the classic Mandarin of the officials in the capital and the simplified characters mandated by Chairman Mao.

Anyway, that afternoon in the Ocean Terminal, a saviour was at hand. The Anglican Archdeacon Cheung, small and neat in his dog collar and purple shirtfront, stepped forward from his place in the receiving line. 'I speak Mandarin,' he said. 'Perhaps I can help.' He listened intently to a long peroration from Abbot Sik. 'He wishes to offer a special Buddhist blessing to Her Majesty the Queen.' There was a hasty reaction from among the entourage. 'Very wrong. Not proper at all. Who knows, it may even be in conflict with her position as head of the Church of England.' The archdeacon offered no advice on this tricky issue but continued mildly, 'Well, anyway, if it would be of assistance I could interpret on the day itself, just as I've been doing now. It would be quite easy. At the appropriate time, I could just come forward, stand between the queen and Abbot Sik, and then go back to my own place afterwards.' This kind offer provoked something approaching panic among the officials. 'No, no, that's impossible. If anyone moves out of line and towards Her Majesty, that person will be perceived as a threat, certainly liable to be tackled and overpowered by the bodyguards and in extreme circumstances, possibly shot.' We should clearly stay in line both physically and theologically and cause no further trouble.

The next rehearsal threw up another tricky issue, from a different quarter although, again, the person involved had seemed rather subdued. This was Mother Joseph of the Little Sisters of the Poor; like Abbot Sik, she was swathed in robes although hers were white and her hair and neck were covered so that one saw only her rather pale face and bright blue eyes. At the end of the afternoon, Mother Joseph asked if she might speak to me privately and, miraculously enough, we did manage to find a secluded spot. 'I want to make a confession to you,' she said. I find it hard to convey how profoundly I felt this request was the wrong way round but I tried to be open minded and assume an accommodating expression, prepared to hear anything. She looked sad. 'I am not Mother Joseph.' She had succeeded in surprising me quite a lot within the course of about thirty seconds. 'If you are not Mother Joseph, then who are you?'

'I am Sister Robina. You see, Mother Joseph is Belgian and she doesn't speak very good English and she is rather shy. When the invitation came for her, she said "Oh, this isn't really meant for me. It would be much better if one of you British girls were to go." And I am Scottish so she picked me. I work in one of the homes that we run for elderly people. A lot of them are confused and call us by all sorts of names and don't know what our real names are so I thought well, this wouldn't be so different from that and it wouldn't matter really. However, as time has gone by, I'm not so sure and I've felt more and more uncomfortable about the whole thing.'

We were already past office hours so in the evening I telephoned Eric Ho, the director of home affairs, who was in charge of this function, and explained the situation. When I had done this, his response was: 'Well, Rachel, all I can say is that these nuns don't seem to know right from wrong.'

Finally, we were at last at the day of the 'Indoor Garden Party' and the small figure of the genuine Elizabeth II was genuinely making her way towards us. Here was a new difficulty. Despite all the preparations, I had not made any allowance for being over-whelmed by a catch in the throat and a buzzing brain that kept diverting me from my duties with thoughts of 'It's the queen. My goodness me, this is the real queen right here and now.' Poor woman, she must be so used to it; at that time, she had already spent more than twenty years continually confronted by this kind of nervousness. Did she guess then that she was one day going to have to celebrate sixty years of this sort of toil? Anyway, I managed to get out everyone's names and a few details about them without any serious mangling and she asked each one soothing, easy to answer questions.

And everything went swimmingly. Sister Robina was introduced as Sister Robina. All the right people had been properly briefed and so when Archdeacon Cheung put himself in position to interpret for the abbot no one had him marked down as a potential assassin and he was just allowed to do his stuff. The abbot's remarks were really very long given the nature of the occasion but the archdeacon translated them graciously but rather briefly and blandly as general good wishes towards Her Majesty and the people of Great Britain. I must say, though, that I have always assumed that it was the forbidden special Buddhist blessing and that the archdeacon saved the day with his diplomacy so that all sides were satisfied. Anyway, our few minutes of glory were quickly over and the queen went off to meet stars of the Cantonese film industry, who had doubtless been less trouble to rehearse.

There were to be no more royal visits for a few years and in the meantime my own little life would see its share of events that were just as momentous as far as I was concerned.

The first was a posting to another job: from the New Territories administration to the Finance Branch in the Government Secretariat. This was taking me even further from the grassroots but it was to be regarded as an honour. Being sent to the Finance Branch was the administrative equivalent of recruitment into the British SAS. It was known for unremitting hard work, so perhaps generations had found it consoling to consider themselves members of an elite as they looked out of their office windows into grey, dark evenings on which other, less privileged people had already been relaxing at home for a couple of hours.

We were in the Colonial Secretariat in Lower Albert Road, the nerve centre of the government, with nothing higher but Government House, home and office of the governor, appropriately located in Upper Albert Road, with a lane running between the two so that it would take less than a minute to go up for a meeting. The governor, naturally, did not descend.

No auditor could have been too critical of our accommodation. It was serviceable but definitely not luxurious. I do not think that there was an artwork anywhere in the entire complex of three wings (East, Main and West) and our sturdy office furniture was mainly constructed by those who in Cantonese slang were known to be 'eating royal rice', i.e., residents of the local gaols. On the other hand, we were fortunate enough to be close to the Botanic Gardens and Lower Albert Road itself was home to fine banyan trees as well as a giant Burmese rosewood outside the front door of the Main Wing so there were always plenty of squirrels and birds, including the noisy cockatoos who were supposed to be descended from pets that had been let free in the confusion of the Japanese invasion of 1941. The entire complex was completely open with no surrounding fences and no guards. Inside, the Security Branch was shut off within a locked steel cage door but otherwise it was perfectly possible to walk around the corridors and knock on any doors. The telephone lines were equally open and there were circulars issued about the need to be particularly careful about Ranjan Marwah, an enterprising journalist on the racy *Star* newspaper, who was very skilled at phoning up naïve civil servants, giving the impression that he was a colleague and extracting all sorts of interesting information from them.

It was not of course just a matter of putting in long hours in the Finance Branch but also the intellectual effort that was expected. The ordeal here was the Tuesday morning sessions with the deputy financial secretary. On those days a queue would form outside his office of Finance Branch staff who had draft papers that needed eventually to be approved by the Finance Committee of the Legislative Council at one of its Friday afternoon meetings. Although the Legislative Council (colloquially known as LegCo) is Hong Kong's equivalent of a parliament and it exercises some of the same functions, particularly the passing of laws, at that time the council's members were all appointed by the governor and were outnumbered by the most senior civil servants, secretaries, in effect ministers, holding various portfolios who were appointed as 'official' members of LegCo. One of LegCo's major functions was to debate and pass the colony's annual budget but during the year there were many reasons to require additional financial approvals, perhaps for new capital expenditure projects or to get supplementary provision to deal with unexpected needs or budget overruns. There were fewer official members of the Finance Committee and it met in private. Papers put to that committee were thus vulnerable to being voted down or put back for revision. It did not happen very often because the appointed members of LegCo were mainly drawn from establishment-minded businessmen and professionals but when it did it was regarded as a great embarrassment to a government that had not been competent enough to put forward watertight proposals.

On Tuesday mornings we had to get an approving initial from the deputy financial secretary or principal assistant financial secretary so that our papers could be issued to the Finance Committee in time for their next meeting. The method was just like an Oxford tutorial except that we did not physically have to read out our drafts. Instead we handed a copy to this senior colleague and sat nervously across the big table as he asked piercing questions about the substance, the wording or the figures. If your answers weren't good enough you suffered the humiliation of taking it away to bring it back the following week in an improved form and, of course, this was no academic exercise that we were involved in.

I was dealing with the entire education budget for Hong Kong and I was aware that if I failed to convince then, say, the programme for building, equipping and staffing the new technical institutes to provide vocational training would be held up. I recall that the high cost of the machinery said to be essential for the courses in printing was a particular stumbling block and I acquired a superficial and temporary expertise in the subject as I went back time after time until the paper was agreed. This was the essence of what we generalist administrative officers were meant to do: to get a grasp of diverse specialisms sufficient to understand whether what was being put to us made any sense and then to translate it into terms clear enough for other intelligent laypeople to understand. This was not something peculiar to Hong Kong; it had been the traditional approach to running the British Empire. It was somehow believed that, if you had studied, say, Greek and Latin Classics at Oxford or Cambridge you had thereby demonstrated the possession of sufficient innate ability to be able to pick up any subject in the realm of government and take an intelligent lead on it. This was understandably infuriating to professional people who were our colleagues and used AO as much as an insult as a factual term. It had however proved effective in practice; the system was quite uniform so, for example, the procedures for applying for more money were always the same even if what we wanted to do with the money could vary. All our papers were written in English in those days; it was taken for granted that anyone involved in any way in the higher reaches of government, whether British or

Chinese, would be sufficiently fluent in the language to be able to cope with that.

It could have all seemed rather bureaucratic but the mid-1970s were the heyday of Hong Kong's social and economic development and so, for instance, my success with the printing machinery played its small part in the creation of a world leading industry that is still renowned for the high quality of the books it produces.

The Tuesday torture sessions were particularly enlightening when Henry Ching was the one to approve the papers. I had the greatest respect for Henry but I wondered whether he was entirely human. He never had a hair out of place and when we were working on Saturday mornings, which we did at least twice a month, he would complete *The Times* crossword, as reprinted in the *South China Morning Post,* with extraordinary speed. He had an uncanny ability to glance at appendices full of figures and unerringly spot which one 'couldn't be quite right'. He was equally precise about the use of language and the logic or otherwise of an argument. To humbly submit a draft to Henry's thoughtful gaze was a great learning experience. The enquiries were as piercing as my former philosophy tutor's but the consequences of getting it wrong were more real than the miscounting of the number of angels on a pinhead.

My own theories about how to do this sort of writing evolved and I boiled it down to four questions to be asked of every single sentence. Is this true? Do I know what it means? Does it add anything of value to this piece of writing? If I am advocating a change of policy, have I clearly explained why it would be justified? It is surprising, or perhaps not, how much can be discarded if these principles are ruthlessly applied!

The Finance Branch year was geared towards production of Hong Kong's annual budget and we worked to a strict schedule to achieve it. The budget would be unveiled in February but the aim, usually met, was that the entire text of the estimates would have been sent off to the Government Printer by Christmas Eve. There was no outsourcing and the Government Printer was a civil servant too. We all managed to keep secret what was in this mighty tome of hundreds of pages in the interval between drafting and publication. It represented the culmination of many weeks of negotiation with individual departments over how much money they would have in the following year, how their approved activities would be described and so on. The finale was a mammoth exercise in proof reading. We would feel as if our eyes were permanently crossed as we checked words and figures over and over again and it would be an unpopular person who suddenly discovered a whole chunk of data which had mysteriously been left out and for which room had to be found, even at the cost of enormous consequential recalculations. Despite the frayed tempers, teamwork prevailed and the expectation of something reliable as a basis for Hong Kong's future growth was met. It was up to the financial secretary to steer the ship in the right direction and make the big decisions on taxation and expenditure but we knew that he couldn't have done it without us!

However significant the preparation of the budget, there were more important events as far as I was concerned. On 3 July 1976 I married Michael Cartland, a fellow administrative officer, who was a few years older than myself. He had spent five years as a district officer in the Solomon Islands, a British protectorate way out in the Pacific Ocean, before coming to Hong Kong in 1972. After a spell in the Social Services Branch of the Colonial Secretariat, he had been made private secretary to the governor, Sir Murray MacLehose.

Michael is a true child of empire. His father, Sir George Cartland, had left Manchester in the depressed 1930s to join the Colonial Service and had gone to the Gold Coast, later renamed Ghana. Although the catarrh that had plagued him since childhood in the smoggy industrial north of England cleared up almost as soon as he reached Africa, it was otherwise far from healthy and he found himself jumping up the seniority list as colleagues met premature deaths through tropical diseases like Blackwater Fever; apocryphal stories told of the medicine cupboards to be opened in extreme circumstances which, in the absence of any remedies, contained only a bottle of champagne intended to make the unfortunate victim's last hours as happy as possible. There were other risks too, such as the need to mediate between warring tribes armed with the sharp pangas that they normally used on their cocoa crops. He ended his career as the last British chief secretary in Uganda before that country gained independence in 1962.

He died, aged ninety-five, in 2008, his long life a vindication of the principle of 'the survival of the fittest'. When we cleared out his study, we found that he had kept all sorts of government papers from his Uganda days, of almost fifty years before. In circumstances so very different from Hong Kong's, they showed the same preoccupations with housing, schools and medical facilities. Those papers now repose in Oxford, kept in acid free folders to preserve them for any scholars who might be interested, by the Bodleian Library of Commonwealth and African Studies, which is accommodated in Rhodes House, just south of my old college, Lady Margaret Hall. The ceremonial sword and pith helmet embellished with the Royal Coat of Arms that were part of his dress uniform perch on top of the bookcase in our sitting room in Hong Kong; they are the same as the Hong Kong administrative officers, the 'cadets', used to have.

Michael and I arranged our wedding in rather a hurry, taking advantage of the governor's sudden decision to take a short holiday, thus leaving the way clear for his staff to do the same. I was given away by David Akers-Jones, my old boss from the New Territories administration and Joyce Bennett assisted at the ceremony. The Independent Commission Against Corruption had been established a couple of years previously and we were conscious of the need to obey all its strictures. These included limits on the value of gifts that civil servants could receive on occasions like weddings and birthdays and all our guests observed this ceiling of HK$400. The only person who breached the rule was the governor himself. As he rushed off, he instructed his ADC, our friend, Denis Shackleton, to 'give Michael a case of champagne'. Denis, making best use of his freedom to decide how this instruction should be carried out, concluded that the best Pol Roger from the Government House cellars would probably fit the bill.

Being married inevitably brought many changes. Once back at work, I was telephoned by someone in the Treasury with whom I'd been dealing on some of the finer points of school financing but who otherwise didn't know me well. He complained about a draft that I'd sent him and said that he'd much preferred the version he'd had earlier from someone called 'Miss Howard'.

Just a few years previously, the system still prevailed under which a female officer who married was forced to give up her place in the 'permanent and pensionable establishment'. The government would give her a marriage gratuity, rather like an old fashioned father handing over a dowry and she might then be employed on month-to-month terms. This was no longer true but at my own choice I decided to change my status to that of an officer on contract. In those days, government pensions were not transferable in any way and one had to work right up to the pensionable age before being able to get a dollar. I was afraid that this would give me insufficient flexibility if, say, Michael's retirement date arrived and we wanted to leave Hong Kong. In the event, this decision affected my career in connection with the arrangements for the transfer of sovereignty from Hong Kong to China, especially since, as it turned out, we never did want to leave.

My marriage also led to a return to the New Territories although this time to live rather than to work and it also had separate but significant impacts on Anna Ding and Joyce Bennett. These all lay just a little way into the future.

CHAPTER FIVE

Creed and People

BY THE MIDDLE OF 1976, I had reached important milestones. I was a married lady and I felt firmly committed to life as an administrative officer in the Hong Kong government. Like so many others, I had thought in the early days that this might prove just to be a temporary phase and that, at some point, I might go 'home'. Although I was developing an ambivalence about what 'home' was anyway, I was settled and comfortable in Hong Kong. It was not just a matter of enjoying it but rather that there was some sort of prevailing philosophy that appealed to my deepest instincts.

It would, of course, be wrong to be too sentimental about Hong Kong and its history. Its foundation lay in the Opium Wars, essentially drug dealing backed up by imperial power, an episode which was hard enough to defend or explain away even in the nineteenth century, and often brushed under the carpet in the twentieth century when those illicit profits had been laundered into legitimate commercial enterprises. It would be wrong also to be too indulgent towards the administrative grade and the Britons who at that time still made up most of its directorate ranks. Although it was blessed with a sort of mythology of the mandarins, supposedly a brilliant cadre imbued with nobility and uprightness, I knew all too well that among my expatriate colleagues there were those who were drunkards, stupid, arrogant or cynical, or a combination of these. Somehow, though, there was enough of something decent to make things, on balance, quite all right.

It is only recently that I have been able to understand better what that was. I found a few words from someone I never knew and who was no longer in Hong Kong when I arrived. Sir David Trench was the predecessor of Sir Murray MacLehose as governor of Hong Kong. He left temporarily during the 1967 riots, but before his departure he made a radio broadcast. In it, he alluded to the violence and abusive language and said, 'It is, of course, difficult for us, brought up to value reason and fairness, and to respect the views of others, to understand what makes people speak and act in the way this minority in our midst has done.'

This sentence represented what it was that made Hong Kong so lovable to me and what seemed to me the engine that drove the best of the administrative service. There is nothing grandiose here, nothing about the 'British way' or the 'Western way' and indeed the whole tone of this short passage is geared towards a cohesive community in which there are common values which do not attach to nationality or ideology. Interestingly, too, there is no reference to prosperity, economic development or the operation of free markets which, as the years went by, came to be touted as an intrinsic part of the Hong Kong success story. Reason, fairness and respect for the views of others . . . wouldn't the whole world like to live in communities that abided by those principles and isn't it rare to be able to do so?

I was led to ponder what the roots were of this value system that I found so attractive and reached some conclusions. First of all, it was connected to things that were strengthening during the nineteenth century, growing in parallel with the less attractive ruthlessness which forced the 'Unequal Treaties' upon a weakened Chinese nation. The importance attached to 'fair play' was nourished by the traditions associated with the team games whose rules British men codified and which both boys and men played with such enthusiasm. Second, the racism and sense of superiority which were such an unpleasant feature of many years of British imperialism were modified by contrary arguments that became a feature of the cultural discourse of the 1930s. Reluctant colonial civil servants like Leonard Woolf and George Orwell influenced to some extent the way in which everyone thought, and produced people who were somewhat less sure of themselves; and all the better for it. Third, service in the Second World War seemed for many to sharpen the

moral sense rather than to erode it, to make people more determined to create more just societies once peace was finally achieved.

This was undeniably a philosophy developed by a narrow section
of the world's population: white middle-class British males. However, once floated out upon Hong Kong harbour, as it were, it
became a boat which was willing to accept many different sorts of
passenger. I was able to get on board with it although my own
background and, come to that, my gender did not necessarily reflect
it and so could local Chinese members of the administrative grade.
In a sense, our own personalities became somewhat subsumed and
we found new and important identities as administrative officers,
which meant more than just routine work done from day to day.
Those of us who were of British origin developed, in some respects,
an ambivalence towards the country in which we had been born
and brought up. If, as sometimes happened, issues arose in which
Hong Kong's interests seemed to be at variance with the UK's we
had not a moment's hesitation in taking the former's part and
fighting for its benefit. Our Chinese colleagues, similarly, looked
to the welfare of the local community as their prime concern.
Although Chinese culture and history was important to them and
their families, contemporary China itself was too shut off to have
much impact on thoughts and feelings, coupled with the fact that
many were the children of those who had escaped to what they
judged would be a better life in Hong Kong.

There were handbooks and circulars telling us how to do our
job, in terms of how to write the variety of official documents,
process them and present them in proper form. At the same time,
there were many things that were not written down but which we
absorbed as the correct way of doing things because of the behaviour
that we could see all around us. Records were important, not just
the files of papers but also the minutes of meetings. Succinct notes
of decisions taken and main points made were normally preferred
to reams of waffle that quoted every little remark. Everyone who
had been at the meeting was given an opportunity to comment and
question, to suggest a more accurate rendering of what had taken
place. Once that had been done, however, the minutes became
sacrosanct. It was your bad luck if the position that you had taken

so firmly turned out to be wrong or misguided; it was completely unacceptable to try and improve the situation by sneakily changing the record.

Another principle that was understood by all was that of 'declaring an interest'. It was basic that you could not be involved in a case where you stood to benefit without letting everyone else understand how it was that you might be considered to be tainted. It was quite straightforward for those of us who had grown up within the system. In 2003, the financial secretary, Antony Leung had to resign because it came out that he had bought a new car for his family in the period between completion of the budget and its publication, and, even though he came to know, from his position of privilege, that the intention was to raise the first registration tax on such cars, he never chose to reveal this apparently unfairly gained advantage. When this information leaked out as a result of active and determined journalism, administrative officers of the old school were shocked to the core. It seemed as if the financial secretary might just as well go out in the street without his trousers on as to ignore something as basic as this. It was noteworthy that Mr Leung had come into the government late in his career and had not had the opportunities we had had to learn certain thought processes over such a long period that they became instinctive.

We also had our own way of discussing things and conducting ourselves. Compared with modern people and perhaps with others of different nationalities also, we were diffident and not outspoken. We were supposed to be truthful without being too blunt and we would try to answer questions; if we didn't know the answer we would say so and offer to come back later with the information. Again, this descended from some nineteenth-century British concept of how a gentleman should behave but in this case there was a particularly good match with traditional Chinese ideas of propriety. That culture probably valued modesty even more than ours did but there was enough common ground for us to achieve in the Hong Kong government a partnership that worked well.

Another common element in our two cultures that made it easier for us to work together was that we each had a more or less equal sense of superiority. Each side felt that over hundreds (in the case of Britain) and thousands (in the case of China) of years we had managed to reach some sort of pinnacle of civilisation. This was in spite of periods of decline experienced by both sides. We could all therefore enjoy a certain quiet self-confidence that helped us to tolerate what we might perceive as the others' oddities.

This Hong Kong government way of doing things made it easier for me to be one of the small number of women in the administrative grade than it might otherwise have been. Even though I was not the only one, there were few enough of us scattered across the various secretariat branches and government departments for me to expect, for many years, a high chance that I would be the only female at any meeting I attended. I feel sure that many of the men I worked with were not comfortable with women being recruited at a senior level. There had been a rather ridiculous practice of informally giving to intelligent women in relatively junior positions a disproportionate amount of responsibility. The prime example of this was Mrs Bolton, the secretary to the quartering officer, who ended up sorting out all sorts of knotty problems. Often, when considering launching a new project, the cry would go up: 'We need to find someone like Mrs Bolton to work here.' By which, I'm afraid, they meant: 'We need to find an able woman whom we can underpay for exercising her skills'. Anyway, their sense of fair play had eventually led the male establishment to try giving some women a chance and their good manners made it difficult for them to voice any misgivings.

Once, after a meeting in the New Territories Administration headquarters, we were standing around in small groups in the conference room, chatting about this and that. I suddenly became aware of a great stream of swear words emanating from the knot of people next to the one of which I was part. The cursing was nothing terrible, 'bloodys' and 'buggers' and so on, and I was not perturbed. Nonetheless, a silence fell; no one said anything but it was as if there was an invisible speech bubble floating at ceiling level: 'John, there is a lady present!' The culprit could obviously read the speech bubble too because he simply said forthrightly, 'Well, if she thinks she's going to do a man's job then she's got to learn to listen to men's talk.' Eyebrows were raised, lips compressed and the floor stared at.

Then someone coughed and suggested lunch and the incident was not mentioned then or at any other time. Nothing else like that ever took place either.

If the values that permeated the Administrative Service were basically sound, we were greatly helped to be effective by some fortunate circumstances.

The system was very much geared to helping the civil service run things with minimum hindrance. As LegCo fulfilled some of the same constitutional functions as the British Parliament the Executive Council (ExCo) was Hong Kong's equivalent of the cabinet, considering all major policy recommendations before steps were taken to implement them or to place them before LegCo, and yet the members of both were essentially the choice of the governor, even if they had to be approved by the Foreign Office in London. The norm was that these would be members of the local community who, whatever their ethnic origins, spoke very fluent English and could easily deal with all the papers, many of them quite technical, being written in that language. The appointed members might offer advice, and sometimes very wise advice it was too, coming as it did from capable businessmen or distinguished professionals but, in the final analysis, the governor would make the decisions and could expect the Executive Council to fall in behind him, while on the Legislative Council he had a majority comprising the senior civil servants, who were the 'official members'. What prevented this strange system from turning into a frightful tyranny, apart from the moral scruples of those who ran it, was that at the end of an admittedly long, trans-oceanic cord was the democratically elected British House of Commons where questions would be raised if it became clear that there was something unsatisfactory going on in Hong Kong and whose members would, if necessary, press the government of the day to take action.

It is quite common to describe the 1970s and 1980s as Hong Kong's Golden Age, a period of immense progress. All the factors that I have described contributed to this, but there was also the great good fortune of having money to play with. Hong Kong remained a low-tax economy throughout but government revenues rose as prosperity increased thanks to the growth of highly profitable industry which in turn was due to its almost insanely hard-working population. Refugees from China with nothing to their names would start off on factory production lines, learn skills, scrape together the money to strike out on their own, put in phenomenal hours, exert every bit of brainpower and imagination they possessed and some would become hugely wealthy themselves while also providing employment for the hundreds of thousands who sought to enter from Mainland China. The result for us in the civil service was that we could look at dreadful living conditions or the lack of desirable facilities and, instead of just wringing our hands, could make a plan to make things better, and get it all done speedily too.

All the same, this was not a blind and mindless process like some sort of chemical reaction in which certain things were brought together and just reacted with each other to produce a predictable outcome. Individuals and the decisions that they made had a crucial impact even if they themselves were also shaped by the influences that prevailed in Hong Kong. I saw some of these people at work and felt the effects of what others did.

Sir Murray MacLehose, later Lord MacLehose of Beoch, was governor from 1971 to 1982, so we are now able to look back on his period in office and take a more considered view on it. Certainly, from the point of view of social change within Hong Kong, it can be judged a considerable success and one for which he deserves a large measure of personal credit, even if some historians argue, probably rightly, that insufficient attention is paid to his predecessor Sir David Trench and the foundations that he laid. With hindsight, too, it seems that MacLehose was too ambitious in the line he took at his historic 1979 meeting with Deng Xiaoping, then vice premier of the People's Republic of China and that as a result difficult foundations were laid for the subsequent discussions on Hong Kong's future as he provoked Deng into making forceful statements about the irrevocability of the principle of the territory's return; but we in Hong Kong at the time, even within the government, were not aware of this as matters surrounding these talks were kept secret from all but a very few and the implications not well understood within the community.

Sir Murray was, by Hong Kong standards, immensely tall, being well over six feet and he was lean without being skinny. This made him a naturally imposing presence and on the rare occasions when he walked through the Central District with just the ever-present bodyguard, he was quickly spotted and a ripple would go through the crowds with a sense that here was someone outstanding and not just as a result of his position. To be governor of Hong Kong, or after 1997, chief executive, was a demanding role, with ceremonial functions as well as political and practical. It was as well that Sir Murray could cut an impressive figure, as some of the clothes that went with the job could easily make the wearer look rather silly. There was, for example, his outfit as chief Scout of Hong Kong, with a Boy Scout beret to be pulled over to one side as well as the governor's dress uniform, the design of which was clearly descended unchanged from the nineteenth century and which was topped with a helmet complete with a plume of ostrich feathers. This was worn only on the most formal of occasions, including arrival in Hong Kong to be sworn into office. Some were a little disappointed that the last governor, Chris Patten, did not keep up the tradition but instead arrived in a lounge suit and never wore the full rig.

The governor always had an ADC, selected from among the officers of the Royal Hong Kong Police Force who looked after the ceremonial and logistic aspects of life at Government House. While my husband, Michael worked as the governor's private secretary, the ADC was Denis Shackleton, who became a good friend of ours. Denis had a similar uniform to the governor's, also with a plumed helmet. It once happened at the passing out parade of graduates of the Prison Officers' Training School that as Denis got out of the official Rolls-Royce, just behind the governor he gave his helmet a slight knock on the roof of the car. This had rather dramatic consequences since it dislodged the plume and as Denis stood to attention in his proper position slightly behind the governor a small shower of white feathers cascaded down to come to rest at his feet.

Sir Murray himself had no particular love of ceremony nor of all these fancy clothes and, as often as possible, would go in shirtsleeves to visit housing estates, youth camps, markets and so on. He positively encouraged civil servants to give up the European style of suit with jacket, collar and tie and instead adopt the 'safari suit', consisting of lightweight trousers with an untucked short sleeved shirt in the same fabric with plenty of pockets. Sadly, however, this practical garment did not prove a long-lived trend; it seemed that people felt more comfortable in the conventional and retreated back into the previous type of attire even though it was warmer, which in Hong Kong's climate led to increased use of air conditioning.

It was, nonetheless, not exactly relaxing to be in Sir Murray's company. There was all the grandeur associated with his office and its trappings. It was jokingly said that there was some special device in the carpet of his study at Government House which ensured that visitors got smaller and smaller as they walked across its great expanse until they reached him behind his desk. He could also be sharply questioning about what was, or was not, going on in the matter of the governing of Hong Kong. He was on a mission to bring about drastic improvements and he would not tolerate any laziness or slackness that might stand in the way of that.

He gave his personal attention to many innovations that shaped present-day Hong Kong and he was deeply involved in what went on. Later on, when I was handling policy on the performing arts, I came across a file dealing with the founding of the Arts Festival. It was a tradition in all British colonies that the governor, and only the governor, should use red ink for his signature and handwritten notes. This file began with a few lines in MacLehose's scarlet scrawl: *I think we should have an Arts Festival. Ask Run Run to come and see me.* Run Run was Sir Run Run Shaw, a noted philanthropist and also by far the most influential figure in film making in Asia and in television in Hong Kong. The business he had built up was internationally significant and the works produced by his studios shaped the Chinese world view in Hong Kong and beyond. The red writing was in evidence again in the next entry in the file, dated a few weeks later: a laconic *Have spoken to Run Run. There will be an Arts Festival.* And indeed there was an arts festival, which in 2012 celebrated its fortieth year with plays, concerts and opera, both Western and Cantonese. In fact, there had been discussion about a possible arts festival for a while among a few people but one can be sure that the push from Government House was decisive.

This direct approach was typical. The first section of the Mass Transit Railway opened in 1979, running down the Kowloon Peninsula and out to the industrial and population centre of Kwun Tong. It was MacLehose who, when shown the plans had pointed out that there was no intersection with the existing lines of the Kowloon-Canton Railway. The designers hastily went back to work and came up with an interchange between the two systems at Kowloon Tong Station.

At that time, there was no direct rail service into China and passengers had to get off at the Hong Kong border station of Lo Wu and walk across the tracks to the China side; such passengers were mainly Hong Kong people visiting relatives in Guangdong Province at the time of the main Chinese festivals, when they would be able to get some time off work and could take across gifts of necessities such as medicines and cooking oil, often carrying them on traditional bamboo yoked poles. The through train service began again in April 1979, thirty years after the political situation in China had led to its cessation. By then, slowly improving economic conditions in China meant that the nature of gifts from Hong Kong was changing and instead of staples, luxuries like television sets were popular. Around that time Michael and I happened to chat to a man who was frothing with indignation: his Mainland relatives had spurned the set that he had brought as it only showed black and white. Intensely irritated, he had swept up the offending article and brought it back into Hong Kong with him, even though this had necessitated a long explanation to the Customs officers who had never before come across such a case. Little did anyone imagine how soon China would become the hub of the world's manufacture of consumer goods!

It was also during the MacLehose era that work began on the country parks that now make up around forty per cent of the total area of Hong Kong. A certain amount of land had to be reserved as water catchment, but it was an inspired idea to develop these areas and then others into recreational areas for hiking, barbecues and so on. In 1972, just before my arrival in Hong Kong, two devastating landslides, one in a squatter area in Sau Mau Ping and one in the upmarket residential district of Kotewall Road, killed a total of 150 people. Nobody knew for sure which slopes were unstable and might lead to other such disasters. MacLehose imported experts and set up a programme to map and stabilise every single vulnerable area. There were other initiatives, notably the Ten Year Housing Plan and the setting up of the Independent Commission Against Corruption which brought enormous changes for the better to people's lives.

Many facets of his personality and bearing struck a chord with the local community, including an assessment that he lived up to some of the highest traditions in Chinese culture by constantly extending himself in public service even at the expense of his own health. He loved to walk in the New Territories and the naming of the MacLehose Hiking Trail upon his retirement was a most appropriate tribute. Unfortunately, while in the hills in September 1975 he fell and broke his leg and it did not mend easily. He also suffered a minor stroke just before his final departure from Hong Kong.

In October every year the governor delivered a policy address, which equated to the British queen's speech at the opening of her Parliament, setting out priorities for the year ahead, especially any new legislation to be brought in. After 1997 the timing of the policy address was changed but it still fulfils the same function for the chief executive of the Special Administrative Region. Each year groups and individuals alike await it with keen interest as what is announced may affect everyone's lives. According to local reckoning, autumn is well underway by then but I always used to feel that the policy address marked the last of the really hot weather and the time to put away summer dresses.

The policy address is nowadays drafted by great teams of staff located in the Central Policy Unit. It is not surprising that it requires so much work as it is a long, fact-filled document supported by annexes and bureau secretaries' own lists of policy pledges. MacLehose used to do it differently though. He would write his speech himself, leaving blanks for the facts that needed to be filled in and send sections of the draft down to the Secretariat for the purpose. This was sometimes challenging for us humble providers as we might not have available the exact information that he had asked for and in those days before computers were widespread we could not always recalculate to give him what he wanted and instead had to try and discreetly and daringly rewrite the draft so that it fitted the data that we actually did have on hand.

The run up to the policy address was busy for all of us but, obviously, more so for the governor who had the benefit, if so it can be considered, of Government House which was a combined residence and office making it convenient if one wanted to come down in the middle of the night and do a bit more work.

One evening in 1975, whether as a result of insomnia or inspiration the governor did decide to start work again on the policy address and opened the heavy office door so that he could go in and get his draft. A security alarm was immediately triggered since it had been set as part of the normal routine when Michael left the office to go home. That might not have mattered as there was a way to turn it off but encumbered by a leg in a plaster cast after his recent hiking accident the governor could not get to the switch in time. The most hideous noise was now resounding throughout Government House. Denis, the ADC, was awakened from a sound sleep in his bachelor quarters in the basement and, as he was trained to do, picked up and prepared his revolver and went racing upstairs. The linked alarm had also sounded in the Central Police Station and alerted a detachment of police officers who came, as they had been trained to do, streaming through the front gate of Government House and arrived just as Denis was kicking open the door to the governor's study, ready to shoot the intruder. Meanwhile, the poor governor had overbalanced and lay on the floor while Lady MacLehose came down from the upper storey to try and find out what on earth was going on. Explanations were given, order was restored fairly quickly and it was decided to treat the entire incident as a great joke even if one not to be repeated.

Untiring as he was, Sir Murray did not work on his own and some of his lieutenants were equally legendary figures as far as we were concerned.

Principal among these was perhaps Sir Jack Cater. Sir Jack was the son of a London policeman and, serving in the Royal Air Force during the Second World War, did not go to university. This lack of a degree as well as his relatively humble origins marked him out from his colleagues when he joined the colonial service in Hong Kong at the end of 1945. He was also marked out by his exceptional energy and ability.

He died in 2006 and at his memorial service in Hong Kong, the appreciation was given by the then chief executive, Donald Tsang, who had been his colleague for many years.

Sir Jack was appointed the first director of agriculture and fisheries in 1964 and before then he had been in charge of Fisheries. Donald's tribute included the following:

> A letter jointly written by some twenty fishermen associations to the then governor on 8 August 1955 is a testament to the high standing in which he was held. I quote:

> 'For many generations we and our ancestors have lived in Hong Kong, earning our living through fishing. Throughout much of this time, we have been looked down upon and despised by the land people, possibly because we were poor and uneducated. This was the position when Mr Cater became officer-in-charge of fisheries. Since that time he has become registrar of co-operatives and director of marketing, and through his able and kind administration the status of the fisherfolk has continually improved and the prejudice against us has disappeared under his benevolent, democratic and altruistic policies. Under Mr Cater's guidance and with his assistance, our fishing industry has prospered and developed. The continuous increase in fish landing; the mechanisation of the fleet; the starting of co-operative societies amongst us; the establishment of the many schools for fishermen's children. All these things and many more are proof of the benefits which we fishermen of Hong Kong have received under his able administration.'

This period was before I had arrived in Hong Kong, although I heard people talking about it, in particular Cater's efforts to get a better standard fishing boat designed. He was more famous as the director of government strategy during the 1967 riots and as the founding head of the Independent Commission Against Corruption but I like this tale of the fisherfolk as it exemplifies the direct, practical problem solving that was the best of what the Hong Kong government did.

Sir Jack was of a normal sort of height but his rather craggy face and slightly hawk-like profile were much photographed and so he was recognised wherever he went. In 1978, he became chief secretary, which meant that when the governor was temporarily away Sir Jack became acting governor with a police bodyguard with him wherever he went, although he did not change his habits in any other way and stayed in his office in Lower Albert Road. There were awed reports from those who had found themselves at weekday lunchtimes in the same queue to buy a sandwich as the governor and his bodyguard. Here was a living example of the principle that administrative officers in their way of life should tend towards the humble rather than the grand.

When Sir Jack was appointed chief secretary he saw all the members of the administrative grade in batches by seniority. When my group was gathered together, all aged around thirty, he told us clearly that he did not mind if we made mistakes 'so long as your batting average is all right'. It was pretty admirable that he took the trouble to see us at all in his office in numbers that were small enough for some sense of intimacy rather than a large scale speech or meeting. It was immensely liberating to be told that mistakes were tolerable, as we were being given scope to take a lot of responsibility or show initiative which might otherwise have been rather unnerving. And his use of cricketing terminology was typical of the entire service, influenced as it was by the way young British men expressed themselves. If we needed something urgently we would always ask for it 'by close of play today' while, on the other hand, 'let's play this one long' we would say about something that it seemed more politic not to deal with immediately.

The third member of the triumvirate of dominating senior figures of my early years in the government was Sir Philip Haddon-Cave, the financial secretary. I think that from time to time there were frictions among these three, but a financial secretary who gives or, perhaps more often, withholds funds for pet projects is bound to be particularly annoying. At the same time, we all acknowledged that his rigour towards our finances kept us in good shape and allowed us to weather storms. For example, when a worldwide crisis arose in 1973 as a result of higher oil prices he immediately had us drawing up pretty drastic lists of areas where we could save money and, in the event, the opening of the Princess Margaret Hospital was held back.

Civil servants normally expected to work hard for Sir Philip, particularly the inner circle in the Finance Branch who helped to draw up Hong Kong's annual budget. They would spend days cooped up in his office with him, relieved by nips of Scotch from his store as the night drew on. The end product would be an immensely long speech that would not only set out taxation and expenditure for the following year but would also provide an in-depth analysis of the underlying economic trends. When we joined Finance Branch we were told as part of our informal briefing that if we did something that resulted in criticism in LegCo's Finance Committee, Sir Philip might be furious in private but in public would defend even the most junior member of his staff. I was lucky enough to have no personal experience of this but I heard stories that bore this out.

In succession to Sir John Cowperthwaite, Sir Philip had maintained the philosophy that it was the duty of government to facilitate trade and industry but not to get deeply involved in it nor in setting its direction as the belief was that it was businessmen who could best make business decisions. This principle was widely described as *laisser-faire* but Sir Philip found this term inadequate for the purpose and invented 'positive non-interventionism' as a substitute. This did not preclude the tremendous expenditures on welfare, public housing and other services for the community that characterised the MacLehose years and beyond. Sir Philip, even when he sanctioned these projects did so mainly from a purist's financial point of view of whether or not they could be afforded and, on principle, refused to develop any emotional attachment to them and so, for example, never visited the new towns that we were building with the money that he allocated to us.

He was deeply loyal to Hong Kong and would champion the territory's interests as against Britain's, if the need arose. There was a story which may or may not have been true, or partly true, about a visiting delegation of British members of parliament who partook too liberally of the farewell drinks before a press conference that they were meant to be holding with Sir Philip at Kai Tak Airport. One went completely missing but was located on the floor inside a locked lavatory cubicle by the financial secretary who climbed over from the adjoining one and unbolted the door from the inside. The unhappy visitors were propped up before the journalists but since their responses to questions were hardly lucid, Sir Philip had to act as interpreter, 'What Mr Smith is suggesting is. . . .' He claimed afterwards that for fairness' sake, he had tried to shape these imaginative renderings in a way that favoured the British point of view, which would have been rather unusual as far as he was concerned.

Devoted though he was to the cause of Hong Kong, this devotion did not extend to its cuisine and whenever he attended a Chinese banquet, the hosts knew that they should supply one portion of steak and chips together with knife and fork, just for him. Later on, he became chief secretary and together with Sir Roger Lobo, the very distinguished executive and legislative councillor, had to visit China on official business. The future of Hong Kong was in the balance and every little thing might help or hinder and so Sir Roger begged him to suspend the custom of a lifetime and join in eating the native cuisine. Sir Philip reluctantly agreed to do so and with eyes half-closed manfully dabbed with his chopsticks at the dish immediately in front of him, eventually managing to get through a considerable quantity. The Chinese official next to him was most impressed: 'Sir Philip, you seem to love ducks' tongues so much while even we Chinese people often find them quite an unusual taste.' Sir Philip caught up with Sir Roger in a corridor outside the banqueting hall and forcibly expressed his displeasure at the ordeal he had undergone but suffered no long term damage as a result.

Sir David Akers-Jones, who as secretary for the New Territories was the boss in my first proper posting, was very different from Sir

Philip when it came to Chinese customs. He represented the breed of administrators who also became scholars and Sinologists. It is impossible to think of David without his wife Jane. They lived for more than ten years in Island House in Tai Po, one of the very nicest government quarters. Built in 1905, it featured airy verandahs and expansive gardens where David and Jane used to hold wonderful barbecue parties for the department's staff. This entertainment was at their own expense but if we were lucky we could sometimes avail ourselves of the departmental boat, used for travelling between the Outlying Islands and around the coastline that were part of the New Territories and hence our responsibility. The boat was the *Sir Cecil Clementi,* named after Hong Kong's governor from 1925 to 1930, another great scholar and also an enthusiastic walker, one of his favourite expeditions being from Turkestan to Kowloon. The *Clementi* had a crew that included a cook, Ah Do, who made chicken curry for anyone who was on board at mealtimes. It was an excellent curry served with a dish of condiments: raisins, dessicated coconut, diced tomatoes, sliced banana and chutney. It never varied in the slightest degree in either recipe or presentation. I once asked Ah Do, tactfully, I hope, whether he could make any other dish. 'Oh yes,' he replied majestically, 'I can make many, many other things. But everyone prefers the curry.'

The other exciting and unusual way in which officials travelled around the New Territories was by helicopter. Nowadays, there is the super efficient and highly professional Government Flying Service but it used not to be quite like that. The Auxiliary Air Force's fleet of helicopters was flown by amateurs. Most of the time they would be young businessmen, bankers or even civil servants of various kinds but as a hobby they had learnt to fly these things and then were called on to ferry us around. One day, David decided that he and I should fly to Lantau Island to get a good view of the proposed site for a private residential and recreational development which would eventually become Discovery Bay, a settlement of some 16,000 people.

We skimmed over a large area on the east coast of the island. It was bare and rather barren, lacking anything much in the way of vegetation apart from scrubby ground cover. From the air, the island looked so big and so undeveloped. There was of course no airport and its later site Chek Lap Kok was a small island covered in banana plantations lying off Lantau itself, and Tung Chung was the location of a historic fort and a few houses rather than a new town to be built to support the airport. It seemed that there could be no harm in tucking away this proposed new resort when there was such a lot of land to spare.

We were on the way back when the young pilot's decidedly plummy tones came over the headphones that were fitted in our flying helmets. 'Awfully sorry, sir, but a red light's flashing and I believe that means there is an emergency. I rather think that I have to find the nearest helipad and make a landing.' The helipad was found and the landing safely made. 'Why,' said David, 'we seem to be right next to the Sha Tsui Detention Centre. Let's pay them a visit.' We accordingly left the pilot to work out what to do with the helicopter and walked across the grass and up to the barbed-wire topped main fence and gate to the institution, which specialised in 'sharp, short, shock' sentences for young offenders, with plenty of physical activity as well as education. The centre's superintendent reacted to this unexpected incursion in a relaxed and welcoming way and led us on a tour of the afternoon's drilling and outdoor exercises before driving us back to the ferry pier in his Land Rover so that we could get home, even if more slowly than we had intended.

Although during my early days in the government there were few female administrative officers it would be wrong to exaggerate this. I took over my post in the New Territories administration from Ophelia Cheung, so pretty in her *cheongsam*s and with a breathy voice. She was also a graduate of Hong Kong University, still a rare distinction and a sign of both cleverness and determination on the part of any girl who achieved it. Ophelia's father had a famous shop that occupied a prominent corner in Wellington Street: Tailor Cheung; he made suits for film stars like William Holden, whose photo was in the shop window. Holden played a major part in the way Hong Kong was perceived around the world, taking the starring male role in the films *The World of Suzie Wong* and *Love is a Many Splendored Thing*; in both cases, the hero of the novel on which the film had been based was an Englishman but reflecting the contemporary dominance of Hollywood, transformed into an American while, in the second case, insult was added to injury by omitting the 'u' from splendoured, despite the fact that it was from an English poet, Francis Thompson, faithfully rendered by Han Suyin in the title of her book.

Ophelia was one of ten siblings and later on she introduced me to her younger brother, Leslie, who became famous as a pop singer in Hong Kong and then throughout the world as an actor in the movie *Farewell My Concubine* which won many international awards and was voted best Chinese film of the twentieth century.

There was another woman down the corridor from me, and that was Anson Chan. She was senior to me but she and I were dealing with different subjects so I was not working for her but would just run into her from time to time. Anson was rather like a school head girl whom one felt that one should dislike a bit because she was so faultless but couldn't possibly because she was also so extremely nice.

People had different approaches to working on files. David Akers-Jones would make very brief comments, often inscrutable, such as an exclamation or question mark, or both together, in the margins or, if he was feeling particularly voluble, a simple *Oh*. Anson, on the other hand, filled pages with well reasoned arguments in her perfectly even handwriting.

Anson was so beautiful that anyone looking at her might have assumed that she would have been the subject of endless office romances but she was, in fact, dedicated to her family, juggling her time to be with her two small children. Her husband, Archie, was an executive with the Caltex Oil Company and they lived in a company quarter on Tsing Yi Island where Caltex had its oil storage facilities. Despite the industrial setting, Hong Kong in the mid-1970s was already so built up that to be able to have, as they did, a separate two-storey house rather than a flat in an apartment block was quite a privilege.

Anson went on to great achievements, being appointed chief secretary in 1993, the first Chinese and the first woman to hold this post, having previously been the first woman to head a government department and then a secretariat branch. She has always been a doughty fighter for women's rights both within and outside the civil service. She was instrumental in the founding of the Association of Senior Female Government Officers, and I am proud to say that I was also one of the signatories of its original registration as a trades union. Our cause was the fact that while we might be achieving equal treatment as far as salary was concerned women on marriage would still lose the other benefits to which they had been entitled when single, especially housing. This was the last gasp of the old argument that a husband provided for a married woman and that what she earned would be more or less 'pin money'. Anson counter-argued fiercely and logically and eventually won the day.

She has garnered plenty of honours along the way, including, from the British, the award of Dame Grand Cross of the Order of St Michael and St George, one of the most prestigious that they have to offer. Anson is really quite tiny and the star of the order is massive. Apparently, she would also be entitled to a full-length blue satin cloak lined with red silk and trimmed with two gigantic tassels. I do not expect to see her in that any time soon as she is one of the least pretentious people that I know as well as one of the friendliest. At the height of her fame and position in Hong Kong you would often see her at social functions plunging into groups of guests, flashing the big smile that had gained her the Chinese nickname of 'forty thousand', because it resembled the *mah jong* tile engraved with that number, and saying simply, 'Hullo, I'm Anson Chan.'

The New Territories administration nurtured not only Anson but also Donald Tsang, the second chief executive of the Hong Kong Special Administrative Region after the handover and the first to be drawn from a civil service background. Donald did a stint as district officer in Sha Tin but I didn't have much to do with him then as I was pursuing a separate path in the Secretariat. I knew him better earlier when he was in the Finance Branch master-minding the Public Works Programme. All the posts in the Finance Branch were demanding but the one that Donald occupied was terrifying. The custom was to pick out someone who was con-sidered particularly able and give them this rather junior post with no extra pay but enormous workload. The incumbent did get a corner office but that was not much of a privilege as it was required to house exceptionally large piles of files, covering every item of capital works, both large and small, which had to be progressed through an agonisingly complicated system before a shovel could hit the earth and work begin. Every piece of paper involved in this tortuous process had to be entirely accurate and, in addition, there would be constant pressure from important figures who wanted to see 'their' projects advanced. As it happened, this was quite a good precursor of Donald's future career which featured both projects requiring incredible amounts of hard work, such as the issuing of full British passports to 50,000 key Hong Kong citizens and their dependants in a move to stem panic after the Tiananmen incident in 1989, and also a distinct specialism in financial subjects, culminating in a term as financial secretary in the tradition of Sir Philip Haddon-Cave. We old timers were shocked and saddened when in 2012 Donald, then chief executive, was accused of having inappropriately accepted favours from wealthy businessmen and became subject to an investigation by the ICAC. At the time of writing, the outcome is not known.

It is quite strange to reflect on the fundamental changes that have taken place over thirty-odd years, which have resulted in a seamless civil-service philosophy being carried out by a team, which despite the usual office in-fighting, was essentially united, being replaced by a fractious political scene which has still not reached its final stage of development. It is tempting to sigh nostalgically for those days when problems seemed more tractable and solutions simpler but it is pointless. Hong Kong was caught up in great flows of history and of economic growth and change that would mean that the challenges that faced us would become ever more complex.

CHAPTER SIX

Mud on our Boots

MICHAEL'S TIME AT GOVERNMENT HOUSE turned out to have unexpected consequences for Joyce Bennett. In the early days of his posting there, the Private Office was faced with a crisis. A luncheon party was shortly to be held and a single lady had dropped out, threatening devastation to the seating plan. Could a suitable replacement be found in time? Michael suggested this missionary priest-cum-Kwun Tong school headmistress whom he had met and who, it turned out, was already slightly known to the governor and his wife. The seating plan was saved and Murray MacLehose got a chance to see Joyce close up, and he liked what he saw. One of the outstanding and unusual aspects of the Mac-Lehose way of doing things was that, to some extent at least, he was willing to accommodate dissenting voices. He had been contemplating for some time the possibility of some appointments to the Legislative Council outside the normal run of the business and professional elite. He did not want to go too far in the direction of the radicals but Joyce, he thought, 'had her head screwed on' as well as a good understanding of life at the grassroots of Hong Kong. Accordingly, the new members of the Legislative Council who were sworn in on 6 October 1976 included Mr Wong Lam, an employee of the Kowloon Motor Bus Company, who had started out as a bus driver and ticket collector, Father Patrick McGovern, a Jesuit priest with a particular interest in workers' rights . . . and the Reverend Miss Joyce Bennett.

This would mean that the police guards would be ushering through the gates of Government House not just the luxurious limousines of the senior unofficials, as we rather oddly termed the

non-civil service members of the Executive and Legislative Councils, as well as the government cars, identifiable by their distinctive
AM number plates and the Government House cars with their
crown insignia, but also Father McGovern's Vespa scooter and
Joyce's bright blue Mini.

Joyce, however, may not have turned out exactly as expected.
She had a round face, blue eyes and a serene and kindly smile. She
was indeed both serene and kindly, but so was Miss Marple and
those in power should have been on their guard. Joyce cared a lot
about what went on in Hong Kong and she was well informed
about the educational field and also about the city's not-so-nice
underbelly. She relished, and used to the full, the ability conferred
by her new position to ask the government difficult questions.

Liz King succeeded me in my Finance Branch post looking after
the education budget. One day, she and Philip Haddon-Cave were
wrestling with a draft answer to one of Joyce's maddening questions
about education policy that demonstrated her knowledge of all the
details including aspects which showed government in a less than
favourable light. Sir Philip was getting rather irritated and turned
to Liz. 'Is it you whose auntie she is?' he asked fiercely. 'No, sir,' she
replied hastily, 'It's not me, sir. It's Rachel, sir, Rachel.'

I'm sure there were many who had reason to be grateful to Joyce
for the various interventions that she made. I myself did, in the
matter of toilet paper. It was an indication of how bad poverty had
been in Hong Kong in the recent past that toilet paper was not
routinely available in the lavatories in government office buildings
on the assumption that it might be pilfered. Instead, we were
allocated individual toilet rolls which we kept safely in a desk
drawer to take with us on our visits to the washroom.

The 'Ladies' in the Government Secretariat as in all government
offices were adequate but basic. Around the time of Joyce's appointment it was felt that there should be at least one upgraded facility
available. Apart from Joyce herself, there were other distinguished
ladies who were likely to visit the Secretariat on business, notably
Dr Joyce Symons, headmistress of the Diocesan Girls School and
a member of both the Legislative and Executive councils, as well as
Ms Lydia Dunn (later Baroness Dunn), a senior executive with the

venerable trading house of John Swire & Sons and also a member of the Legislative and Executive councils. Accordingly, a 'Senior Ladies' was established, only accessible with a key and fitted out with tiles and basins that looked as if they had come from an ordinary sanitary fittings supplier rather than being leftovers from one of our correctional institutions. These facilities were also open to 'senior ladies' within the administration and since there weren't so many of us around the bar for admission was set rather low and I found that I too was entitled to use this smart new facility. The only drawback was that although the mindset about tiles and taps had changed, that regarding toilet paper had not, which could be decidedly annoying. Joyce Bennett noticed the deficiency too and, being Joyce, was not content to let it pass. She tracked down the relevant bureaucrats and told them, nicely but firmly, that she expected something better. Consequently, that washroom became a pleasure to visit; in addition to all the new fittings and decoration there were always at least three spare toilet rolls on the top of every cistern!

Michael and I were both working on Hong Kong Island: he in Government House on Upper Albert Road and I in the Secretariat on Lower Albert Road. Although our hours were long and things could seem stressful from day to day we were able to have enjoyable leisure times. At school, I had been a complete and hopeless duffer at any kind of sports but Michael taught me to swim. We used to go down to the sea almost every evening, to Deep Water Bay. Often, our visits used to coincide with those of YK (later Sir YK) Pao who also used to like a nightly dip. He would arrive in a chauffeur driven car but otherwise his demeanour was very unostentatious and he would exchange friendly greetings with the regular beachgoers. He had no bodyguards or other companions and, like us, would swim to and from the platforms that were anchored about forty metres from the beach. At the time, the company, World-Wide Shipping, which he had founded was by far the world's largest commercial shipowner and his personal wealth was correspondingly large. Swimming mastered, I went on to learn how to water ski, also in Deep Water Bay, but this was at week-ends, with a little commercial speedboat and driver that could be hired by the hour. There were

no rules or regulations controlling this pastime and we relied on
the skill of the driver to avoid accidents but the waters were not
crowded, which reduced the risks.

The Hong Kong government's salary structure had built into it
an arrangement that could pay out like a fruit machine. This was
'acting' usually 'up' but sometimes 'sideways' instead of or in
addition to 'up'; the 'up' might also be 'doubling up' or 'doubling
down'. This simply meant doing the job of somebody or the
somebodies who were not around, and getting paid for it. The
calculations were complicated sums but because senior people were
still often going away for an overseas leave of a few months at a
time, the lump sum that you could get in this way could be a good
bonus on the normal annual salary. These possibilities were something very much of that era and earlier, more or less disappearing
altogether as leaves became shorter and rules were tightened up.
However, Michael had had acting pay for four months before he
went to Government House, doubling up for his boss in the
Secretariat and earning an extra $20,000 which led us to believe
that we had enough money to consider buying a boat of our own.

The Bull and Bear was a converted ship's lifeboat and it came
complete with its own mooring as well as a speedboat that could
be used for water skiing and we added a Laser dinghy that Michael
had been using for sailing at the Royal Hong Kong Yacht Club. All
this was not as plutocratic as it may sound. We brought in friends
as partners to help out with the costs and since in those days the
water was clear and unpolluted it did not matter that our vessel did
not have the capacity to go very far as we could do a lot in the bays
of Hong Kong Island and by motoring the short distances to
Lamma and Po Toi Islands, where we could hike in the cooler
weather when swimming and water skiing were not so appealing.

We took on a 'boat boy', Wong Chi-ming. Chi-ming lived in
public housing in the fishing port of Aberdeen with his extended
family but he had been brought up living on boats. His family were
Tanka or boat people, against whom Hong Kong Cantonese had a
traditional prejudice. Like most such prejudices, there was no
reason for it even though the boat people were somewhat ethnically
different and certainly had a quite different way of life, based on

their fishing and other maritime activities. It was said that boat people never came ashore at all during their lifetimes. The gaudily decorated floating restaurants in Aberdeen Harbour, offering Chinese cuisine that appealed to Western tourists, took their inspiration from the boat people's wedding boats. Certainly, Chiming was completely and utterly at home on the water and was never even slightly unnerved by the roughest weather conditions.

He was skilled at purchasing and preparing seafood: big juicy prawns served with a soy sauce with diced chilli floating in it or small but delicious winkles. Sometimes we would eat like that or at one of the restaurants at Sok Kwu Wan on Lamma Island, not as numerous or as commercial as now. Our favourite had a young waitress who was usually wearing a T-shirt inscribed with the words 'Sweet Girl', and she was. More often, though, we would arrange our catering on a pot-luck basis, with everyone bringing a contribution to the feast. Our friend Anton Irving, a young biologist who had been recruited from the UK to help realise the government's plan for a network of country parks, was a talented amateur chef. 'I love you, Anton,' Anna Ding would cry passionately, 'You always make two puddings.' Anna herself learnt to water ski within a couple of afternoons; the coordination and balance that had stood her in good stead in her days as a racing car driver made her a natural performer at this new sport and she took the more difficult option of balancing on a single ski.

However, these days came to an end rather quickly. Michael's posting at Government House was over and the governor took an interest in what would happen to him next. 'Michael,' he said, 'should get mud on his boots.' The muddiest place that the personnel people could think of was Yuen Long in the northwest New Territories. He was appointed district officer there in an area which was still largely rural, centred on the ancient market town of Yuen Long, which was being rather gradually developed into a secondary new town. It was bordered to the north by China and to the west by Deep Bay, the other side of which was also China. As an administrative district, it had formerly comprised the *chat heung*, (seven districts), strongholds of the powerful Man and Tang clans. However one of the seven had recently been split off to form the major new town of Tuen Mun with a projected population big enough to merit a district officer of its own.

The district officers were the backbone of the long-established way of governing the British Empire, taking responsibility for administering sometimes vast tracts of land, including acting as the local magistrate. In the mid-1970s, Hong Kong district officers had lost their role as magistrates but retained significant powers in land administration and related matters. The DO was very much seen as the channel of communication between people and government in his district and it was this aspect that the later created City District Officer scheme aimed to emulate.

In the past, the expectation had been that the district officer would live in his (always 'his', of course) district and suitable quarters had been provided for that purpose. As a consequence of the splitting of the district, the Yuen Long house was now in Tuen Mun but we thought that we should go and live there so that Michael could do the job fully rather than just commuting in from the very different atmosphere of residential Hong Kong Island even if that meant that it would not be practical to keep our boat.

Our new address was 'Dunrose, 18½ Miles Castle Peak Road', which described our location exactly. We were 18½ miles from North Kowloon towards Castle Peak, as Tuen Mun had previously been known before reverting to its original name. We were next door to Perowne Barracks and during our period of residence it was the Gurkha Engineers who were stationed there. We used to be invited over sometimes especially for the festival of Dussehra which fell during the pleasant autumn season. We would sit in armchairs in a great marquee with silver tankards of Pimm's to hand to watch the 'Nautch girls' performing their exotic dances: in fact, Gurkha soldiers in drag as this was considered better than putting respectably married wives on display in this erotic show. The high point came with the beheading and sacrifice of a bullock, which was fortunately carried out far offstage.

Our own house was called 'Dunrose' in accordance with the old fashioned English custom of combining the names of a married couple. Yes, the district officer's quarter had originally been owned by Duncan and Rose, a retired missionary couple who had lived there in the 1920s. They had built the house to suit their own needs, which were not the same as their successors'. They had only one large bedroom and so when David Akers-Jones was district officer Yuen Long he had blocked off part of the hallway to accommodate his children. There were open grates in the spacious sitting/dining room and in the winter we laid fires with the 'coal' which we bought in bags from the Yuen Long market although it seemed more like charcoal and burnt up very quickly. A wide verandah ran around the house and it could accommodate tables, chairs, barbecue and dartboard. The entire house and verandah were raised on a network of pipes, which served as a damp course. Behind the house was a range of low outbuildings which could be used for storage and for staff quarters, at least once they had been thoroughly cleaned as they seemed to have housed chickens at one time.

The house was rather hot as it had a flat roof and was located at the bottom of a hillside where it caught no breeze. We had an air conditioner in our bedroom but otherwise only ceiling fans.

It was the garden, however, that was the jewel of Dunrose. There was a tennis court which had become rather dilapidated but we did a deal with the Gurkha Engineers and, in return for shared usage, they provided the labour to resurface it. There was a little pond where a red-eared turtle lived and a strawberry patch planted by the Akers-Joneses. We also had a flagpole where the Union Jack was raised every day. I was at home on the day Earl Mountbatten was murdered by Irish terrorists and I got a call from David, telling me the news and asking me to lower the flag to half mast.

What I loved most were the trees and shrubs. Even their names were euphonious: azalea, hibiscus, sleeping hibiscus, guava, dragon's eye, foxglove tree, the fragrant white jade orchid tree and the great Flame of the Forest with its scarlet flowers in season. I sometimes wonder whether on our deathbeds we are allowed to go back to some place we have loved very much in life. I would go back to the garden at Dunrose. And it would be the only way to travel there now since the site is occupied by two towers of luxury apartment blocks, and the garden all gone.

I was still working in the Secretariat but I had been transferred out of the Finance Branch as it was reckoned that I could not combine the necessary hours with the long journey from our new home, not to mention the commitment to social functions in the district.

I was now in the Environment Branch, working on transport policy and I had plenty of opportunities for real-world sampling of various different forms. There was no rail link of any kind and the buses had limited routes which were of no real help to me. A major component of my journey was the ferry between the industrial town of Tsuen Wan, further down the Castle Peak Road, and Hong Kong Island. In the mornings Michael could give me a lift to the ferry pier but I made my own way back in the evenings. My walk from the pier to the main road took me past some interesting shops, notably streets specialising in paper offerings to be burnt as part of traditional rituals for the deceased, a practice more common then than now. These were things to be used in the afterlife and so there were elaborate houses and cars, crafted out of coloured paper on a bamboo framework. Coincidentally, I assume, there was also a clustering of practitioners specialising in the treatment of haemorrhoids. Their consulting rooms were usually on upper floors but at ground level they had large and graphic photographs demonstrating exactly what frightful excrescences they could deal with. I eventually reached the terminus of the minibus that would take me all the way home so long as I was quick enough at yelling out that I wanted to get off as we neared Dunrose, which was not a well-known destination. Occasionally, this unexpected request startled the driver so much that he put on the brakes fiercely and I would stumble and fall as I was walking down the bus. His reaction would be immediate and practical. 'No compensation!' he would cry just in case I was tempted to claim that I had suffered injury as a result of his hastiness.

We felt that we needed some help in the house and we first tried employing Kitty, a girl of seventeen from a village near Yuen Long. We thought that we could offer her a nice little suite of self-contained rooms for her use but she didn't much like it as she was used to a room full of siblings and found the solitude unnerving. She enjoyed the work, especially learning to cook but decided that she would rather have a more ordinary way of life and see people her own age.

We then went to the other end of the spectrum and found Ah Fung, a widow in her late fifties who wore the black trousers and sparkling white tight top of the traditional amah. She had lost her husband and also her brother during the Japanese occupation of Hong Kong; the latter had been shot out of hand by an army officer because he was apparently failing to bring quickly enough the water that he had been ordered to get. Such tragedies had not been uncommon among the civilian population. Ah Fung was completely illiterate but in compensation she had developed an outstanding memory. She remembered things by position or by number and once she had counted up how many items there were in a shopping list she never forgot one. She had worked for many Western families and could make all sorts of tricky things like soufflés as well as a perfect English fried breakfast. In other ways, she was quite traditional. We spoke to each other in Cantonese and it was important to her to establish that Michael had an older brother so that she could call me by the proper term for the wife of the second son of the household.

We didn't need to take on a gardener. Since this was a government property, upkeep of the garden was seen as a central responsibility and the gardener was a member of the civil service. Mr Ho was a local man and he was, in fact, rather well off thanks to the vegetable farm that he owned. His income was probably better than ours and his car was certainly smarter. If any friends happened to visit while it was there they supposed that we had splashed out on the new vehicle in our driveway but I suppose that there was some sort of reflected glory in the situation. I once asked Mr Ho why he bothered with this gardening job and he explained that it was the thought of the civil service pension that attracted him. He was a charming person, always calm and imperturbable, with his life organised to his satisfaction. This was certainly true of his approach to our garden. On the other side of the Castle Peak Road, which was close to the sea and the beach, there was a mansion owned by the business tycoon Mr Henry Fok Ying-tung who had a diligent gardener working there by the name of Ah Baak. Mr Fok very rarely visited and presumably regarded it as an investment and, indeed, all the property around there greatly increased in value as the development of Tuen Mun improved the transport links and astute developers saw the potential for hotels, houses and flats. Anyway, Ah Baak could easily manage to do all he had to do to look after the grounds of Mr Fok's house and still have time to spare so he came to a mutually beneficial arrangement with Mr Ho. Ah Baak raised an ever-changing selection of plants in large ornamental pots in return for being treated every now and again to a *dim sum* lunch in Yuen Long town. Everyone was satisfied. The district officer's residence looked as it should and Mr Ho had more time for his own preferred activities of drinking rice wine, taking naps in the outbuilding that he had fitted out as a comfortable office, and flirting outrageously with Ah Fung, who said that she didn't care for his behaviour although I always had the impression from her blushes and simpers that she didn't really mind.

It was while we were living in Dunrose that I experienced the first of what I thought of as 'the breath-holding events'. I can identify three of these during my time in Hong Kong. These were times when most of the community seemed to be as one, focusing on a drama that seemed to have the potential to overturn our entire way of life and plunge us into deep crisis. Strangely enough, in each case fever pitch was reached over a week-end and by the Monday it seemed in each case that some sort of resolution was being reached.

The week-end in question was that of 29 and 30 October 1977 and the *casus belli* was the Independent Commission Against Corruption. The organisation had been in existence since 1974 and it had demonstrated that it was not going to go away, be merely cosmetic in its operations, or susceptible to manipulation by the corrupt. It was also apparent that the ICAC had come into being at a time when the public were ready to offer it wholehearted support to end the misery of having to offer a bribe for every little thing that they needed. During 1977 the ICAC was taking determined action against the 'Fruit Market Syndicate', a powerful Kowloon drug trafficking gang protected by crooked police. This sent a real signal that even the most entrenched criminals could not expect their cosy way of life to continue. It rattled those clever kingpins who had for so long been making money far in excess of their government salaries. It also unnerved the 'small potatoes'. There were plenty of police officers who had accepted relatively trivial sums of money simply because that was just part of the way of life. Such people might well not know exactly where the money they received came from; it was doled out by the controlling syndicates to ensure a web of complicity. These little guys could, however, read the words of the new anti-corruption legislation and see what the ICAC was doing and they were frightened and resentful.

On Friday 28 October about 2,000 police officers went to the police headquarters in Wan Chai, Hong Kong Island to deliver a petition of complaint to the commissioner, the head of the force. The headquarters of the ICAC was not far away in Hutchison House, rented commercial premises in the Central business district and about forty of the protesters went on there and violently stormed the offices. They were only partially successful but they did quite extensive damage and beat up some ICAC staff. Other police eventually came to the rescue of the ICAC personnel who had had to barricade themselves in. The community was in shock.

The end of October in Hong Kong normally has some of the best weather of the whole year and the most suitable for hiking. Accordingly, Sunday 30 October had been designated as the day for the New Territories Community Chest 'Walk for Millions', a mass participation charity fund raising function. A district officer was regarded as the government representative in his district and was expected to be aware of the ceremonial aspects of his role and to support 'good causes', especially something as major as this. We were scheduled to take part and we planned to go the whole distance rather than being there for the opening and about ten minutes afterwards before going home, which was what official guests sometimes did. We walked at the front together with John Grieve, the district police commander for the New Territories.

There were thousands of participants and the atmosphere was electric, although not with the fun and socialisation of an enjoyable outing. The thought shared by everyone but which could barely be uttered was 'police mutiny'. We walked with John and went over the possibilities. There were stories of refusal to perform routine duties. Were these true and, if so, what might it portend? What would a widespread police mutiny look like and what would the consequences be? Could the British Army units stationed in Hong Kong take over at least some of the work of the police? If so, how would it be arranged? Perhaps because Michael and I were young we were not afraid. Instead, we felt wound up and energised for whatever the developments in the days ahead might be.

In the event it was the old people, not us, who had to put in the hard work and make the difficult decisions. There was a series of intensive meetings at the highest levels of the governor and Executive Council. On 5 November it was announced that there would be a partial amnesty for corruption offences. What it came down to was that from then the ICAC would not act on complaints and possible offences that had taken place before 1 January 1977, although exceptions could be made in cases so heinous that it would be 'unthinkable' not to act. There were some purists who felt that this announcement was tantamount to letting the guilty escape well-deserved punishment, but most Hong Kong citizens thought that this was a reasonable compromise and that, given the mood of the police and the crucial importance of basic law and order, nothing else could have been done. It also turned out that the ongoing fight against corruption was not fatally wounded nor even undermined and Hong Kong continued its steady progress towards an international reputation for negligible levels of bribery.

This was quite characteristic of Hong Kong: a major crisis defused in less than a week! Life reverted to normal and soon it would be Christmas, a lovely festival at Dunrose thanks to the poinsettias that Mr Ho conjured up and the excellent space that we had for holding a party. The air was crisp and cool without being too cold and we were looking forward to the break since, unlike the forthcoming Chinese New Year celebrations, we had no commitments in Yuen Long apart from the office party with its standard catering of fruit salad with prawns in a sharp flavoured mayonnaise as well as barbecued suckling pig, some beer, but not too much, and the entertainment of a lengthy lucky draw for prizes of a value moderate enough not to alarm the ICAC.

Since we had moved out from Hong Kong Island, Anna Ding had been at something of a loose end. She came out to see us sometimes but she missed the regular boating so she joined the Victoria Recreation Club, a long established institution that had its own small strip of private beach in Deep Water Bay as well as a restaurant providing simple dishes of noodles and so on. She had her own water ski and she would occasionally hire the speedboat moored on the other side of the bay and zip around, showing off her prowess and recapturing some of what she had liked about our expeditions.

Anyway, on Christmas Day we had a total of about twelve, including Anna, for lunch. As everyone lay around in the stupor induced by roast turkey and Christmas pudding, Anna surprised us by saying that she would have to leave shortly because 'a friend' was coming to pick her up in a car. At this point, history becomes a bit unreliable as there are two conflicting accounts. We say that we just happened to be out in the garden when she left while 'the friend' always claimed that we were hiding behind a tree in order to satisfy our curiosity. Which of these versions is correct can never now be established but what is certain is that when we saw a gentleman of what we considered to be quite advanced years wearing a natty pair of driving gloves as he manoeuvred his open-top sports car up our driveway, we said more or less simultaneously, 'Why, it's Arthur Starling!' And then Anna was whisked away in her carriage by her cavalier.

Arthur had been our neighbour in the same block of flats before we left for the New Territories and we knew a bit about him as he was also a civil servant. Later on, we got to hear more of his intriguing life story, which encapsulated so much of twentieth century British history and was also closely linked to the development of Hong Kong. Arthur had been born in 1918 in London, a true Cockney whose accent could be heard faintly until the end of his life. He was someone with a range of accomplishments. He was a cunning tennis player until well into his eighties and had a good singing voice and stage presence. In the amateur musical shows put on in Hong Kong, he was a natural for songs from *My Fair Lady*. He would play to perfection Alfred P. Doolittle, the Cockney dustman in the part made famous by Stanley Holloway. And indeed his life had some similarities to Holloway's even though he was some thirty years younger and his war was the Second World War rather than the first.

Like Holloway, he started life as a clerk although his work was in hospitals. Because he was in the Territorial Army he was swept up into the war effort right from 1939. Arthur was among the troops rescued from Dunkirk and, fittingly enough, he came back to England in a requisitioned Thames pleasure steamer. After a stint in Home Defence at the time when invasion by Hitler was a real possibility he became a 'Desert Rat', in the Eighth Army, whose victory at El Alamein was a crucial turning point. He was not part of the force that re-took France in 1944 but he was always mildly resentful of the soubriquet of 'D-Day Dodger' that was applied to soldiers like him who were instead sent to Italy. The Anzio landings had been a gruelling experience, at least as difficult as that of the soldiers who invaded Normandy a few months later. Arthur would speak freely about what had happened to him during the war but when he reached Italy and the desperation that the Allied troops had found among the civilian population in Naples his eyes would always slightly change focus as if he was still seeing something that he really did not want to see.

Arthur was a colour sergeant by the end of the war but he did not wish to stay in the army: after all, for its duration, he had seen hardly anything of his young wife, Molly. He returned to hospital administration and worked first in London, then in the colony of British Guiana before finally arriving in Hong Kong in 1958. He rose to become chief hospital secretary and after retiring from that took a new position, helping his old friend Dr Gerald Choa, who had been the director of medical and health services, to plan the new Prince of Wales Teaching Hospital at Sha Tin. Life should have been perfect but Arthur was a widower, Molly having quite unexpectedly suffered a fatal heart attack several years before.

He started going to the nearby Victoria Recreation Club and it was there that he saw a sea goddess dropping into the water as she finished her ski and then found her sunbathing on the beach towel beside his.

Just over a year after he picked her up from our Christmas party Anna Ding and Arthur Starling were married in the City Hall registry with Michael as one of the witnesses. There was a slight delay when Anna was required to read something off a card as part of the ceremony as her ensemble did not include anything as unglamorous as a pair of reading glasses but Arthur loaned his and they proved to suit her very well. They had a reception at the Foreign Correspondents' Club and a few weeks later we had an evening party for them at Dunrose. I couldn't run to a wedding cake but I did make sherry trifles decorated with 'A's picked out in silver balls.

There had been a gap between Anna's wedding and our party for her because I was busy with other things. Our first child, James Howard Cartland, was born on 29 April 1979 and afterwards I took nine months off work. Standard maternity leave is 'four weeks before, six weeks after' but I negotiated something better, albeit unpaid, with Donald Tsang, who was then handling personnel matters for the administrative grade, another thankless task handed to him because he was good at his job. This one involved not piles and piles of files but listening to processions of people either sad or angry because they had not been given the promotion or the posting that they had been hoping for. With all those extra weeks at home, I was able to experience life at Dunrose to the full.

We had quite a bit of wildlife in the garden. We had our own cat and dog who hated each other so much that we had to make a sort of Berlin Wall arrangement to keep one (BadCat, the cat and her offspring Sinbad and Mogbad) in the back portion and the other (Pippa, the dog) in the front. There were numerous frogs, one of which took up residence under the dog's water bowl on the verandah as well as a bright green Bamboo Pit Viper that hung in a small shrub outside the kitchen window.

When our friend Hamish Macleod, later financial secretary, brought his family to visit we provided some unplanned excitement for their young children since as we sat on the verandah their son spotted a cobra rearing up on the lawn with a frog's legs sticking out of its mouth and flailing furiously. There was only one possible end to such an unequal struggle and from that day the hollow at the base of Pippa's bowl was no longer occupied so we were able to identify the victim exactly.

On a weekday not so long after this incident Ah Fung told me that Mr Ho wanted to see me in the garden. 'Come and look at this,' he said and took me to crouch down by one of the exits from the damp course that ran under the house. This was a pipe about a foot high and once my eyes had got used to the contrast of the darkness inside it and the bright sun outside I realised that what we were seeing was a cobra, probably the frog-swallower, its body protruding from its coils for almost the full height of the pipe, its hood extended and its eyes glittering. Mr Ho and I watched it together for a while in a kind of trance, as if there was some sort of reverse snake charming going on. However, it did not take much thought to conclude that this was actually a dangerous snake and it would be better to proceed accordingly.

I went inside and called the police. A team of six officers arrived who seemed to be some sort of specialist unit. They assessed the situation and asked if we had any old newspapers. These they screwed up and placed at all the entries of the damp course apart from the one closest to where the cobra was coiled. The officers lined up on either side of this exit but well back; they were armed with long bamboo canes. One man then went round and lit the newspaper balls. As the smoke began to penetrate the network of pipes the snake slithered towards the only remaining exit and as it emerged was efficiently beaten to death. It was big, almost six feet in length, and it was buried in the hillside behind the house.

The leading personalities in Yuen Long were closely linked to the land through generations of having been settled in that area. Fish farming was particularly lucrative as was rice importing and dealing. Some school principals also had particular standing and influence within the community. A member of the respected Man clan had shown an extraordinary streak of entrepreneurialism and set up a charter airline business, taking backwards and forwards the large numbers, particularly from the New Territories, who tried their luck as workers in the Chinese restaurants of Europe and North America. Eupo Air proudly proclaimed on its advertising material and business cards: *Head Office San Tin, New Territories* (which was, as it happened, a village of quite moderate size), branch offices London and New York.

Yuen Long was still largely a world unto itself and successive district officers figured in local lore. More recent DOs had their photographs transferred onto white tiles and enshrined on the wall of the Town Hall. The residents often mentioned David Akers-Jones who had gone on to greater things with responsibilities for the entire New Territories but he was considered in some way to be permanently and particularly Yuen Long's own. They also spoke in awe of 'Two Gun Fraser', a former police officer who had been made district officer and who had done much to curb the lawlessness that had set in during the Japanese occupation when ordinary day-to-day government in this relatively remote area was more or less absent. There was a thrilling tale of Fraser coming along with his two guns, even though he did not fire them, to intervene in the nick of time as a couple accused of adultery were about to suffer the traditional punishment of being forced into a bamboo container normally used for carrying pigs and then drowned in the village pond.

Even if that kind of drama was no more the relationship between the district officer and the local people could have its flashpoints. There could be disputes over rural committee elections, government compensation, land and building proposals and projects that might have bad effects on *fung shui* and therefore threaten the health and prosperity of whole villages. Sometimes, the government was not loved by some people and at one point while I was at home with the baby the police advised that they would like to step up security at our home. In practice, this meant that every day at around 10 a.m. a policeman on a motor bike would putter up our driveway, stop to sign the report book kept in a box outside our back door and do a U-turn back down the drive. This was a nice little marker in the day's routine but I always wondered how effective it really was as a form of protection since any vengeful person was left with approximately twenty-three hours and fifty-five minutes available for wreaking havoc. But fortunately no one ever decided to take advantage of this opportunity.

Although we lived in Dunrose for a while longer, by the middle of 1979 it was no longer as district officer Yuen Long and family. Michael had been very suddenly transferred to the Security Branch. The reason for that was a new crisis hitting Hong Kong: that of the arrival of thousands of 'boat people' fleeing Vietnam. This had been going on in fairly manageable numbers since 1975 as Vietnamese looked for a safer place to live in the aftermath of the US withdrawal from Vietnam, after which the Viet Cong had united the country and set up a new communist government. In 1979, however, it seemed that the Viet Cong were embarking on a systematic programme of ethnic cleansing of the Chinese population of Vietnam. Motivated by a mixture of fear and hope for a better life, Vietnamese, particularly those of Chinese origin, took to the sea in very risky conditions, in vessels that were often not fit to make the voyage, at the mercy of those whom they had bribed to get a place on board and in danger of pirate attacks. It is estimated that as many as half a million of the people who left Vietnam never made landfall in any recipient country, presumably all lost at sea.

Hong Kong was the destination that these boat people tried to reach because it was known that the Hong Kong government's policy was to allow them to land and then provide food and accommodation, at a basic level, and also to make efforts to arrange resettlement in developed countries. On the Hong Kong side, it was immensely challenging to establish facilities quickly enough for the flood of refugees arriving and there were subsidiary worries such as the infectious diseases they might be bringing to Hong Kong including possibly even bubonic plague. The chiefs in the Security Branch dealing with all this were more or less worn out but would almost certainly have to go on dealing with these problems for the long term. So that they could take some leave

Michael was drafted in temporarily as deputy secretary for security. It was another of those occasions when being singled out as someone with the capability to do a difficult job well also meant being given an extra dose of stress and strain.

Just as Michael took over, one of the most notorious incidents in the saga of the Vietnamese boat people in Hong Kong took place. A ship originally called the *Ky Lu,* later transformed into the *Skyluck* had arrived from Vietnam in the early part of 1979 with about 2,700 refugees on board. There was no space for them in the refugee camps that had been set up and grave (justified) doubts about the captain's story that this was a normal freighter that had happened to pick up a lot of people on the high seas rather than a profiteering operation. The *Skyluck* was therefore required to anchor and was guarded by police boats, with food and water being provided by the Hong Kong government for those on board. This situation had lasted for about four months when the *Skyluck*'s passengers took matters into their own hands by petrol bombing the police boats and cutting their vessel's anchor chains so that it drifted and ended up on the rocks on Lamma Island. Dealing with the aftermath was Michael's very first task. Emergency accommodation was found by requisitioning the new prison that had been about to open at Chi Ma Wan on Lantau Island. He had an extremely busy few months, dealing with the arrival of refugees, the facilities for those already here and attempts to find resettlement countries. As time went by, the government's processes and procedures became more settled and less improvised but Vietnamese boat people were a problem of some sizeable scale until about the early 1990s, by which time the situation in Vietnam was such that people could return there, resettlement countries had already accepted many thousands and the remainder were integrated into the Hong Kong community.

During this period, Michael had two places of business: his day-to-day office on the fifth floor of the Secretariat, close to the chief secretary and political adviser, and a command centre for emergencies in Victoria Barracks which still occupied a prime site in Central. It was to the latter he went on 2 August 1979 because a typhoon was threatening. This was Hope, a mildly ridiculous official name for what turned out to be one of the more severe typhoons to affect us. The observatory's typhoon signalling system has a designation of ten for its severest storms but rarely has to get up there and even a number eight signal will stop all but the most essential activity. Hope powered her way through signals eight, nine and up to ten within the course of a few hours that morning and, as it turned out, affected the New Territories particularly badly. Hope was so fast! It only took about half an hour for the fierce winds and rain that she brought to knock out Dunrose's telephone line and water and electricity supply as well as devastating the garden with bushes and smaller trees uprooted and blown about as well as branches from the larger ones. Debris lay everywhere including right across the driveway. At one point, Ah Fung and I tried to open the back door, literally clinging to each other, but could not stand and were more or less blown back in.

In my years in Hong Kong I have been through many typhoons and it has become a routine to listen to the observatory's reports and follow all the well developed procedures for dealing with these tropical storms. Hope was different though. Not only were its effects particularly severe but it was also my only experience of being in the eye of the storm, which was really striking. As the eye passed over the house in the middle of the afternoon a dead calm suddenly fell and the winds dropped. I walked through the garden, that was so different from what it had been only the day before, to our neighbours at Perowne Barracks. They still had working telephones and so I was able to report the damage that we had suffered to our essential services. I had just enough time to do this before the storm started up again although with somewhat less power than before. Michael was able to get home that evening and by then, amazingly enough, there were already workers from the emergency teams there restoring water, electricity and telephone. I don't believe that we were specially privileged; this was the way that the utilities trained their staff to respond.

The garden was a different matter though. Day after day went by and it still looked a mess. Mr Ho occupied himself in righting the pot plants, standing them up again, patting and tweaking them so that they at least were in a better state. He was completely ignoring the heaps of trees, bushes and branches which might to some have seemed a more pressing problem. By now, though, I knew better than to question Mr Ho. Saturday came and Michael was lucky enough not to have to go to work so we were sleeping in when I heard a commotion in the garden. Going to investigate, I found five teenage girls working away, cooperating to lug heavy branches to one side, collecting basketfuls of debris and generally restoring the garden as far as possible. Mr Ho stood to one side, quietly observing and every now and then offering a word of advice or instruction. He was never one for excessive explanation. 'My daughters,' he said laconically. 'They were at school during the week.'

We were able to take some leave ourselves in November, which was not the best month to visit Europe. We would have a baby of six months with us and we planned to take my parents away on holiday even though my father was by then using a wheelchair. We had decided that the most practical thing to do would be to rent a house in France and we went to the Alps because, in a rather bookish way, I had done some research and made the improbable finding that this region had more hours of sunshine in November than any other part of France. I think the trip was a success. My parents were very game even though my mother found the mountains rather overwhelming and the corkscrewing roads made her travel sick while my father was quite shocked by some aspects of French life: 'Fifteen bob for the *Daily Mail*,' he grumbled, not having come to terms with the British conversion to decimal coinage or the laws of supply and demand in a small town that entertained only occasional tourists. Michael and I enjoyed the novelty of seeing up close a traditional rural way of life, based on cattle raising. Perhaps we would have paid more attention, or to different things, if we had realised that quite soon we would ourselves be living on the other side of those self-same mountains.

CHAPTER SEVEN

Hong Kong Waters and Geneva

WE HAD TO LEAVE DUNROSE and come back to a more ordinary life on Hong Kong Island. Ah Fung decided that Mr Ho and his smart car would be ideal for transporting some of the smaller kitchen items that she wanted to be sure not to lose and to have ready to hand as we were settling in. Like many Hong Kongers, Mr Ho's life took place in a fairly geographically restricted area and trips to Hong Kong Island were something that he rarely, if ever, undertook. Still, he was in thrall to Ah Fung's charms and at her behest would make efforts that he would not otherwise have contemplated. This, however, was a decision that both probably came to regret. When they eventually arrived at our new flat both looked worn out and Ah Fung was quite emotional.

'He drove so, so slowly. I kept telling him to drive faster but he wouldn't.' Since their route had taken them along the Tuen Mun Highway, which was the first of Hong Kong's motorway or express-way type roads this must have been pretty unsettling for other road users too. 'In the end,' she continued, 'I was so exhausted that I told him that he would have to manage on his own for a bit and I closed my eyes to take a rest. When I opened them again we were driving round and round inside Lai Chi Kok bus terminus!' This was at a point probably at most a third of the total journey which allowed one to gauge how protracted the first section must have been. Anyway, they safely reached their destination but there was another annoyance for Ah Fung as she unpacked the cooking utensils and spotted the pin-up calendar left behind by the last occupant. Unusually for her, she lapsed into English. 'Very naughty,' she sniffed. 'No pants.'

Thanks to timely advice from Anna Ding, we were able to buy *Tiki,* the junk which the New Zealand Insurance Company was replacing with a newer one. It was quite common for medium-sized companies to own such a boat that its staff could enjoy at week-ends and public holidays. Michael had a post in the Trade Department and, as it turned out, international trade negotiation was to become his specialty for the remainder of his career, although with diversions into Social Welfare and Financial Services.

I was sent to the Economic Services Branch, where my main duty was overseeing the implementation of the report of the Advisory Committee on Diversification although I also fitted in some other subjects such as oil and gas supply. The Advisory Committee was an example of the sort of the thing that, I think, the Hong Kong government did rather well. It started out with a problem that at least some members of the community saw as a serious one that needed to be tackled for the good of Hong Kong. In this case, it was the concern that the economy was over dependent on its long-established manufacturing industries and the feeling that there should be an examination of the possibility of a more diverse economy and of the means to make such changes. There was a network of committees to consider all the different facets of the question and at the end a report of almost five hundred pages, admittedly in rather large print, was published, transparently making recommendations and explaining the reasoning for them. Everyone was given an opportunity to comment and the Executive Council, the equivalent of the Cabinet, endorsed the recommendations and asked for six-monthly progress reports.

The recommendations covered all sorts of subjects including some, such as the expansion of technical education, which at first sight did not seem to have a direct connection. To an extent, also, it was a gathering together of ideas, such as the building of a convention centre, which had been in the air for a while but needed a push and official endorsement to get them moving. The principle was always to facilitate the initiatives of entrepreneurs. There was to be no departure from 'positive non-interventionism', no 'picking winners' and offering of direct help to key industries. The wisdom of this was proved by what happened to the offshore oil industry.

It was then supposed that there was great promise in the development of oilfields in the South China Sea and we devoted thought
and attention to the question of how we might assist. In the event,
there was not as much potential for that industry as had been
supposed but because of our essentially 'hands off' approach this
caused negligible pain to the public finances.

The report itself could be considered the offspring of Yeung
Kai-yin (KY), who was still in the Economics Service Branch, and
who was a person of enormous energy. The branch also had within
its purview the finances and governance of the Mass Transit Railway
Corporation, which had been set up in 1975. There was an entire
filing cabinet devoted to all the complexities of the setting up
process and a cursory glance would suggest that every piece of paper
with in it had been inscribed by KY in his geometric, completely
even handwriting, normally in royal blue fountain pen ink. KY had
served a long apprenticeship in Finance Branch and he had clearly
a great affection for its forms and procedures. He had been part of
the group that drew up the budget with Philip Haddon-Cave and
it seemed that he admired Sir Philip's way of working because
whenever there was anything of the slightest importance to be
drafted he would gather as many of the branch staff as he reasonably
could into his office, sit us in a semi-circle around his desk and ask
every now and again for a nugget of information or a suggestion
for a word. He was facilitated in this approach by an extraordinary
ability, which I have never seen in anyone else, to write as legibly
and evenly upside down as upright. This meant that those sitting
on the other side of the desk could see the draft as it progressed
instead of waiting for him to finish a section and then pass it across.
However, even this magical display could pall a bit after a few hours
or, as sometimes happened, pretty much the whole day although
with suitable breaks every now and again. When he was not drafting
KY could have a volatile temper and items of office equipment
would go sailing across the room. His secretary did not always take
this lightly but would chuck things back so his office would become
a war zone of flying staplers and telephone directories. Added to
that was his chain smoking and the fug it produced. KY was an

irritating, intensely lovable human being whose nit-picking diligence rendered great services to the community of Hong Kong.

Towards the end of 1982, on 23 October to be precise, we welcomed
the younger of our two children: Caroline Joyce, her second name
a tribute to the redoubtable Reverend Miss Bennett. This time
around, I was a bit more used to babies, what they looked like and
how they behaved. By putting together paid leave due to me and
some negotiated unpaid leave I was again able to take more than
the standard maternity allowance although this time I thought that
six months should be enough. All the same a break as long as that
could not be filled in by a temporary substitute so I had to expect
a posting. This was down the corridor and up a couple of floors,
to the Health and Welfare Branch.

In the Health and Welfare Branch my new boss was Henry
Ching, with whom I had previously worked in Finance Branch.
My area was medical policy and we were doing some potentially
fascinating things. We recognised that our hospital services were
not reaching our expectation of the sort of service that we should
be able to render to our citizens. We administrative officers began
looking thoroughly at the existing situation. And this was not just
riffling through papers. We went to hospitals, from tiny St John
Hospital on Cheung Chau Island, which was as much a nursing
home as what was normally considered to be a hospital, to the
Queen Elizabeth Hospital, a maze of a place with all kinds of
specialties. Queen Elizabeth suffered from overflowing demand
which led to corridors full of camp beds, for many years a shame
and a cause of obsessive concern in our provision of hospital services
in all the major hospitals. There were ancillary facilities too to
understand and visit, mortuaries and laboratories and so on.

The process we began then culminated in the setting up of the
Hospital Authority in 1990 and significant improvements. Subsequently, though, different problems have emerged. Around 1997
a public debate sponsored by the government began on how the
medical services should be financed, with the underlying assumption that some sort of social insurance scheme had to be introduced

as it would not be practical to continue the existing system under which health services are largely financed from general revenue, with minimal charges levied on the individual user. Some fifteen years later the issue has made no meaningful progress while sucking up quantities of time and energy. At the same time, patients, particularly in the poorer parts of Hong Kong, experience crowded wards and clinics as well as overworked doctors and nurses. A career in the Hong Kong government has, overall, been deeply satisfying but it is frustrating to have been part of a team that tackled a problem and achieved some success and then to see the same or similar things reappearing.

It was a nice diversion to concentrate on a literally concrete subject: the proposal to build a hospital at the eastern end of Hong Kong Island. We had plenty of data to show how unsatisfactory, indeed how life threatening, it was that the critically ill and emergency cases had to be taken by ambulance right to the other side of Hong Kong Island to get to Queen Mary Hospital. Dr TY Chau of the Medical and Health Department and I together waged one of those paper wars beloved of bureaucrats to get agreement for that hospital. We rebutted every counter-argument, produced any information requested almost before it had been asked for and eventually the 'enemy' succumbed. The enemy of course was the Finance Branch, our very own colleagues just like us; indeed it was entirely possible that I would go back there myself one day and would find myself rigorously guarding Hong Kong's treasury and turning down projects. As it was though, we got the Pamela Youde Nethersole Eastern District Hospital. Some fifteen years later, I underwent a minor operation there myself and as I settled down on my day bed and waited for the anaesthetist, I could not suppress a small feeling of extra entitlement. 'This is *my* hospital,' I thought.

Another major crusade we were engaged in was the campaign against smoking. Although I did some work on it the main protagonists were the two deputy secretaries, first John Chambers and then Geoff Barnes together with Judith Mackay, a local doctor who was later described by the tobacco companies as 'the most dangerous woman in the world'. The fruits of such exercises are not seen immediately but by 2012 Hong Kong had the world's lowest smoking rate.

Throughout that period in the early 1980s everyone in Hong Kong was suffering from enormous psychological pressure. It was the knowledge that the moment had finally come, the discussions were underway which would decide what would happen to Hong Kong after the New Territories lease expired in 1997. Although we went on with our lives, working at things that had nothing to do with The Future, that in fact seemed to assume that the status quo would continue forever, this was always in the back of our minds. It was like having a close relative who was sick with recovery uncertain. There was not much substance to discuss as what was going on was being conducted in secret. In the absence of solid information symbols and portents became invested with meaning. In September 1982 Mrs Thatcher, the British Prime Minister, in Beijing for the critical meeting that would initiate the negotiations, stumbled and fell on the steps of the Great Hall of the People. Hong Kong was horrified. Some middle-class adolescents had their lives changed forever by that day as their parents suddenly decided that it would be safer to send them away for their schooling.

If there was little substantial information available there was plenty of speculation and, Hong Kong being what it is, a certain amount of lateral thinking about alternatives.

A favourite surmise about the outcome of the negotiations was that Britain would be allowed to keep running Hong Kong on some sort of 'management contract' and that essentially everything would remain exactly as before. There was no clarity about how such an arrangement could be worked out in practice. Furthermore, a moment's realistic analysis would have shown that this was hopelessly optimistic. China's great historic wounds were connected with the foundation of Hong Kong which was a consequence of the humiliating Opium Wars, seen, among other things, as a sign of China's weakness in relation to the power of the West. It was unthinkable that the opportunity would not be taken to right this wrong and regain Hong Kong.

Some expatriate civil servants had a suggestion that was perhaps more realistic in concept, even if also difficult to put into practice. Their idea was that the Hong Kong civil service should put an advertisement into, say, the *Economist,* offering to hire themselves out as a unit to any small country that might like to avail itself of a capable administration. It was a fantasy but rather a charming one. It would surely have been fascinating to try and build a new Hong Kong somewhere else and to work out what were the essential components of its success and how these might be replicated.

I also came across a few local businessmen who reacted in a typically Hong Kong manner. Hong Kong was foundering because of the terms of a lease, which was an essentially commercial, contractual document. Why couldn't Hong Kong take a leaf out of this book and buy an island somewhere and reestablish itself? I was asked, apparently in all seriousness, about the characteristics of various British islands such as the Isle of Wight, Isle of Man and the Channel Islands group. Needless to say, this was another one that never got off the drawing board.

The months dragged by in this uncomfortable state. Hong Kong was accustomed to a free flow of information and it was odd for those of us outside the small circle involved in the negotiations to become like the classic 'China Watchers' trying to extract some meaning from the enigmatic comments that did find their way into the press and mostly drawing rather pessimistic conclusions. At the time Hong Kong had a floating exchange rate and the political pessimism was mirrored in the downward slide of the value of the Hong Kong dollar. By the end of September 1983 it took HK$9.6 to buy one US dollar and the main focus of Hong Kong's anxiety switched from the political to the economic.

Hong Kong is heavily dependent on imports to maintain its way of life and these were shooting up in price. Once again, the community, without any specific organisation, demonstrated a collective consciousness that feared the same things and drew the same conclusions. The week-end of 24 and 25 September 1983 was another of those times when Hong Kong as if one held its breath and this time the phrase that captured the fears was 'valueless currency'. It was as if some invisible, inaudible but quite plain message had gone out on the Saturday to strip the supermarkets. The goods most in demand seemed to be rice and toilet paper and determined shoppers were wheeling trolleys stacked with these as well as other things along the pavements.

We had been invited to bring our children along on the Sunday for a day's boating with Chris Cheng, a local industrialist, and his family. Since his boat was moored out at Sai Kung, a long and inconvenient drive from our home, he would kindly send a car to pick us up. He apologised that on this occasion it would be rather an old one. His mother was worried about the security situation and was not at all keen about him going out but if he was to do so she had asked that he try not to draw attention to himself with a flashy car. Indeed, in the group gathered on the boat the talk was all about safety and security. The consensus was that there was no need to panic yet but if one had been thinking about a holiday away from Hong Kong it might be a good time to take it. When we got home we received a phone call from Michael's parents, who had been living in Australia since 1968. They had seen media reports of the situation in Hong Kong and Barrie, his father, said that, if we wanted to, we could send the children down to them so that if things worsened we would be able to stay in Hong Kong and do whatever was needed without having the worry of looking after a young family as well. Born in 1912 and having worked mainly overseas since his mid-twenties Barrie was accustomed to living with danger and trying to react in the most sensible way.

Things did not worsen. Instead they got very much better, at least as far the potential problem of our having a steeply devaluing currency was concerned. While we had been floating in Hong Kong waters emergency meetings had been convened on the exchange rate. A statement was issued by Douggie Blye, the secretary for monetary affairs, and Hong Kong in the strange way its collective psyche operated, decided that this was sufficiently reassuring and began to believe, and behave, as if the problem would be fixed.

By a great piece of good fortune the government had a solution to hand. John Greenwood, a young economist working in the private sector, had proposed that the Hong Kong dollar should be pegged to the US dollar as a better alternative than free floating for a small economy like Hong Kong's with no central bank of its own. This simple concept required intensive thinking through as to how exactly it could be operated. It required the cooperation of the note-issuing banks who would be responsible for the technicalities of smoothing out minor fluctuations in the exchange rate around the chosen value of 'the peg' of US$1 to HK$7.8. Despite these efforts the scheme might have failed anyway for lack of public confidence in the new arrangement. If it had failed, the next option would probably have been to abandon the Hong Kong dollar altogether and to try to run the city on the basis of US dollars. We were lucky enough not to have to try that option nor any others. The peg arrangement was announced on 15 October; it held as soon as it was introduced and became the mainstay of Hong Kong's monetary policy. Hong Kong relaxed and went back to its normal business of trying to spin its Hong Kong dollars into more of the same.

Nearly ten years later when the Hong Kong Monetary Authority was established its first head always travelled in a government car with the number plate of 'AM 78'. Some supposed that if that ever changed we should take it as a sign that perhaps the peg is finally about to be abandoned!

Our own lives were in a state of flux too and, again, the cause was a posting for Michael. He was now quite experienced in international trade policy and it was decided that he should head the Hong Kong Government Office in Geneva, which was principally occupied with representing Hong Kong's interests in the General Agreement on Tariffs and Trade, the GATT, which had formed the basis for the conduct of world trade since it had come into effect in 1947 and which, like many international bodies, had its headquarters in the Swiss city. When we went to Geneva the Hong Kong government representatives operated under the umbrella of the British delegation, although Hong Kong ran its own trade policy and the Hong Kong Office in Geneva reported only to Hong Kong. Hong Kong's status in Geneva was to be significantly changed as was the nature of the GATT itself, and Michael would play a major part in both these developments but that all lay in the future.

We gave up the flat that we had just moved into, sold our boat and packed up our things for a move to Switzerland. The following four years would be very different from my previous experiences. The Hong Kong government could not offer me a post there and so I would be taking unpaid leave and sampling what it meant to be a diplomatic wife. We settled into Nyon, a small town in the Geneva commuter belt but an ancient one, with traces of Roman settlement and a medieval centre, taking over the house that the government had been renting for Michael's predecessor. Like all decently sized Swiss houses it came with its own nuclear fallout shelter as required by law. In our case, this doubled up as the laundry room; if we had stuck to the rules we should have had it equipped with drinking water and basic supplies to see us through an attack but instead we took up the storage space with washing powder and fabric softener. Down in the network of cellars reached through a trapdoor in the garage floor we also possessed a *carnotzet*, something that was rarer to find in a private home than a fallout shelter. It was a wood panelled room, decorated with posters of mountain scenes and intended for the consumption of Swiss cheese specialties such as fondue and raclette.

During our stay there we discovered quite a lot about Switzerland but its culture is surprisingly complex and there was much to learn. The population is not so much greater than Hong Kong's but four different languages are spoken: German, French, Italian and Romansch, this last being the mother tongue of fewer than one per cent of the Swiss. Geneva, Nyon and all the places that we normally visited were in the French-speaking area, la Suisse Romande. Since Geneva was so much a city of international organisations, it was just about possible to manage with no French, relying on English instead but it would have been very limiting. Portsmouth High School taught French in the way normal for an academic school in the 1960s. Consequently, I had read Racine, Molière and so on in the original texts but had studied comparatively little in the way of day-to-day phrases and conversation. But the Portsmouth approach turned out to be a very sound one. I had a strong foundation in French grammar and adding in new bits of vocabulary was not such a difficult task.

The atmosphere in Geneva was quite cool. This applied not just to the weather which, indeed, in the summer was delightfully warm with the sun sparkling on the lake as the steamships took trippers between Switzerland and France. Life was as regular as the steamers' time-table. The busy, chaotic rest of the world seemed as far away as in a dream or in some other dimension. Events in Hong Kong which just a short while before had been so gripping and so personal came to seem as if behind a light veil which robbed them of some of their drama and made them seem more humdrum.

It was in this 'Geneva state of mind' that I followed from a distance the continuing negotiations over Hong Kong's future and their conclusion in the Sino-British Joint Declaration signed in September 1984. This brief document was a descendant of the philosophy of 'one country, two systems' which would allow China to resume sovereignty over Hong Kong while at the same time allowing the latter to maintain its very different way of life. Hong Kong would become a Special Administrative Region of China, enjoying 'a high degree of autonomy' and with 'Hong Kong people ruling Hong Kong'. This was all to be enshrined in a set of laws which would remain unchanged for fifty years, until 2047. There was much trumpeting of how the aim was to preserve Hong Kong's 'stability and prosperity'. 'Well,' I thought, 'that sounds as if it might be all right. It's probably the best deal that could have been reached given that Chinese national pride and modern Britain's comparative weakness made a reversion of sovereignty inevitable. It might work.'

I was, anyway, rather preoccupied with family matters, being the non-working mother of two small children. We had a trip to London around this time for the christening of our daughter, Caroline. We particularly wanted the service to be conducted by Joyce Bennett. She had baptised James in St John's Cathedral in Hong Kong when he was six months old but when Caroline was that age Joyce was busy preparing for her retirement and return to the UK.

Joyce was now in a situation which could have been quite disheartening. In Hong Kong she was very clearly a person of respectability and high social standing: a member of the Legislative Council, a school principal and a serving Anglican priest. She had thought of remaining in Hong Kong but her Bishop told her that he believed that there was more that needed to be done back in the land of her birth. However, on her return, she was confronted with a great deal of opposition from within the church to her continuing to operate as a priest since the Anglican Church in England did not at that time ordain women as priests and did not do so until 1994. Joyce consequently spent more than ten years speaking up for the ordination of women and being regarded by some as an irritant and by some with rather more anger than that. She was not one whit disturbed but sailed on full of confidence, determination and good humour. It seemed to me that perhaps Sir Murray MacLehose and Sir Philip Haddon-Cave should have written to the bishops and archbishops warning them that resistance was useless and that they would save themselves a lot of time by doing whatever it was that Joyce told them was the right thing.

She had bought a house in Buckinghamshire which she shared with Mary, her goddaughter, a Hong Kong girl, but was spending a lot of time in London. She was on call as a Cantonese interpreter for the Metropolitan Police and was also ministering to the Chinese congregation at the historic church of St Martin-in-the-Fields which has survived the days when it really was surrounded by fields and is now at the corner of Trafalgar Square in one of the busiest parts of London. This was Joyce's toe in the door of the English church since there was a desperate need for a Chinese speaker and it could hardly be argued that she was not well qualified in that respect. There had been all sorts of arcane arguments about how she was to be described and what she might and might not be allowed to do. 'But, after all,' she said, with her look of wide-eyed innocence and her mischievous grin 'they don't know what's going on once we're all speaking Cantonese.'

We arranged for Caroline to be baptised during the normal Sunday afternoon service that Joyce held in St Martin's crypt. Michael almost failed to be present for his daughter's christening.

He had been at a meeting in Mexico to discuss the regulation of the international textiles trade. His plane back was delayed and his luggage was lost at the transit stop in Houston. British Caledonian, the airline concerned, had very decently given him some cash to buy replacement clothes. (They went out of business a few years later. Perhaps being so fair towards their passengers was not a paying proposition.) Tired and jet lagged, but wearing a nice new sweater, he was in his position by the font. Joyce was very considerate towards our guests who were attending the service, which was normally entirely in Cantonese. Instead, she gave a section by section consecutive translation into English. In the circumstances, this was quite hard on Michael whose eyelids drooped and almost closed as he began to sway on his feet but luckily he managed to recover himself and stay awake and upright for the remainder of the ceremony.

We briefly attended the usual post-service refreshments with the rest of the congregation who were Chinese speakers who would make long journeys in order to worship in their own language. It suddenly seemed as if we were back in Hong Kong. I was particularly impressed by the cakes on offer. They seemed to have come straight out of Maxim's, the chain of Hong Kong bakeries, specialising in decoration with great swirls of buttercream and jams in jewel colours. They were presumably sourced from somewhere in London's Chinatown. We went on to our own party in a flat we were renting during our holiday. My father enjoyed himself hugely including the process of getting there, which had required four strong guests to manhandle his wheelchair up the small flight of steps that led to the building.

Not long after this, I was able briefly to rediscover my identity as a Hong Kong civil servant. We managed to persuade the government that it would be highly desirable if I could have a sort of refamiliarisation week back in Hong Kong with a programme of briefings and visits. It was marvellous for me to catch up with everyone and everything and to feel revitalised by Hong Kong's pace, energy and its love of life including all its ridiculous and ironic aspects.

On one day during that week I had a government car to go to the New Territories and, on the way back, decided that I could reasonably make a small diversion and take a look at Dunrose, which I knew to be unoccupied. We went to the top of the driveway and already there was Mr Ho's familiar lemon yellow car, looking as smart as ever it had done. Rules and procedures meant that even if there was no one living there the garden must be properly maintained by the person employed to do so. We parked behind Mr Ho's car and I went through the familiar wire gate into the front garden and saw him, his head protected by his battered but serviceable straw hat, raking up the scarlet petals from under the Flame of the Forest tree. He looked up and smiled tranquilly. 'Hullo, how are you?' he said in an even tone. It had been several years since we had seen each other at all and yet he evinced no surprise at this surely unexpected appearance. 'Mr Ho, do you remember me? Do you know who I am?' His eyes crinkled in amusement at my stupidity. 'Of course, I know who you are. Where are you living now? Still on Hong Kong Island?' I brought him up to date on our doings although I don't know that he was very impressed by the mention of Switzerland: nowhere outside the northwest New Territories really counted much at all.

We chatted pleasantly a while longer and then we parted. I have never seen Mr Ho since nor do I know what happened to him but I hope he has had many years of contentment on his government pension. Dunrose also I never saw again. There was a practice of sometimes allocating temporarily unused government accommodation to non-profit-making organisations and so in the 1990s Jackie Pullinger's St Stephen's Society was given the use of our former home since one of the by-products of the Joint Declaration on the future of Hong Kong had been a consensus on the future of the Kowloon Walled City, ending years of stalemate. Britain and China agreed that the Walled City should be cleared and demolished and replaced by a public park.

The Joint Declaration was like the large outline of a picture and for years afterwards there was complex and often stressful work to be done on the colouring in. This was not decoration or trivial detail; how well this process, which involved officials from China and the United Kingdom supported by the Hong Kong administration, was carried out would to a large extent determine how effectively the Joint Declaration would be implemented and how the citizens of Hong Kong would fare after 1997. The truth of this can be seen in the ongoing difficulties over the right of abode in Hong Kong of children born in Hong Kong of Mainland Chinese. The relevant part of the Basic Law is ambiguously written and there are views that the rights that it apparently gives are not in Hong Kong's best interests because of fears of uncontrollable population increase. The Beijing government has been asked to interpret the Basic Law in order to make things clearer but there is an inbuilt resistance to interpretations or, worse, amendment of the Basic Law since this seems a threat to the principle of 'Hong Kong people ruling Hong Kong'.

A piece of this follow up action which affected us directly concerned the future conduct of Hong Kong's international trade relations. The Joint Declaration had stipulated that Hong Kong could maintain and develop economic and cultural relations and agreements with states, regions and relevant international organisations on its own. The ability to conduct international trade relations was fundamental to Hong Kong's economic well-being and the General Agreement on Tariffs and Trade was the appropriate multilateral contractual forum that set the rules by which its members conducted their trade with each other and which provided a mechanism for the settlement of disputes.

What was now required was the 'colouring in' that would allow Hong Kong to move from being a rather unusual offshoot of the UK delegation in the GATT to being a contracting party in its own right. Fortuitously there was an appropriate procedure in the 1947 GATT articles that provided for dependent territories to do just that. All that was needed was for the UK delegation to make a declaration in the GATT to the effect that Hong Kong had a separate customs territory and full autonomy in the conduct of its external commercial relations. The fact that these precise words had already appeared in the Joint Declaration greatly helped the discussions that now had to take place in early 1986 with the GATT legal authorities in Geneva and between China, the UK and Hong Kong in Beijing. The upshot was that the UK declaration was made on a day in April 1986 and the Chinese delegation also made a declaration on the same day to the effect that the conditions on which Hong Kong had become a GATT member would continue to apply beyond 1997. Strictly speaking this latter declaration was not a legal requirement and China was not itself a contracting party at the time, only an observer, but nevertheless it was a welcome reassurance to the international community of China's commitment to honour the terms of the Joint Declaration and it helped to dispel any doubts that contracting parties might have had about what would happen beyond 1997.

In the event Hong Kong's accession passed without comment and at the next meeting of the GATT Council Michael sat with the Hong Kong delegation between Hungary and Haiti. This, however, was not quite the end of the story. If Hong Kong had full autonomy it needed to be seen to have it. Again it was fortuitous that diplomats in Geneva do not owe their diplomatic status to the Vienna Convention, for the simple reason that Geneva is not the capital of Switzerland. Rather, an equivalent status is granted in Geneva by the Swiss authorities as a matter of courtesy and purely at their own discretion. They saw fit to exercise that discretion to grant that status to the members of the Hong Kong delegation and, most visibly, allocated a dedicated number for the CD number plates on their cars so that they should no longer be thought of as belonging to the UK Mission.

There was perhaps some discomfort on the part of the British diplomats in Geneva to find part of the Empire slipping away in such obvious fashion especially as Michael could now raise Hong Kong's own flag (name plate) at meetings and say his piece while the UK delegation had to remain silent as only the commission's spokesman could speak on behalf of the members of the European Community (as it then was).

Nonetheless, cordial relationships were forged. The UK Mission was kind enough to give us one of the stock of books of condolence that they kept when in December of that year we received the shocking news from Hong Kong that Sir Edward Youde, the highly popular and much respected governor who had succeeded Murray

MacLehose in 1982 had died in his sleep while on an official visit to Beijing. We would not have known where to obtain one otherwise. Sometimes we were able to help out with our own special knowledge. The housekeeper at the UK mission sensibly showed us the proposed menu for a dinner for the Chinese ambassador. We were able to advise that we were not aware of any Chinese person who would think of a cold soup as anything other than unnatural and a penance to have to eat and that the proposed main course of lamb was risky too as many found that to have a quite repulsive taste and smell. We also tried to be a friendly presence for those in the Chinese mission, who were often quite new to Geneva and could find the mechanics of life in a French-speaking city baffling.

Anguishing over a dinner party menu was quite typical of our new way of life. Our friend Joan Plaisted, an American diplomat, popped in to see us one day and when she said that she really had to be on her way our young son asked why. 'James,' she said solemnly, 'I am going to eat for my country.' And there was a lot of that going on! We recognised that this was something that we had to accept as part of the job since we didn't want Hong Kong to be seen as somehow not fitting in. Luckily for us, though, Hong Kong was more interested in the substance of what went on during the day rather than the style of what went on in the evenings so we didn't have to worry too much about being judged on the clothes we wore or by the standards of some pretentious protocol.

Small talk was difficult for all diplomats in Geneva. It was a multilateral post rather than, say, being a representative in the Swiss capital of Berne to Switzerland and the Swiss government. The day-to-day business was that of mingling with representatives from almost every country in the world and trying to assert one's own position in the international organisations that had their headquarters there. The evenings' business was to meet up with these same diplomats on a social level and to try not to offend anyone. It was a salutary lesson in how potentially tactless normal conversation can be among a restricted circle, with unconsciously held prejudices and stereotypes cropping up rather frequently.

Over the years, a lexicon of 'safe subjects' seemed to have developed, recognised by all even if not written down anywhere.

Assisting this process was the fact that Geneva's business time table was quite rigid with dampened activity, and therefore opportunities for holiday breaks, in the summer and at Easter and Christmas. In addition, most people who were posted there made at least some attempt to ski and to go to the mountains at week-ends. There was thus quite a lot of scope to ask fellow guests whether they had been away yet, or had plans to go away and, depending on the time of year, whether they had yet started skiing or whether they had stopped in the face of warmer weather.

As a result of a fall at home I broke my wrist which necessitated several weeks in plaster. I felt that I should have continued with a fake cast for a bit longer as a kind of public service as it had clearly been such a Godsend for so many. Their faces lit up when they saw me at dinners. Something new but non-controversial to talk about! And there was so much to ask! How had I done it? (It was June and so not very likely to be a skiing injury, which cut off an otherwise fertile line of enquiry.) Was it a bad break? Which hospital had I gone to? When would the plaster come off? And so on, and so on. My accident had taken place while Michael was away in Hawaii for discussions on the Hong Kong/US textiles agreement. This seemed to add a little twinge of resentment to the painful wrist although, to be fair, I knew that these expeditions to exotic places were for the protagonists mainly a blur of jet lag exacerbated by sleeplessness as it seemed to be a point of honour not to settle any issue until the last possible moment.

Geneva was, understandably, regarded as a desirable place to live and a diplomatic posting there was an enviable one. Various countries whose governments' records were not regarded as, ahem, spotless, would seem to keep large presences there, with staff perhaps related to the head of state and not noticeably active in the normal business of meetings and so on.

Some of the world's ultra wealthy also found the mansions that dotted the shores of Lake Geneva a good place to put down roots for at least part of the year. Our son, James, was of primary school age and attended an international school where some of his class-mates certainly came into this category. He wanted to know whether his friend, Mohammed, could come and play. He could as far as I was concerned but it turned out there was an obstacle; Mohammed had to 'ask his driver'. Negotiations over dates, times and routes between me and the driver were successfully conducted through these two small intermediaries and on the appointed day a very large Swiss muffled up in a greatcoat arrived with a shy and slight six-year-old in tow and came to collect him again a few hours later.

As with all children, they had of themselves no concept of race or nationality and played together, happily or not, simply dependent on their individual tastes and personalities. There were, apparently, students originating from over a hundred different countries and the school decided to use this as a basis for an educational experience. There was to be a celebration on this theme one Saturday afternoon and all mothers were asked to produce some typical homemade snacks. I was glad of my dual claims since English fruitcake was much easier to knock up than Chinese *dim sum.* The food and the entertainment all seemed to be well received but there were negative, and surely unintended, consequences as for weeks afterwards the playground descended into warring factions taking reference from all these suddenly discovered differences. James came home one day, full of indignation. 'Mummy, England is bigger than America, isn't it?' 'No, James, I honestly can't say that. On the other hand, though, England once owned America and America never owned England,' I told him, thus making, I suppose, my little contribution to international disharmony and discord.

I was able to keep Hong Kong's end up too. Once when I went to meet him, I was approached by another boy who boldly asked, 'Do you eat snakes?' I thought of the many bowls of warming snake and chicken soup topped off with Chinese crispy croutons and white chrysanthemum petals that I had downed over the years and was able to say promptly that this was indeed the case. My interlocutor went rushing over to the group of his peers who were waiting for the answer. 'He wasn't telling stories. His mother does eat snakes.' Perhaps I would have been asked to provide a demonstration at the following year's 'International Fair' but I believe that another one was never held.

Switzerland itself, the community in which we were living, had its peculiarities too. I should hastily say that our overall view was positive. We liked it so much that we bought a flat in an Alpine village and return there often to enjoy its peace and beauty. I think that the Swiss system of government is a model for the rest of the world. There is so much political harmony and consensus that it is rare to know anything much about the names and personalities of political figures, so quietly are they getting on with running the country. Unlike most governments, even the most ostensibly democratic, the Swiss actually trust their citizens and decide matters great, small and medium sized by referenda, many of which originate from popular initiatives. The trust is repaid by a sense of responsibility that, for example, leads to majority votes against longer holidays.

There is a sense of civic pride and a cohesion about acceptable ways of behaviour, that become ingrained habits. There is a price paid for this by non-Swiss who do not have the cultural norms hardwired into them from childhood in the way that native Swiss do. Whenever foreigners who have lived in Switzerland get together they begin, after a while, to swop stories about the difficulties they faced in assimilating and the trouble they got into along the way.

The Swiss were in advance of many other countries when it came to concepts like separating rubbish and recycling and in the mid-1980s that could be a problem area for newcomers. Those who either wilfully or carelessly mixed up categories of garbage or dumped it in the wrong place could find themselves subject to a home visit from a government functionary. 'But how did you know where to find me?' 'We sorted through the grass clippings that you had put in the receptacle for purely household waste and discovered that in amongst them were letters addressed to you here' would be a typical explanation.

Almost every citizen would play a part in enforcement of the rules. The neighbours would come out as noon on Saturday approached ready to point out that washing one's car was not permissible after this time. The police would turn up at a late-night party, having been alerted to it by a guest who had left fifteen minutes before. We were fortunate in that the services of a gardener were included in the cost of the house that was rented for us but other foreigners who were responsible for their own gardens received anxious telephone calls from local residents reminding them that the statutory date by which all trees and shrubs were required to be trimmed was not far off. We became accustomed to the regular visits from the representative of the office of the 'Contrôle des Habitants', checking up on the details of who was living in the house and who had been living there and always most interested in our predecessors' dog, probably because I was so vague about who its new owners were and so no cross-referencing was possible.

Leaving the country could be risky. There were tales of those who on their return were detained at the airport because of some traffic violation that they were not even aware of having committed. When we ourselves moved back to Hong Kong we became the subject of urgent messages passed on through the Swiss Consulate asking the whereabouts of the original number plate of a car that we had owned, sold and which had since been re-registered. Thankfully, Michael's successor as head of the Geneva Office was able to locate it at the back of the shelf in the garage of the house which he had also taken over from us and so we could return it and restore our good name.

We gradually became a bit more Swiss ourselves. We became familiar enough with the rules, regulations and customs to avoid any clashes with the authorities. All the same, I was homesick for Hong Kong. Our house had a wonderful view across Lake Geneva to Mont Blanc but, perversely, I yearned for the pleasure of being able to walk in a teeming street where I would quickly bump into some acquaintance or another who would be bound to have an outrageous or outrageously amusing or brilliantly hopeful story to tell. Hong Kong was full of life in all its craziness, and I missed it.

We were due to return at the end of 1987 and I wanted to find out what job I might be able to go to. I telephoned Wilfred Wong who was now in the personnel post previously occupied by Donald Tsang. It was clearly a case of 'out of sight, out of mind' as he seemed to barely remember who I was and rather doubtful about what I might be able to do. We agreed that he would cast around and I would phone again in about a week. Things were very different then. He told me that he had discovered that I was really quite 'postable'. To describe a civil servant as 'postable' is about the highest compliment that can be paid without venturing into areas liable to accusations of sexual harassment. It meant that you were not a pariah and bosses wanted to have you in their offices. Wilfred was now actually giving me two options: one dealing with transport and one with the arts.

I had been in transport policy some seven years previously. I had found dealing with the personalities involved in say the establishment of the Mass Transit Railway as riveting as any of Trollope's novels, and the economics of the franchise arrangements that we had in place to provide much of our enviable public transport system were interesting too. On the other hand, roads and bridges and so on left me cold. I have a very poor sense of direction and had not felt comfortable with the complex mathematical models used in transport planning. The arts, however, I loved and I thought that the working days would be as enjoyable as any period of leisure if that was what I was going to be occupied with. And so I said 'yes' to Wilfred's second option and, indeed, it proved a good decision as far as I was concerned.

CHAPTER EIGHT

Arts, Heritage and Hope Deferred

WHEN I HEARD ABOUT IT IN GENEVA, my new post, responsibility for policy on culture in the Municipal Services Branch, sounded as if it should be the epitome of sedateness. I would essentially be looking after the performing arts and built heritage.

'Old buildings. How nice.' The main group that I would be dealing with would be the Antiquities Advisory Board. What a genteel ring that had to it, summoning up visions of dustiness, scholars and venerable libraries. Soon after my return I attended my first meeting of the board. In my entire previous government career, I had never before attended such a meeting, one which seemed so constantly to be on the edge of descending into physical violence. Had something changed in the four years I had been away either in myself or in Hong Kong? Had I become too sensitive or was everything in this city now tinged with hysteria? Neither was really true; it was just that nice old buildings aroused furious passions which was not, after all, such a very bad thing.

The particular cause of the passions was the Ohel Leah Synagogue situated in Robinson Road, a middle-class residential street in the Mid-Levels, that decidedly middle-class part of Hong Kong Island. On examination, it was not surprising that feelings were running so high because the circumstances surrounding the case summed up some of the most characteristic features of Hong Kong.

The synagogue was less than ninety years old and although its external architecture had a certain amount of charm it would not have seemed outstanding in any European city. This was Hong

Kong, however, where there was almost nothing left that was more than about twenty or thirty years old, and in the urban area almost every building seemed to be a characterless multi-storey. This was also Hong Kong which was deprived of development land in desirable areas and the synagogue and its surrounds could be transformed into lucrative residential high-rises. This was also Hong Kong where heritage consciousness was still quite low; pragmatism ruled and many would say, in rather pejorative tones, 'It's just an old building, after all.'

The problem was that the Jewish community (although there was not total unanimity on this) wanted to dispose of their synagogue. The community would benefit financially from a proposal from Swires, the Hong Kong conglomerate second only to Jardines in history and influence, to use the site for a massive residential development. The conservation lobby believed that there was only one possible course for the government to follow and that was to insist on preservation. From our point of view, it was not so simple and the complications were of the kind that have constantly bedevilled heritage issues in Hong Kong. It comes down to what right, if any, government has to impose its will on the legitimate owners of private property. The normal way out of such dilemmas and particularly in Hong Kong would be by some sort of exchange of money to compensate the owners for whatever loss they have to bear. This, however, would come up against another aspect of Hong Kong life: the economics that make the developers so keen to have a historic site would mean that fair compensation to the owners would cost the government billions and it is perfectly legitimate to ask whether that is the best possible use of public money or whether citizens would not rather see new schools, hospitals and so on.

The controversy over the synagogue dragged on for months and months and was pretty unpleasant, with court cases being launched and accusations of collusion and bitterness and broken relationships between those who were on different sides of the debate. Gradually, a solution began to emerge. Swire bought other nearby properties which gave them more flexibility as to how they could develop the site and an elaborate plan was devised that allowed the synagogue to be saved while new residential buildings also could be erected. It was a good solution, even if not perfect since the synagogue now looks quite overshadowed by the giant blocks behind it. There were other beneficial effects that lasted for years: the painful arguments and the heightened emotions had made the public begin to think about heritage and to give more weight to the idea our historic buildings might be worth preserving. It did not however solve the problem that still exists of the lack of a systematic approach to conserving buildings that belong to individuals or groups for whom the financial benefit foregone is enormous if they do not knock down and develop their sites to the maximum. And, arguably, the government is wrong if it tries either to coerce or to pay market price for such buildings.

Things are sometimes easier in the New Territories. There is more pride of ownership going back hundreds of years and villagers will not want to see the destruction of temples, ancestral halls and the study rooms that enshrine the importance of the old imperial examination system to the traditional social and economic hierarchy. Soon after I took over my new post I went to look at what was going on at Tai Fu Tai, an old mandarin's mansion hidden away in Yuen Long District. The Antiquities and Monuments Office and the small but enthusiastic team of government conservation architects as well as the specialist contractors they employed were cooperating on a beautiful restoration. Workmen were frying bamboo nails in great woks to harden them, recreating techniques from the time of original construction in the mid-nineteenth century. Other craftsmen were deploying their skills on delicate carvings, plasterwork and stained glass producing a setting worthy of its grand former inhabitants.

When it was all done we invited David Wilson, who had succeeded Edward Youde as governor and was, like Sir Edward, a noted Sinologist, to officiate at the opening. The dignitary who had built Tai Fu Tai came from the Man clan and the village elders still took an interest in what went on there. They consulted the *Tung Chiu*, the traditional almanac and recommended the uniquely auspicious day for the ceremony. Sadly, the governor had something else on that day but, never mind, the elders looked in the *Tung Chiu* again and came up with a list of two dozen dates that were just as good or, indeed, they said any day that suited the governor would probably be all right. By whatever means, we ended up with a perfect day in November 1988.

Tai Fu Tai may well be the prettiest, but dotted all around the New Territories are interesting buildings that reflect centuries of Chinese culture. In that word 'dotted' lies the weakness though. They are fairly difficult to get to and to impatient Hong Kongers may not seem worth the effort of the journey. We have to accept that we do not have an equivalent of Versailles that will definitely draw tourists. There are some cases, too of unfortunate juxtapositions, notably the Ping Shan Pagoda, a fascinating piece of six-hundred-year-old architecture nestled incongruously at the foot of skyscrapers which overshadow it and may lead some to assume that the pagoda itself is just a recently constructed fake.

I also had under my charge a giant jigsaw puzzle. Murray House had been one of the very first colonial buildings to be erected in Hong Kong. Ever since the 1840s it had occupied a prime corner site in Central, for most of its life being used as a British officers' mess and then latterly as the headquarters of the Rating and Valuation Department although it was the subject of an exorcism ceremony required apparently as a result of its wartime use as a Japanese interrogation centre which was said to have led to its being haunted. It was nonetheless almost universally agreed to be strikingly attractive, built by the Royal Engineers with a practical colonnaded design that was charming in its simplicity. It was so special that when it was agreed that the land on which it stood could be used for the new Bank of China headquarters there was not a dismissive decision simply to demolish Murray House. Instead, the rather extraordinary plan was conceived that it should be dismantled stone by stone and the stones all meticulously numbered and stored so that the entire building could be reassembled at some later date. This was done in 1983 and all 3,000 pieces were stored in a couple of giant huts by the Tai Tam Reservoir. I often asked if we were sure that they were indeed all there and was always assured that this was the case.

All the same, no one had ever had the faintest idea what to do with all those stones apart from keeping them tagged and ready in their storage huts. There was no plan as to where, whether or when they might be reassembled until the deputy director of housing said that he had a public housing estate that might do. Said just like that it seemed unlikely but further examination made me think it wasn't such a bad idea after all. By 1988, Hong Kong had experienced some years of very solid prosperity and the government did not feel the need to cut the corners in anything it did including construction of public housing. Furthermore, the particular estate that was being suggested was not run of the mill either. Great progress had been made in rehousing squatters but there were a few areas which remained to be cleared and one of these was in Stanley, a historic area on the south side of Hong Kong Island which was otherwise a high-class residential area, a traditional village based on a fishing community and a market which had become a tourist attraction. Ma Hang, the public housing estate that would be built so that these squatters could be accommodated in it, would be low rise, high quality in construction and with a boundary that stretched right down to the sea and included within its perimeter a piazza area and a historic temple. The concept was that Murray House might be re-erected right at the seaward side of this boundary.

This seemed no worse than the only alternative on offer which was continued storage and so I pursued it through to approval. By the time of the successful reconstruction, I was no longer dealing with the subject. The jigsaw of three thousand pieces was successfully put together again. It still needed about 150 more stones for the project so some that fitted in had to be sourced. Chimneys were added from the former Mental Hospital in Sai Ying Poon at the western end of Hong Kong Island which was a building that had been left to deteriorate so much that it could not be preserved and all that could be done was to retain the façade as part of the design of the community centre that replaced it and to salvage some architectural features. The new Murray House was opened by Tony Miller with whom I had had my first experiences of the Hong Kong government in September 1972 in his grown up-capacity of director of housing.

Later on there was another reconstruction next to Murray House when the Edwardian Blake Pier which had originally also been in

Central was repositioned there. The whole thing was therefore more or less a mish-mash. And yet, thousands of visitors seem happy enough with the result and I don't blame them. The buildings are attractive enough in their own right and in a position that shows them off to best advantage and seems a natural setting for them as if they might always have been there. Blake Pier is used as a pier for ferries to Po Toi Island and Murray House accommodates a variety of restaurants. The atmosphere is cheerful and busy.

The 'heritage' side of my portfolio of subjects therefore presented some conceptual challenges such as optimum use of buildings that have been preserved, as well as the approach to historic buildings in private hands. These challenges remain but the community's pride and interest in its own history is growing aided by the determined efforts of some individuals and pressure groups, and that is really the key to making better progress.

Even if I could not find entirely satisfactory answers to these policy issues I did all the same reap the personal benefits that I had envisaged when I first heard about the post. Often during the working day I was quite legitimately doing things that I would have chosen as leisure activities and I spent many happy hours talking to historians and fossicking in the remains of Hong Kong's past.

This was also true of the other side of my schedule of duties with its responsibilities for the arts. It was fun to go to performances and to get to know the creative people behind them. In one case, both sides came together as the Hong Kong Festival Fringe had been operating for about four years in a heritage building, which had formerly been the headquarters of the Dairy Farm Company, built in the early years of the twentieth century and part of a business operation which encompassed a herd of dairy cattle kept in cowsheds near Hong Kong University as well as great blocks of ice brought by ship from America for the wealthy consumers of Hong Kong. The Fringe had originally been conceived as an adjunct to the annual Arts Festival but it quickly evolved into being also 'an open platform for the arts' where at any time of the year artists could put on performances and exhibitions on terms that were more flexible and more reasonably priced than anywhere else in Hong Kong. It was run by the idealistic Benny Chia together with

Catherine Lau who provided the practical underpinning for the creative inspirations.

I supposed that Benny in particular would soon be on the move. Hong Kong offered so many opportunities for a well educated person like him to find a stable job that paid well rather than being involved in the scrabbling for resources that was an intrinsic feature of a small unsubsidised arts venue. Of course, I was wrong. At the time of writing, the Fringe has been with us for almost thirty years and Benny and Catherine have been there throughout. Its finances improved somewhat when we were able to get a restaurant set up there. Benny and Catherine had located an Australian woman called Michelle Garnaut who wanted to set up there and would pay the Fringe for being able to do so. First we had to convince the board of the Fringe that this was a legitimate use of its space and that it would enhance its basic functions as an arts centre rather than detracting from them. The government owned the building and leased it to the Fringe for a peppercorn rent and so the next task was to persuade the departments concerned that it would be all right to let the Fringe keep the money that they got from Michelle since this would be subsidising the arts rather than giving anyone an improper benefit. All this was done and over the next twenty years 'M at the Fringe' became one of Hong Kong's best known eating places and gave Michelle the base later on to expand to Shanghai and open 'M on the Bund' there.

It was all quite strange. We were only five years away from the currency crisis when it had seemed as if the entire economy was about to implode. Looking to the future, there was less than ten years left before the reversion to China about which many still felt anxious. At the same time, though, there was a great gushing stream of optimism and energy. And it seemed as if luck was on our side too. Things mostly seemed to turn out well and anyone who had a good idea seemed to be able to find a way to bring it to life. A young English girl turned up in my office one day. She had been in Hong Kong for three weeks and wanted to do something that involved 'young people and the arts'. We had a very pleasant chat about the possibilities but I thought it was all pretty hopeless really. She was Lindsey McAlister and twenty years later she is the director of the Hong Kong Youth Arts Foundation which she set up and which puts on arts-related projects for about 800,000 young people every year.

Back in 1988, it was relatively easy to help the arts community in Hong Kong. There weren't too many of them, they were mostly dedicated and visionary and all they needed was some cash to grease the wheels. Potentially, the most serious problem was that they would prove unable to spend all the extra money that they got. This could be really annoying! Some arts group would explain piteously how poor they were and how much they could achieve if they had a more generous government subsidy. We could go into battle on their behalf with the Finance Branch, explaining how the community would benefit as a result of a more liberal attitude on their part. If we succeeded we would feel triumphant as if we had won some sort of competition ourselves but our triumph would be turned to humiliation if our protégés proved unable to live up to their promises and a significant unspent balance was left at the end of the financial year. We would then become subject to all sorts of self-righteous reprimands for our folly that had resulted in 'wasting taxpayers' money'.

There were a couple of occasions on which we had to go to the Finance Committee of the Legislative Council to get emergency grants to avoid the collapse of pillars of Hong Kong's nascent arts scene.

The Hong Kong Arts Festival had established itself as a sort of cultural fulcrum for Hong Kong. It was the major opportunity each year to see high quality performance from overseas which was a nurturing influence and inspiration for our own arts groups. It had become a social highlight, which perhaps had some negative connotations since it was questionable whether the function of the arts was really to allow wealthy people to put on expensive clothes and meet up with others of the same ilk. Yet this also was a sign that the arts and culture were considered some sort of essential component of respectable society and that was no bad thing if we wanted to claim a share of the community's resources.

The Arts Festival had signed up the Vienna Philharmonic, then as now regarded as one of the world's very best orchestras. What a treat! Unfortunately, the festival's management had negotiated a contract that was, in those pre-Euro days, denominated in Austrian schillings and that had, as was the wont with Germanic currencies, got stronger and stronger. This strengthening had been so marked that what had been expensive but affordable had become so costly that it threatened the very survival of the Arts Festival, which did not hold substantial financial reserves. We managed to persuade Finance Committee to give us supplementary funding so that the hole was plugged but the festival's problems were not over.

The festival's general manager had resigned and left Hong Kong and a young arts administrator named Tseng Sun-man had been appointed in his place. Sun-man was confronted with a really difficult situation and while he had had no part in its creation it was up to him to clear it up. The Vienna Philharmonic had been and gone and their performance had been a great success but it turned out that there had been no planning to speak of for the next arts festival. It seemed as if it might be quite impossible to have an arts festival at all. To organise a festival of this type and magnitude requires a long lead time. Distinguished artists have schedules that are filled up years in advance and, in the case of Hong Kong, in order to minimise travelling costs, as far as possible groups should be booked who already have plans to tour in the region: in those days going down to Australia or perhaps to Japan, as it would have been unimaginable that there could be regular performances of this calibre in Mainland China.

It was a desperate situation but luck came to our aid again and we were also assisted by some determined people. The festival had been employing an 'international adviser' named Joe Seelig but he should have been called Joe Steely as he now stepped into the breach. He managed to put together a programme for us, comprised mostly of things that he had spotted at the Edinburgh Festival and its fringe, with a heavy emphasis on mime groups. He presented this to us at various meetings and if anyone there began to demur on the grounds, say, that his suggestions might not go down well with the more conservative tendency among the festival-going public his eyes would take on a dangerous glint, his lips would compress and he would point out that if we wanted any festival at all there was no alternative to taking what we could get.

Tseng Sun-man kept his nerve. He took the package that Joe and he had managed to put together. He led his team to market the festival as this time having a different, avant garde theme. It proved to be one of the best received festivals ever.

The other group who needed an emergency grant was the Hong Kong Ballet. In their case, there was no dramatic cause. It seemed that the Ballet had just been over optimistic and had counted on a level of donations and sponsorship that were never forthcoming. The company was only a few years old and again had insufficient reserves to weather any but the most minor of financial difficulties.

There ensued a debate about whether Hong Kong needed a ballet company at all. Wasn't it an unjustified luxury when so few ordinary people were likely to be interested in its activities? One of the most convincing counter-arguments focused on the need for a strong cultural infrastructure to support the students and graduates of the newly opened Academy for Performing Arts. Modern dance was comparatively strong thanks to the extraordinary efforts of Willy Tsao who set up the City Contemporary Dance Company in the premises formerly occupied by his family's textile factory. In those days, we had an autonomous Urban Council with their own finances from the revenue of household rates and they could take a generous attitude towards their performing companies: the Chinese Orchestra, Repertory Theatre and Chinese Dance Company. In the end, the case in favour of the Ballet prevailed and as the years went by it became well established and renowned for the high standard of its performances.

The academy stands on the waterfront at Wan Chai. Its design is visually arresting, with the main external wall divided by struts into a pattern of triangles. Quite often, I used to walk home past the academy building: it would be all lit up and in each of the triangles you could see, say, first a dancer in practice leotards jumping and pirouetting, then a violinist and then a still figure practising on a Chinese flute. It was an unselfconscious display of youthful hope, concentration and energy. Inside, I knew, there were more wonders: gigantic Greek gods constructed of pâpier machë and meticulously accurate costumes for entire European villages of the eighteenth century, all the work of the students in the School of Technical Arts.

The academy had been the gift of the Jockey Club to the community to celebrate the club's centenary. The Royal Hong Kong Jockey Club was at that time making plenty of money from its monopoly on horserace betting and the relationship with the government was very good. Quite apart from the taxes that they paid they had lots left over for large-scale donations. They had asked the governor, Sir Edward Youde, what he would like for their birthday and this had been his answer.

I was involved in many different issues connected with the academy but one of the most pressing was the engagement of a new director. The choice was a man named John Hosier who had immediately before been director of the UK's prestigious Guildhall School of Music and Drama. There was risk on both sides in taking on a middle-aged person who, however distinguished in his own milieu, had no experience of working in Hong Kong and in an organisation so closely tied to the Hong Kong government. The subtle but real differences in culture could make it difficult for an outsider to achieve as much as hoped for. Gus Chui, the secretary for recreation and culture, was sure that Hosier was the right man for the job but his target was more doubtful. He explained his eventual decision to accept the appointment as the result of a variation of a Chinese Water Torture. He said that for a period of weeks during the summer he would, as he walked the streets of London, often become aware of a small figure behind him and when he turned round he would find Gus anxiously urging him, 'Oh please come to Hong Kong. Please do.' And so he did, and the academy flourished under his care.

We would muse about things that we did not think were realistic possibilities: a second orchestra in addition to the Hong Kong Philharmonic, an opera company, even. What we had already seemed rather at risk, let alone hoping for more. And yet, in due course, it all came to pass.

I had only just over a year to enjoy this wonderful job and then was torn away for a posting but one that meant a promotion so I could hardly complain. I stayed in the Municipal Services Branch but became a Deputy Secretary with a very different schedule of responsibilities. The Municipal Services Branch looked after policy and any common issues for the Regional and Urban Councils which in the New Territories and the urban area respectively provided a variety of services ranging from the Health Inspectorate to libraries to crematoria to refuse collection to beaches to theatres and so on and so on.

What the councils did required an army of staff with different sorts of skills. We in the branch dealt with things like promotion and conditions of work. This meant that I had the new experience of negotiating with staff association representatives, in effect civil service trades unions. I found that my deficient Cantonese stood me in good stead. I had never learnt any swear words apart from a couple of the most basic so I quite undeservedly gained the admiration of the staff on our side for the phlegmatic way in which I reacted to torrents of abuse. The truth was that the more imaginative and colourful attacks on my competence, intelligence, morals, ancestry and so on were quite wasted on my ignorant ears.

I came to the conclusion that most of those who put themselves forward to represent their fellow workers had immense stamina and staying power, able to tolerate hour after hour in our rather dreary conference room in a remorseless strategy of attrition. This was not true of every group. The librarians told me that they found these consultations with management rather trying. 'We prefer to be quieter,' they said. 'That's what we're used to in our line of work.'

We were now well into 1989 and this was to prove a momentous year for Hong Kong as well as for many parts of the world. The movements in Europe that would end or significantly change communist governments were creating ripples that washed the shores of Hong Kong. It was impossible to escape awareness that entire societies were reaching turning points in their history.

In April reports began to come out of China of some sort of student unrest in the wake of the death of Hu Yaobang, a respected reformist leader who had been sacked a couple of years previously, apparently forced out by more conservative elements in the Communist Party. From the middle of April onwards there was intense activity, spearheaded by students but also attracting workers and others. Tiananmen Square, one of the best known sites in Beijing and indeed in the entire country, where massive official parades and ceremonies were held now became the location of a protest camp. There was so much going on and reliable news from China was not easily come by but it seemed as if there was a real possibility of a dialogue between the protestors and the leadership and, as in Europe, the beginning of a process that would lead to democracy in China. At least that was how it was perceived in Hong Kong.

Hong Kong went mad with hope. It was like a collective intoxication and the most unlikely people were caught up in it, even if later on they might try to deny or downplay what had happened during that period. Michael was working in the Trade and Industry Branch and we knew many industrialists and attended many functions organised by them. Hardheaded businessmen would arrive at these events with their faces glowing. Out on the street or on the Mass Transit Railway they had stuffed banknotes into the collecting boxes for donations to go to support the protestors in Tiananmen. Everywhere there were people taking up such collections. Were they genuine? Probably mostly yes; there were no reports of frauds and scams and there was such a widespread mood of dedication to the ideals of the Tiananmen protesters that for once few in Hong Kong would have taken an opportunity to make easy money by shady means. Whether the enormous sums got to their intended beneficiaries and did them any good is another question altogether. This giving was something that Hong Kong people could grasp onto as a way to participate in the great events taking place in the motherland to the north. Attention was focused on Mainland China but there was also an underlying calculation that a democratic system there would make our own future less risky, would indeed lead to the most optimistic predictions that we could come up with for ourselves being fulfilled.

In any May in any year Hong Kong is likely to be subject to heavy rainfalls but this was particularly true in 1989. There is always an edge of danger in weather conditions like these and a typhoon

that month resulted in landslides, flooding and fatalities in Hong
Kong. As the month wore on, euphoria transmuted into feverish
tension. Martial law was declared in Beijing and the young leaders
of the protest did not seem to be as united or as effective as before.
Students from the Central Academy of Fine Arts hastily created a
statue, the 'Goddess of Democracy' and erected it in Tiananmen
in an effort to strengthen the resolve of those who were staying in
the Square. Hong Kong, through formal and informal channels
and through some sort of weird telepathic communication that
seemed to have developed, knew that things were no longer going
well.

A vigil was to be held in Hong Kong in support of the Tiananmen students, led by Szeto Wah and Martin Lee, the two most
prominent figures in the democracy movement in Hong Kong and
with their own Goddess of Democracy statue as its centrepiece.
They wanted to make use of Victoria Park, which was controlled
by the Urban Services Department and was the largest public park
on Hong Kong Island, with many different sports facilities and
often used for major community activities such as the flower selling
fair at Lunar New Year.

My office was also on Hong Kong Island, in Wan Chai, not so
far from Victoria Park although it was not somewhere I could easily
have walked to because of the way the road network was laid out.
In the same office building as me were the chiefs of various grades
such as the health inspectors, librarians and also the park keepers,
known in our bureaucratic language as amenities officers. Farley
Ma was the chief amenities officer, having risen through the ranks
on account of his knowledge, personal qualities and job performance. Farley was a very reliable person and I thought that I might
spend some time with him as the afternoon wore on because he
would be likely to know what was happening.

We began to get disconcerting messages and phone calls. The
marchers with Martin Lee and Szeto Wah at their head were being
refused admission to Victoria Park. There were, apparently, two
linked problems. First, there had been no application made in the
proper form for this use of the park and, second, there was anxiety
that the crowd might damage the football pitches. Any outsider

observing what was going on might well have concluded that there was some deliberate, Machiavellian strategy aimed at frustrating the march. Farley and I knew that it was more plausible that this problem was genuinely being looked at only through the prism of procedures for park usage. 'I don't think we can leave things like this, do you?' Farley was an expert gardener, devoted to the cultivation of trees and flowers and by nature thoughtful, almost meditative. He was also known and respected by all the front-line staff. If an extreme situation called for some unconventional jumping over lines of authority and hierarchy then Farley could do it. 'I think I'll make some phone calls,' he said. I left him to it and shortly afterwards the demonstrators were allowed into the park and that particular source of tension was defused.

By the beginning of the last week in May the mood in Hong Kong was deeply gloomy. Michael and I went to a trade association dinner, attended by many leading industrialists. There was no more talk of donations for the Tiananmen protesters. News from Beijing was drying up but there was a consensus in Hong Kong. Reprisals were about to begin although no one knew exactly when or what form they would take. Our community held its breath in a period of painful, helpless waiting.

On Sunday 4 June we went out on the boat of our friend Raymond Liu. Raymond was the younger son of Casey and Lena Liu who had been among the first people I had met in Hong Kong. He and his brother had been educated overseas, originally sent to England as a safety measure during the 1967 riots. Both had returned to live in Hong Kong and Raymond had become a successful entrepreneur in his own right.

We were away from any sources of news but as soon as we got back in the early evening, we knew. Every taxi on the road had a black ribbon tied to its radio antenna. I thought idly how strange it was that they all seemed to have ribbons of exactly the same type, tied in the same way and wondered where they had got them from and for how long they had been keeping them ready. Groups of people were congregating in stunned silence. Many seemed to be gravitating towards the Cenotaph, located in the heart of the city and which had been since 1923 a memorial to those who had died in battle. It was a copy of the memorial in London, the 'empty tomb', designed by Sir Edwin Lutyens, but the Hong Kong version had an addition of eight Chinese characters, the meaning of which could be translated as 'Their brave spirits never fade, their legacy endures forever'.

In the early hours of that morning in Beijing tanks and soldiers had gone in. There is debate even now on casualty numbers and where exactly the attacks took place. What was certain was that Tiananmen Square had been cleared, the Goddess of Democracy statue had been overthrown and destroyed and unarmed young people had been killed and injured.

On the next day I followed my usual morning routine and on my way to work took our daughter to her school bus stop. She was at a primary school for international students and some of the parents did not know Hong Kong well or had not lived here long. They were frightened. Overnight, the police had been out in the nightclub area of Mong Kok dealing with looting since it seemed that some criminals and triad gangs had decided to take advantage of the unsettled atmosphere. 'I've told my daughter not to catch anybody's eye. I think that the locals will turn on us expatriates,' said one of the mothers waiting for the bus. 'No,' I told her. 'I don't think you need to worry about that.' What had happened in Mong Kok seemed so unrepresentative of the generally prevailing mood, which was deeply solemn.

There had been an instinctive decision by more or less the entire local population to wear black that day. My office was awash with grief: not polite lip biting with moistened eyes but breaking down in racking sobs. So many of us were parents and those who had been killed were young idealists; it was that identification which made it particularly poignant.

At the same time there was urgent work to be done. Even if we knew that there was no danger from within the local community we did not know what was happening in Mainland China or how the situation there might develop. Every part of government there-fore had to prepare to deal with possible crises. My own area of responsibility was food supply security and I began to activate a contingency plan. This was based on the traditional assumption

that Hong Kong's food supply was essentially dependent on China
and that if there was unrest within the Mainland we might find
ourselves running out of basic foodstuffs. We discovered that our
sources of supply were already so diversified that this was not in
fact a very serious risk. If necessary, the market itself would quite
easily adjust and rely more on other sources for imports. Furthermore, after a short period of confusion it became clear that the
Beijing government was firmly in control and there would be no
such drastic effects on life in Hong Kong.

Nonetheless, it was hardly surprising that I found that it was well
into the evening before I felt I could leave work. To get some
exercise, I used to change into casual clothes and then walk home.
As I got closer to the Peak I noticed that the sky was clear and bright
and the air surprisingly fresh; Hong Kong did not seem the urban,
man-made creation that it usually did. The lines that Shakespeare
had put into Juliet's mouth drifted into my head:

> . . . when he shall die,
> Take him and cut him out in little stars,
> And he will make the face of heaven so fine
> That all the world will be in love with night,
> And pay no worship to the garish sun.

For a fleeting moment, it felt as if the Tiananmen students were
truly there in the profusion of lights shining above the earth and
that, in some sense, they were not dead and would never die.

Over the following days, there were efforts to rekindle the
embers of Hong Kong support for the democracy movement in
China. Fax machines were the newest kind of technology, the
Internet not being in widespread use until a few years later. The
suggestion was relayed from person to person: 'If you know someone in China with a fax machine, maybe even just a business
contact, send them an account of what happened on June 4 so that
the information will gradually spread through the country.' However, this initiative petered out as stories emerged of soldiers being
sent to guard fax machines and it was realised that this initiative
might endanger those who received the faxes.

Separately, some Hong Kong people were involved in helping dissidents to escape from China but that was something about which it was better not to know too much, either then or now. The ignorant could not by careless talk unwittingly give away secrets.

There had been enormous marches in solidarity with the Tiananmen protesters and now there would be ceremonies to remember those who had lost their lives. The vigils on 4 June became an annual event, attracting thousands of people to Victoria Park and giving news editors around the world a ready-made story about the one place in China where the massacre was commemorated as well as an opportunity for tasteful photographs of the faces of earnest young people illuminated by candlelight.

Those who would never have considered themselves to be political activists but had briefly been galvanised into participation during the hectic months of the Tiananmen protests were no longer so visible. Most Hong Kongers were just a generation or two from being refugees and those recent memories had inured them to believe in the prevalence of sorrow, suffering and loss. It was up to individuals and families to work out their own survival strategies in this uncertain world, always aware of the fragility of the framework of their lives. The events of those roller coaster months in which hope had been allowed to emerge had been deeply unsettling. Those citizens whose ambitions had seemed to be entirely bound up in conventional ideas of success and who had found themselves, to their surprise, briefly caught up in a fever of entirely different concerns that were on a higher plane, bore their disappointment with resignation. The scar remained, though, and even if it faded somewhat as weeks, months and years passed it did not disappear altogether.

CHAPTER NINE

Clashes of the Titans

WHAT HAPPENED IN AND AROUND Tiananmen Square on 4 June 1989 had many after effects. Worldwide confidence in Hong Kong was shaken and as at the time of the 1967 riots some sages decided to write the place off, pronounce it not a good investment risk and so on.

There had long been a view that Britain had not been doing enough to live up to its responsibilities towards the people of Hong Kong and in particular that it was not sufficiently willing to provide a 'safe haven' for those who felt that they had to leave. Some suggested that the best way would be to enable anyone to exchange a Hong Kong Identity Card for a full British passport with the right to live in the UK. It would indeed have been an effective way of ensuring that the Chinese government lived up to the letter and the spirit of the Joint Declaration, since if not they would be faced with a ghost town but the British government judged it would be political suicide as far as their electorate was concerned. What was offered in the end was a total of 50,000 full British passports to be mainly allocated to people whose services were considered vital to the continued functioning of Hong Kong or whose employment or personal history was such that they might believe themselves in some way to be at risk from the new régime. Donald Tsang, with his well-known capacity for hard work and organisational skills, was drafted into a new post to set up and administer this scheme.

It is unknowable how many actually used their British passports to settle in that country. Anecdotal evidence suggests that the number was comparatively small. I met a man who had a passport because of his service in the Police Tactical Unit. He went to go and have a look at his potential new home and, essentially, got as far as the London Underground Railway. He contrasted the dirt, the indiscipline of the passengers and the long delays with his experience of our Mass Transit Railway and decided that he would take his chance on Hong Kong. Others who could not get one of the allocated British passports or had reservations about going there tended to prefer Canada, mainly Vancouver or Toronto. Taking this course, though, also required sacrifices. I had anguished conversations with colleagues who had reached the top of the tree in their profession and were now contemplating starting all over again in some backwater in British Columbia. Some became 'astronauts', with wife and children settled overseas in order to secure residency while the husband and father worked in Hong Kong where it was easier for him to earn money and flew to see his family as often as he could.

The government decided that another component of its response should be a programme of major works that would demonstrate that Hong Kong's leaders believed that the territory had a future. The cynical gave the package the nickname 'The Rose Garden', with its connotations of something highly attractive but almost impossible to achieve. The works were not brand-new ideas but rather proposals that had been around for a while but needed some impetus to get them underway. The most significant was the replacement of Kai Tak Airport by Chek Lap Kok, which required extensive reclamation off North Lantau and construction of a network of roads and bridges as well as the Airport Express railway line to move goods and passengers to and from the urban area. There was associated expansion of the container port and, separately, development of the universities on the argument that Hong Kong young thereby would not need to emigrate to access higher education at home.

Something else that was given a bit of a push as part of this process was implementation of the report of the Broadcasting Review Board. This had been published in 1985 and its recommendations were being brought into being at a fairly moderate pace. One of these was that a cable television broadcaster should be licensed to produce and distribute programmes in Hong Kong. The particular reason that it was thought worthy of the Rose Garden was that as things stood it was being built by a consortium of multi-national companies, and thus an example of faith from the private sector and from overseas as well as from within Hong Kong. At the same time, the government had one of its periodic fits of reorganisation. The Municipal Services Branch, where I had been working, disappeared; some of its functions were distributed around the government while a new Recreation and Culture Branch retained the responsibilities for arts, sports and heritage and took on broadcasting policy and the latter, I was told, would now be for me to look after. I would sit in the same office but have entirely different kinds of files arriving in the in tray and new people to work with. This sort of thing happened quite a lot.

By and large, I liked all the things that I did in the Hong Kong government but I quite possibly enjoyed the next few years the most. The broadcasting licensing and regulation that we embarked on proved intellectually challenging and developed into a drama that involved some of the most influential and powerful personalities in Hong Kong.

I had to begin by gaining some sort of understanding of the subjects on which I was supposed to be taking a lead. MH Au of the Telecommunications Authority, who was to prove an especially valuable ally over the years ahead, patiently gave me an introductory guide to the science of broadcasting, helped by a handy diagram of the radio spectrum. 'Wow, MH, it says "microwave" there. Is that a mistake?' 'No, those are the microwaves that can be used for transmission rather than cooking food.'

Although I spent the bulk of my time on broadcasting my schedule also covered the film industry and film censorship. The Motion Picture Industry Association sent me a selection of representative local films to watch and the Television and Entertainment Licensing Authority arranged a viewing for me. The purpose of this was so that I could see samples of what was considered to fall most appropriately into the various censorship categories. As a result, I can say that probably the least erotic experience that anyone can have is to watch a whole lot of clips from pornographic movies on a wet Wednesday morning in the company of a group of solemn civil servants. We also saw quite a lot of violent Hong Kong–produced stuff, which I did find quite stomach churning, particularly a local variation on the Sweeney Todd story, apparently based on a real case, in which murder victims were turned into *dim sum* in disgustingly gory detail. Then we switched to some Japanese pornography which was 'dirty' in every sense in that mud always seemed to be part of the set-up. It was quite a relief that the next clip seemed mainly to feature a character reciting a charming little poem that featured willows, bamboo and boats floating by. I noticed, however, that my companions who had sat phlegmatically through all the sex and bloodshed were now gripping the arms of their chairs, pursing their lips and knitting their brows. 'Very difficult,' they explained. 'Triad initiation ceremonies. We have a specialist police officer who comes in to advise us on this sort of thing. We have to be careful about anything that's too accurate or schoolchildren will be copying them for their gangs.'

In fact, the censorship system was well established and ran itself pretty smoothly. Hong Kong's films were world famous thanks to movie moguls like Sir Run Run Shaw and actors like Jackie Chan. Around the periphery, there were plenty of tales of thugs, rackets and intimidation but it was hard to find anyone who was willing to come forward with specifics. We did manage to lay the foundations for a Film Office to try and help with things like making location shooting easier. An awful lot of attention had to be given, however, to what might be called the 'STAR Wars', the licensing of cable television as complicated by the presence of a new satellite television broadcaster.

Despite our best efforts our little corner of the Rose Garden was not flourishing. The multi-national consortium expected to provide cable TV was quietly falling apart. It was a matter of an incompatible marriage, with four partners rather than two and the cultural differences of its multi-nationalism didn't help either. It was fascinating to see how unalike the American and Hong Kong/British attitudes were, with the former wanting everything to be completely litigation proof while the latter were more prepared to leave things a little vague and hope for the best. The Hong Kong partners were Sun Hung Kai Properties and the Wharf Group, representing two of the biggest family fortunes in Hong Kong. It was really excessively optimistic to imagine that all these big beasts could have quietly lain down together and produced television programmes. Failure would not be explained in those terms, however, but rather would be taken as a strong signal that Hong Kong itself had become an unworkable concept.

Into this unstable situation came Richard, the younger son of Li Ka-shing. KS Li was the wealthiest man in Hong Kong and high up on any world list of the rich and powerful, all achieved by his own efforts and abilities from beginnings so humble that he was not even able to complete secondary school. By late 1989, Mr Li's companies such as Cheung Kong and Hutchison had major interests both in Hong Kong and overseas in the retail industry, ports operation, property and many other types of business including telecommunications. This last made a move into broadcasting quite a natural one, given the similarity of the technologies used for the two purposes. Richard Li was twenty-four years old, just back from studies in Canada. He was assigned some of his father's most able lieutenants, including Simon Murray and Robert Chan. The plan was to open up a satellite television broadcaster that would get its transmission capacity by bouncing off Asiasat, which was launched in April 1990 and the footprint of which covered an enormous swathe of Asia, including Hong Kong. The consortium charged with setting up the new cable TV network was disconcerted by the arrival of what was potentially a powerful new competitor.

This complex new situation meant that within a short space of time we had to sort out a suitable licence for STAR, the first ever Asia-wide satellite broadcaster, watch the cable TV consortium falling to bits, limit the damage from that as far as possible, re-tender the cable television franchise with conditions that were fair to both satellite and cable broadcasters and then issue a licence to the successful bidder. The effects were really remarkable in their speed and scale. The STAR offering included a BBC World Service television channel and there were stories of villagers in obscure parts of Kazakhstan clubbing together to buy a satellite dish so as to see news from the outside world, albeit in English. Freakishly enough, manufacture of satellite dishes became a valuable offshoot industry for the People's Liberation Army which was supposed to be financially self-supporting as far as it could. There were rumours of clashes in Beijing between government factions who wanted to clamp down ever more severely on this information free-for-all and the military who opposed the possible reduction in a valuable source of revenue.

We were doing a few other things too, including running a bidding exercise for a new commercial radio station, bringing in complex legislative amendments covering nominee shareholding in television companies, securing an agreement with the BBC to continue a radio relay of the World Service after 1997, drawing up plans for a possible corporatisation of our public service broadcaster, Radio Television Hong Kong and seeing off an attempt by Rupert Murdoch's News International Corporation to buy a chunk of our home broadcaster, TVB, since such a sale was considered not to be consistent with our rules on foreign ownership of broadcasters.

The last of these exercises gave me an experience of sexism, of a type I had not experienced for many years. Negotiations were being conducted on Murdoch's behalf by Sam Chisholm, his number two. At a meeting, my boss, James So, pointed out that I would soon be in London and could visit the Murdoch satellite television channel, BSkyB. 'Good,' said Chisholm with a wolfish grin. 'We'll show her the shopping channel. She'll like that.' I hope that my responding glare was suitably disdainful.

In the event, I did tour BSkyB with their managing director, Gary Davey, who was an entirely reasonable person. We didn't look at the shopping channel but we did look at the ranks of steel boxes like filing cabinets which are vital bits of technology for all satellite television stations but are rather dull to stare at. Gary himself came to Hong Kong soon afterwards to run STAR TV which in a corporate twist and turn Murdoch had bought off Richard Li for a phenomenally large sum which led to Richard being dubbed 'Superboy' by the Hong Kong popular press. We regulators had no problem with this transaction since we thought of STAR not as a home broadcaster but a Pan Asian one which happened to be based in Hong Kong, which was a nice contribution to our economy.

To build up a great fortune by one's own efforts requires extraordinary talents and personal qualities. That may not be so true of
those who have climbed the corporate hierarchy to reach the top
but they will still possess an aura of wealth and power. The civil
servants on the other side of the table may not be as clever but they
must not allow themselves to be overawed. We had to hone our
abilities to let 'all men count with you, but none too much'. In the
case of the 'STAR Wars' we were caught between two of the most
powerful conglomerates in Hong Kong, Hutchison and the Wharf
Group, which eventually became the sole (and successful) bidder
for the cable TV licence.

'Without fear or favour' had to be a daily watchword, not a
slogan tagged on as an appealing afterthought. We were given solid
support by the Broadcasting Authority, the statutory body set up
to regulate licensees and to advise generally on broadcasting policy.
Hong Kong followed the British practice of roping in what were
colloquially known as 'the great and the good' to serve on advisory
and regulatory boards. Perhaps nowadays people are busier and find
it impossible to carve out time for a form of public service which
can be stressful and time consuming but with no reward other than
an official Christmas card, invitation to whatever kind of Chinese
New Year party the parent government department holds, and the
distant possibility of an honour, a 'bottle cap' as medals are known
in local Chinese slang.

We were fortunate in the then members of the Broadcasting
Authority; they were a cohesive group, helpful, humorous and
reassuring. Much of that was surely due to their chairman, Sir Roger
Lobo, definitely one of the greatest and the best. Sir Roger was the
son of Pedro Lobo, a distinguished Macau businessman and philanthropist. Macau in its time had been probably more complex than
Hong Kong: a Portuguese colony in which the colonists stayed and
inter-married with the local population but, however many generations they were away from actually living in Portugal still thought
of themselves as Portuguese.

Although Sir Roger retained his links with Macau he had mainly
been active within Hong Kong, both as a businessman and in
public life where he had been senior member of the Executive and

Legislative Councils. His words were few but always worth hearing. His years as a trusted adviser probably meant that he knew more secrets than anyone else in Hong Kong but he was far too discreet to spill any scandalous beans. His acquaintanceship with the famous would become more apparent through his astonishing talent for mimicry. As we waited for everyone to assemble so that some long and difficult meeting could start he would have us in stitches with his impersonations. Particularly funny was his account of Margaret Thatcher, whom he had seen in action when she summoned the Hong Kong Executive Council to 10 Downing Street to seek their views on Hong Kong's future. She may have been impatient and bossy but she seemed to have had a genuine sense of responsibility towards the people of Hong Kong.

We civil servants also needed to be hardworking and thoughtful. A visitor from the US administration asked me how many people I had working on cable television licensing and regulation. 'Oh,' I said, 'we've a very small team. There are four of us.' He was stunned. 'When you began that sentence, I thought that you were going to say "forty". That's what I'd call a small team.' In fact, we relied on many other civil servants in related functions: lawyers and tele-communications engineers and the administrative officers in the Economic Services Branch who dealt with telecommunications policy, since in the case of a fibre-optic network there was an intimate relationship between provision of television and telephony services. We could even ask advice from the 'father of fibre optics', Professor Charles Kao, then the vice chancellor of the Chinese University of Hong Kong. He was a charming man who wore his accomplishments lightly but those who were knowledgeable in the field told us that he had completely revolutionised telecommunications by replacing copper wire by glass fibre. This was principally work that he had done in an unglamorous London suburb in the 1960s. He had a young family then and his wife sometimes mildly grumbled about his long hours: 'You're not going to win the Nobel Prize, you know,' she joked. That is, however, just what he did in 2009.

We were in situations where circumstances changed quickly and where there was activity going on at the highest level which in Hong Kong meant the Executive Council, our equivalent of the Cabinet, always referred to by us as ExCo.

Very late one Friday afternoon I came away from the chief secretary's office with instructions to rewrite an ExCo memorandum and to do it more or less overnight. This was a dispiriting thought from every point of view; I was not at all sure how I could manage the logistics alone quite apart from the daunting amount of composition to be done. Shelley Lee had invited me to a casual dinner in a restaurant near the office. Shelley had been my contemporary in the administrative grade ever since 1972 and she and I were at that time deputies in the Recreation and Culture Branch with responsibility, respectively, for sports and arts and broadcasting. I decided that I might as well just drop in and eat something even if it meant that I would be even later in starting on the drafting.

When I did eventually get back to the office I was surprised to see lights shining in the windows. I unlocked the outer door and walked in to find Philip Chan, a young administrative officer who was a member of our team and who greeted me with his usual beaming smile. 'I knew you were going off to that meeting and I thought that I'd better stay here in case there is anything else that has to be done. I've asked a secretary to stay behind too.' This last was particularly important since in those years around 1990 we administrators had only a vague idea as to how to operate our own office equipment. We relied on others to type and print out our documents.

Philip and I worked together producing a new draft paper on the lines that I had been told to do. Things that were to be submitted to ExCo had to follow strict guidelines on format and wording and the file also had to show that relevant people in the government had seen the draft and agreed to it. In this case, Liz Bosher had to sign off on it. This was the married name of the Liz King who had joined the government at the same time as I and was now the deputy secretary for economic services, responsible for telecommunications policy, which was closely connected with our subjects.

It was about 11 p.m. but I phoned Liz at home and she kindly agreed to come down. She read through our draft and made a few suggestions for small changes in wording, which we were happy to accept. Emboldened, she began to suggest quite major surgery, dividing up paragraphs and moving them here and there. We told her firmly that she had better think again. It was not a question of whether her suggestions would be improvements or not. We were equipped with word processors, which were pretty advanced as far as contemporary technology went but very limited compared with the personal computers that came later. From the typing point of view, it would be a major undertaking if we were to do as she proposed and we had to finish the thing before the deadline.

The new broadcasting policies we were creating were generally of some interest to academics who were experts in broadcasting regulation, which was a specialised subject of its own. They would analyse closely what we did and often come up with extraordinarily elaborate hypotheses about the reasons for it, imputing to us all sorts of Machiavellian thinking. If I ever had the opportunity I would try to explain that we weren't as clever as they seemed to believe and a proportion of what was produced was the outcome of a late night feeling of 'That's good enough and we really can't do any more'.

Liz left us and Philip and I began checking every word and figure to make sure that we had not carelessly let in some awful error. By about 2 a.m. we decided that we had done enough even on that process as we were beginning to be unable to make any sense of the words. I asked Philip if he could do one more thing. In those days, all government offices operated on Saturday mornings and civil servants were required to come in at least on alternate Saturdays although many of us would come in more often than that as the relatively quiet atmosphere was good for catching up on anything that had been put on one side during the week. Philip gathered up an armful of ExCo papers, all in the proper format as laid down in the guidelines and manuals. He would minimise his sleep so that he could deliver them to the council's office the first thing the next day. Of such are bureaucrats' triumphs made!

It was around this time that my seven-year-old daughter was brought to my office one evening. We were going to see a show together but I had just a few things that I had to finish first. Caroline watched for a while with narrowed eyes and, once she had worked out what was going on, delivered her verdict. 'You have *such* an easy job. You just take the books out of that box,' indicating the files in the In Tray, 'write your name on them and put them in the other box,' indicating the Out Tray. '*I* could do your job. Everyone in my class could do your job.' Beginning to fear a preemptive strike on my executive office chair, I hastily decided that all those urgent things really could wait and that with no further delay we should set off for *My Fair Lady*.

Once the original consortium to provide cable TV had fallen apart we had to draw up conditions for a whole new tender and put it up for bidding. As it turned out, the Wharf Group was the only bidder but we still had to decide whether their proposal was acceptable and, once that was done, draft detailed licence conditions and negotiate them with the Wharf representatives.

This process took a straight thirty-seven hours, from 6 p.m. one evening until 7 a.m. on the next day but one, all spent in the not particularly congenial surroundings of our office conference room. This was an occasion when we became painfully aware of the small numbers that we were able to deploy. We had a single lawyer on our side but it was the inimitable Charles Barr, who would never let late hours or his counterparts' impatience get in the way of a good wrangle about where to place a semi-colon.

I did not sleep at any point during the negotiation but that was not so hard as no actual brainwork was required of me. My only function was to ensure that everyone kept going since we had immutable deadlines to meet so it was vital that no individual got tired and disenchanted enough to give up and go home. During the early hours of the last day the group's mood had got so bad that I began to fear that we really were not going to make the final stretch. I asked David Webb, an administrative officer on our team, to go to the 7-Eleven store at the bottom of the building and buy a bottle of Scotch. I knew that there was no government claim form that I could fit this one into and, accordingly, that this was going to be my personal donation to the cause of television licensing in Hong Kong. 'David,' I said, 'if you end up getting Johnnie Walker no need to splash out on the Black Label. The Red will do.' The cheaper product was duly bought and poured out in small tots, enough to liven everyone up but not enough to send them under the table.

For me a novel aspect of this particular post was relentless interest on the part of the media in what we were doing. There had always been a few people from the press who were interested in efforts to preserve old buildings but I had not before had the experience of handling a subject where developments were being breathlessly watched day by day by the entire press pack.

Overall, I liked journalists. It was a career that I had aspired to when I was a teenager and one that my sister had actually pursued. I believed that the press fulfilled a useful social function and that it was part of government's responsibility to treat them fairly and to respond to them promptly and as fully as we could. I flattered myself that I had a cordial relationship with those who were following the broadcasting policy stories. The advantage of this was that they would swallow the small white lies that I told them on the rare occasions when I judged that to do so was in the best interests of Hong Kong.

I attended a useful training course organised by the government on how to handle the media. As tends to be the way of such things, I did not get this opportunity until after I had been facing the reality for several months, floundering along as best I could. One of my fellow students was Eric Lockyear, a senior police officer and the then head of the Police Public Relations Bureau. 'Oh,' I moaned during the class discussion, 'I hate it when you go to some event and a gaggle of reporters cluster around you and you can't get away.' 'Well,' said Eric drily and unarguably, 'it's not as bad as being shot at.' There were, anyway, I learned, answers to my problem such as ensuring that you left a little bit of room to manoeuvre by never standing with one's back literally to the wall but always about a foot away from it and, if things got really grim, just walking away so that the panting scrum had to walk with you, firing questions as they went.

I discovered from what we were taught and from what I encountered in real life that each medium needed to be handled in a different way.

Television was undoubtedly the most powerful. Being rendered in two dimensions from the shoulders up somehow made you more alive, as far as most people were concerned, than walking around, visible from head to heels. 'I saw you on the television,' they would say in awe, 'you must be very busy.' In the street, I would sometimes be aware that strangers were glancing at me, wondering if they knew me as some sort of genuine acquaintance. I once shared a lift in an office building with a couple who presumably didn't realise that I could understand Cantonese and were arguing fiercely about whether or not they had seen me on the news the night before. Unfortunately, before I could settle it for them, we reached their floor and they walked out briskly, each still refusing to budge from firmly held opposing positions on this question, which can surely not have been of any great relevance to their lives.

That remark, 'I saw you on the television', was rather revealing. I proved for myself the validity of the research that has found that television viewers overwhelmingly focus on the appearance of the people that they are looking at, may have an idea broadly about what the subject under discussion is but can almost never recall the specifics. Friends would tell me tactfully, and my hairdresser in anguished tones, if my hair had not been at its best during some TV programme. I came to realise that if I had an hour in hand before an interview on a tricky topic that time was always better spent in the beauty salon rather than trying to brush up my knowledge of the subject. It was best to make fairly simple points and if the interviewer was aggressive and interrupted your answers you could just smile sweetly in the knowledge that he was probably giving viewers the impression of being a nasty bully. The worst thing that could happen was in a prerecorded interview which gave a presenter bent on mischief a chance to cut it into chunks, interpose others' remarks and throw in a few sarcastic comments for good measure. There was no Internet and no YouTube and so the consolation was that any disaster would float off into the ether and soon be forgotten.

Not surprisingly, radio was pretty much the opposite of appearing on TV. What you looked like didn't matter at all, which was great. In fact, if it was the kind of programme where they phoned you up at home you could sound authoritative even while sitting in an armchair wearing comfy slippers and dressing gown. Dealing with the substance was trickier though. Silence is the deadly enemy of the radio broadcaster since even a few moments without anything happening will make the listener wonder whether there is something wrong with his set or with you. It is easy, too, to unthinkingly refer to something that needs to be seen. I once did a briefing on new radio frequencies. 'Let me just run through this map,' I said grandly while the poor interviewer pointed frantically at the word 'Radio' on his equipment bag until I finally tumbled to the problem and started again. 'I can describe the boundaries of the areas affected by these changes. . . .'

With the print media, it came down to a question of trust. 'Let's go off the record,' they would say, sounding like spoony schoolboys suggesting a walk down Lovers' Lane. I had learnt to be rather disbelieving of these would-be Lotharios with printing ink on their fingers. They often didn't mean badly but Hong Kong journalists and the newspapers they worked for were not always very sophisticated and the things they were asking about were often complex and had become hopelessly garbled by the time they hit the printed page.

There were exceptions. Ray Snoddy of the UK's *Financial Times* had been dealing with broadcasting matters for far longer than I and, although I didn't admit it, I learnt a lot from him on occasions when I was meant to be the one supplying the answers. Kevin Lau of the *Economic Journal* genuinely saw journalism as a vocation, especially at a time when it seemed quite possible that in future freedom of the press would have to be fiercely defended. He was admirably assiduous and would work hard to assemble a mosaic of information and then ask so charmingly for the last missing piece that it was a pleasure to give it. At the *South China Morning Post* the news editorial team of Ann Quon and Fanny Wong were reliable backstops; they had a great instinct for something that was about to go into the paper and yet did not sound quite right and were conscientious when it came to trying to track down the correct thing and getting it in even as their deadline for going to press was looming.

All the same, I did find many of the print journalists quite baffling. 'Why?' I found myself often asking. 'Why did you call me up at home at 3 a.m. about something that seemed so trivial that it could surely have waited until tomorrow?' 'Why, after we had spent so long on that briefing on the issues, did your article still contain a lot of misinterpretations and misrepresentations of the government's position?' 'Why did your piece in this morning's paper have a headline that was completely at variance with its substance?' 'I am an ordinary civil servant. Why do you want to know all these weird things about my personal life, like how much money I am proposing to spend over Chinese New Year?'

To all these enquiries there was only ever one answer: 'My editor made me do it.'

In all these encounters with the press the information officers were our guardian angels. They were professional journalists, recruited into the Government's Information Services Department and rewarded with this rather pedestrian title. It was the information officers who drafted our press releases, who worked with us on the answers to the sheaves of questions submitted by fax and shepherded us through press conferences, being the ones to decide when it was safe to utter the welcome words 'Last question now please'.

The things that I was dealing with were sensitive enough sometimes to require consulting with the governor's information coordinator, Kerry McGlynn. Kerry was an old friend who had been with the government for a long time, in fact we had first got to know him about fifteen years before when he was in the New Territories administration. The job of an information officer could be rather mundane but Kerry was now in clover, since as the governor's press secretary he could go back to his professional roots as a journalist in Australia and wheel and deal with the media.

The reason was that since 1992 we had had a new governor and one with a very different outlook and background from his predecessors. Traditionally, governors came from within the ranks of the Colonial Service: it was the top of the tree, the biggest possible promotion. By the early 1970s the British Empire had already shrunk down to Hong Kong together with some small island territories in the Pacific, the Caribbean and the Atlantic. Between 1971 and 1992 the governors of Hong Kong had been drawn from diplomats in the British Foreign Office who had a special knowledge of China. David Wilson, later Lord Wilson of Tillyorn, was the last of these. The rumours were that powerful Hong Kong businessmen with UK links who had influence with the British government had requested the foreign secretary that Wilson's successor should be a political heavyweight who could ensure that Hong Kong's position was understood and supported by London.

If those rumours were true then the businessmen could not complain that they had not been listened to. The governor appointed in 1992 who would serve right through until 1 July 1997 and the reversion of sovereignty to China was Chris Patten, formerly the chairman of the ruling Conservative Party and a close ally of the prime minister, John Major.

Given a hundred and fifty years of connection, many Britons had friends or family who had lived in Hong Kong for longer or shorter periods, but the UK and the world generally had shown little sustained interest in the place. It would only break the surface of others' consciousness at times of crisis such as the 1967 riots or Tiananmen Square in 1989. On occasions there was a tendency to see the city through a veil that conferred on it an air of mystery and intrigue rather than the more mundane reality of a city of millions of normal hardworking people who happened to be Chinese living in what the author Richard Hughes described as a 'Borrowed Place, Borrowed Time'.

The transfer of sovereignty was a rarity, a prepackaged historical event. Unlike, say, an assassination, the date on which it would take place was known well in advance and its potential significance was undoubted. It would have been more or less inevitable that Kerry would have been very busy as more and more international attention was paid in the years running up to 1997 but there were features of Patten and his governorship that intensified the focus on him and Hong Kong.

First of all, he was a professional politician which was something that Hong Kong had never been exposed to. Civil servants put on the spot in public fora like the Legislative Council answered questions carefully but rather stodgily. They offered as many facts and explanations as they could and if there was something that they didn't know they would pledge to deliver supplementary information in writing later on. Governors and other senior officials attended social functions in order to encourage worthwhile community activities and would display interest in the buildings they were opening or the districts they were visiting. To the population at large they were the office of the governor, the queen's representative in Hong Kong, as much or more than they were individuals with their own characteristics.

Chris Patten was not like that. Although he could quickly master a complex brief he would respond ebulliently to any query whether or not it had formed part of his preparations for the event. He established a public personality as an enthusiast for the many options for high quality eating that Hong Kong offered. The most obscure seafood restaurants on outlying islands all seemed to acquire a photograph of the grinning proprietor standing next to the governor who had been sampling his wares. Patten gave a fresh impetus to the Hong Kong egg tart industry and queues of overseas tourists would form at his favourite bakery. He was probably the only British official who had a widely and openly used nickname. He had been given the official surname of 'Pang' as it was the closest Chinese name to his own but popularly this had 'fei', meaning 'fat', placed before it. Given the Chinese appreciation of their cuisine this was a compliment rather than otherwise.

Second, and perhaps to our surprise, Patten became embroiled in a war of words with China and this became an important story in the Hong Kong and overseas media in the last five years of British sovereignty. In his first policy address in 1992 he announced proposals for major changes to arrangements for election to the Legislative Council. Hong Kong had never been democratic in any normally understood meaning of the term. Improper use of power had been constrained to some extent by the criticism that it would have caused of an elected British government that did not play fair by its colony. There existed a free press, freedom of religion, the right of peaceful protest and, generally, freedom to express one's views as well as a fair and reliable legal and judicial system. There were elections for the Urban and Regional Councils which were responsible for the municipal services that kept the territory running, particularly in the fields of health and hygiene. However, until 1985, the Legislative Council, which as its name suggests is responsible for passing laws, budgets and generally fulfilling parliamentary functions, was entirely appointed and the governor was under no requirement to make it representative of anything. Between 1985 and 1992 small doses of quasi-democracy were introduced with the establishment of 'functional constituencies' to reflect the views of professions and industry sectors as well as a limited number of seats elected on a geographical basis.

There were several components in Governor Patten's package of political reform plans but the one that grabbed our attention was the proposal to overhaul the functional constituency system so that the Legislative Council became closer to one elected by 'normal' democratic means. The electorates in the existing functional constituencies would be changed so that it would be the workers in the industries concerned, not just a small group of industry leaders, who would be entitled to vote. Furthermore, nine new functional constituencies were to be introduced with electorates defined broadly enough to ensure that every employed person would be able to vote. It was proposed that these new arrangements would be put in place for the next LegCo elections in 1995.

There was enormous enthusiasm for these plans. Hong Kong was a sophisticated, well-educated community and it seemed a cruel insult that we could not exercise rights so common in the developed world and choose our parliamentary representatives. It was, unfortunately, rather reminiscent of the keenness in the early 1980s for the suggestion that Britain should go on running Hong Kong under some sort of management contract: ideas with many attractions but that would never be acceptable to China, which had become, really, the only power that mattered.

In 1839 and 1840 the fighting might of the British navy could casually overpower the best efforts of their Chinese counterparts and in the late nineteenth century the British could almost offhand-edly successfully demand a considerable piece of Chinese land in the form of the New Territories and in 1898 sign off on a lease to hold it despite lack of clarity about what would take place when the term of that lease ended. Whether or not it is true as a general principle, power had certainly grown out of the barrels of Britain's vastly more efficient guns. That was then and in the late 1990s the UK had little more than moral suasion to deploy.

The Chinese side was clearly not at all impressed by these unexpected proposals nor by the manner in which they had been presented. Those of us who were not deeply involved in discussions in the run up to 1997 normally had little real idea of what was going on. Two messages did consistently leak out however. First, that the negotiations were always tough and the atmosphere rather un-friendly and, second, that the Chinese side had a deep rooted belief that the British had some sort of cunning stratagem that would allow them, as it were, to wrap up the wealth of Hong Kong in a red spotted handkerchief and spirit it back to London. There were even wild stories going around that the British architect Norman Foster had designed the headquarters of the Hongkong and Shang-hai Banking Corporation which stood at the heart of Hong Kong's business district in such a way that the upper floors could be detached and sent back to the UK! It is not likely that anyone seriously believed this but that it could even be suggested indicated the mistrust that some felt.

The governor made an unproductive official visit to Beijing and the Chinese side began a barrage of graphic insults against Chris Patten ('sly lawyer', 'sinner of a thousand years', 'a prostitute who erected a monument to her own chastity' and, more mystifyingly, 'Tango dancer') and also began to set up their own parallel arran-gements for advisory bodies and forms of government after it. The possibly rather dry subject of the composition of the Executive and Legislative Councils had habitually attracted colourful metaphors. Previously, we had spoken of the 'through train', the ideal political settlement that would essentially be the same before and after 1 July 1997. Now the Chinese and their supporters told us about the 'second stove' that they were setting up, rather like a couple on bad terms with each other where one moves out of the shared home to a new and separate establishment.

The administrative grade of the government was arranged in 'liaison groups' which brought together about fifteen junior and middle ranking colleagues. I was the convenor of one of these groups and what normally happened was that we would get together for a casual lunch, talk about things related to our employment conditions and then I would relay our views to the Civil Service Branch, which looked after personnel matters. We never felt that our opinions had much impact but we enjoyed getting together and chatting. However, at this time we were asked to report specifically on our groups' response to the political situation.

The reactions that I came across were, I believe, quite typical. There was appreciation and approval for the package announced by the governor in October 1992 but this changed surprisingly quickly. Pragmatism took over. The consensus was: 'It's a nice idea but it's not going to work and that's all that is to be said'. Hong Kong Chinese and Britons had cultural similarities that had allowed us to develop a good working partnership but except in extreme circumstances Chinese were less confrontational than the British. If they found something that they didn't agree with they were more likely to shrug their shoulders and turn away rather than risking an unpleasant argument.

We enjoyed casting our votes in the 1995 LegCo elections; it was the closest that we had got to the sort of process that was a cornerstone of Western democracies and we made conscientious choices about who we thought would best represent us. All the same, there was no sense of exhilaration as we expected that the Chinese would roll back these reforms once they resumed sovereignty. In those years Hong Kong politics was not a personally engaging process. It was more like a hobby for those who took an interest in the twists and turns and intricacies of the constitutional debates.

Eventually, the Chinese organised a small circle election for the 'chief executive' to lead Hong Kong after the handover. The voters were four hundred prominent locals who were broadly sympathetic to the Beijing government. Their choice was Mr Tung Chee-hwa, a businessman who worked in the shipping company that his father had founded. His manner was kindly and avuncular and generally the community was accepting of the outcome, even if regretful that the millions of the adult population had been given no role in bringing it about. He was known as a 'Chinese patriot' but was totally assimilated into Western culture, having graduated from Liverpool University in 1960 and ever since a supporter of their famous football team. Others knew his wife, Betty, through her voluntary work for the Red Cross. It was not surprising that Tung had previously been a Patten appointee on the Executive Council.

During the early 1990s Michael was fighting his own battles, more or less against the whole world. His posts in the Hong Kong government were successively director of social welfare and secretary for financial services but he was spending much time in the familiar surroundings of Geneva. The 'Uruguay Round' was the world's largest ever trade negotiation and, among other things, it created the World Trade Organisation as a development of the General Agreement on Tariffs and Trade. Michael had participated in the meeting at Punta del Este in Uruguay in 1986 that launched the round but had not been part of the most recent discussions until Peter Sutherland, the newly elected director general of the GATT, sent a Mayday message to Chris Patten. The talks were foundering and Sutherland's solution was to appoint four 'friends of the chair', experienced and respected trade negotiators who would act as his *consigliere,* undertaking the private deal brokering that he hoped would end the deadlock. He wanted Michael to be one of these and the governor agreed, given the international importance of what was at stake. Sutherland's strategy proved itself and the Uruguay Round was successfully concluded in late 1993.

Thus, the past was returning and poking its way into the present. That would be a theme for the next few years too.

CHAPTER TEN

Snakes and Ladders

I SPENT A LITTLE OVER FOUR YEARS looking after broadcasting policy. That was a good length of time. It was long enough to get to understand the subjects and to become acquainted with the personalities but not so long as to become pigeonholed and no longer a generalist administrator. For administrators, promotions and postings went together and that was all right because our work was generic and skills in writing papers for ExCo and so on were transferable.

This practice also applied to other grades where it was not so suitable. For example, the museums were run as a division of a government department, as was the Antiquities and Monuments Office, which presented us with dilemmas over posting and promotions. How could we give a specialist restorer of ceramics or an archaeologist a merited promotion if they would then no longer be the 'right' grade for the perhaps sole post in which they could exercise their unique skills? We would end up either with square pegs in round holes or people accepting that in order to do the things that they could do best and liked the most they would have to forego advancement opportunities. The situation could have been resolved by floating off our museums and small specialist units so that they could employ their own staff but this was never pursued while I was in the government.

We were still relying on an approach which had been effective when we were a government of 'bright ideas': someone would have an inspiration, draw up some possibly fairly rough plans, get some money from the Legislative Council and put a young administrative officer in charge of setting the thing up and running it until his or her next posting came up. This was the case, for example, with the Music Office which was set up in 1977 and provided children from any background with extraordinary opportunities to learn Chinese and Western orchestral instruments, to play these in groups and to sing in choirs. Occasionally, there would be a variation and the founding administrative officer would stay with the organisation. Thus, Ophelia Cheung, whom I had first met in the New Territories administration, set up the Consumer Council in 1974 and then stayed as its head when it became a subvented organisation.

At the beginning of 1994, though, none of these things were happening to me. I was going to become commissioner for Recreation and Culture. I was now going to be in charge of not only arts and heritage but also sports and recreational activities, which extended as far as responsibility for the safety of fairground rides and cable cars: in other words, the normal sort of mixed bag for any administrative officer post.

An area in which it was relatively easy to make immediate progress was that of heritage buildings. The lacerating public controversy over the preservation of the synagogue some five years previously had led to a heightened sensitivity towards the issue and a more receptive attitude towards preservation. My colleagues in the Antiquities and Monuments Office and I decided to take every advantage of this and began collecting up as many worthwhile buildings as we could and getting them gazetted under the Antiquities and Monuments Ordinance, which would give them very significant protection against ever being torn down or altered. The process required approval by ExCo and every time we succeeded it felt as if we were philatelists who had just obtained a valuable stamp for our collection. We went for the easier targets of buildings that were in public sector ownership but even these were not entirely straightforward since in some cases they were on prime sites with great redevelopment potential and hence preservation meant a big loss of revenue for the government. We triumphantly bagged some of the most recognisable buildings of the colonial era, a hundred years old or more which in Hong Kong terms amounted to almost unimaginable venerability. They included the Central Police Station, the old Central Prison and Magistracy, the historic exteriors at Hong Kong University and Government House itself. The one about which we felt the most elated was the former Marine Police headquarters in Tsim Sha Tsui. We had hardly dared to hope that we would be able to keep this gracious building, constructed in 1884, since it was located in one of Hong Kong's most prosperous commercial areas. In the end, it was a bittersweet victory since although the building was preserved, some ten years later it was put out to tender and allowed to be converted into a hotel and shopping mall. This might not in itself have been too bad since it is good to see old buildings being reused rather than left as sterile and infrequently visited museums but the developer was somehow allowed to destroy the glorious grounds where ancient trees had provided a tranquil and secluded setting that was so much in keeping with the historic site.

As well as adding to the list of preserved buildings we were also busy restoring what we already had, although always aiming to do so in a way which did not undermine the integrity of the original buildings. My personal favourite among these projects was the Yi Tai Shu Yuen at Kam Tin in Yuen Long. It was another reminder of the central role that the civil service examinations, with a total history of some 1,300 years, had played in imperial China. This study hall, built in the nineteenth century, was supposed to be under the beneficent influence of the two gods of literary and martial virtue and they had apparently proved very effective in ensuring good results for those who were educated there. What I particularly loved about it was the 'White Stone Lane' in front of the building and running alongside it and which had been carefully reconstructed. Historically, this had been such a prominent feature that the students of the Shu Yuen were known as the 'Scholars of the White Stone Lane' and it was easy to imagine them making their way along there like the cast in a play, a rich diversity of attitudes, aspirations and ambitions.

For some two thousand years, China had revered scholars and scholarship but there had been, to put it politely, more ambivalence towards the sports which made up the other half of my new portfolio. Archery and horsemanship were gentlemanly pursuits and there was fluctuating enthusiasm for training in the military arts so as to be able to defend the empire. On the other hand, the more common view may have been expressed in the tale of the upper-class Chinese who asked a tennis playing Briton why he did not employ servants to undertake this unpleasant exertion on his behalf. Many young Hong Kongers liked playing sports like soccer, table tennis and badminton but generally parents preferred to see their children doing well academically before progressing to some stable, respectable profession or employment. Hong Kong had relatively little in the way of sports facilities when compared with other places with longer traditions and more space. It was difficult to turn the conflicting requirements of 'sport for all' and 'development of elite athletes' into a coherent policy.

The indefatigable Gus Chui who had persuaded John Hosier to take on the Academy for Performing Arts had scored another coup. His persistence had been rewarded by Sir William Purves, group chairman of the Hongkong and Shanghai Banking Corporation, agreeing to take on the chairmanship of the Sports Development Board, which could make grants to local sports associations to carry out their activities. The total amount to be allocated was, frankly, trivial but it was an education, not to mention an entertainment, to see the piercing Purves intellect and disdain for nonsense, flummery and obfuscation turned with laser-like intensity onto requests for tiny grants for obscure sports. This was after all the legendary approach which had provided the funding for some of Hong Kong's greatest industrial successes from beginnings in tiny backstreet factories. We would have to admit that in the sporting field we did not achieve as many successes although we all cheered on Lee Lai Shan, our champion windsurfer from the island of Cheung Chau and the whole community celebrated when she won Hong Kong's first ever Olympic medal: a gold no less, at Atlanta in 1996.

The year 1995 proved to be exceptionally busy. I had one of those 'instant expert' experiences and this time my new special subject was 'shark attacks and how to prevent them'. Deaths caused by sharks were far from unknown in Hong Kong, even though they had become part of history rather than a current phenomenon. As refugees left communist China for Hong Kong one of the most popular, although dangerous, routes was to swim across Mirs Bay or Deep Bay where the distances were the shortest although these were, nonetheless, long and arduous journeys. Young men would tie inner tubes or something else buoyant to themselves and launch off towards the dream of prosperity or simply of enough to eat every day. Many made it and some did indeed see their dreams coming true, raising a next generation who knew of economic hardship only through their fathers' stories. Others did not and the state of the corpses washed ashore on our side showed that sharks were responsible for at least some of these deaths. Since nobody knew how many of these 'freedom swimmers' set out and from where, there could be no accurate tally of victims, but the received wisdom, partly gleaned from the assessments of the Hong Kong police and the British soldiers who patrolled the border, was that there were many and sharks congregated in those areas where the yield was rich.

The Hong Kong government's attitude towards the migrants had a uniquely British tang to it, harking back to playground and public school games. It was called the 'touch base' policy and meant that an illegal immigrant who was captured within the rural border area would be sent back to Mainland China while those who made it to the urban area and established themselves there could stay and become Hong Kong citizens. It was little wonder that thousands thought it might be worth taking the risk. By 1980, however, this bizarre game had become impossible to sustain. Despite our booming economy, we really could no longer absorb the numbers who were turning up. Abolition of the 'touch base' policy was announced together with arrangements for those who were already here to sign up and get Hong Kong Identity Cards. There were massive lines snaking along the pavements by the issuing offices but no unrest as there was a justified belief that the Immigration Department would be capable of handling this enormous administrative exercise. The rest of us got used to the new legislation that was introduced as a corollary and required ID cards to be carried at all times.

The stories about the well-fed sharks of Mirs Bay became a thing of the past. The predators were still reckoned to be a threat in Hong Kong although not a tremendously serious one. Swimmers at the gazetted beaches which had lifeguards would from time to time be summoned out of the water by loudhailers and warning flags would be hoisted because there had been a shark sighting. There were occasional attacks, sometimes fatal ones, mainly at isolated bays and beaches in the eastern New Territories and each one led to some public panic but the overall feeling was that the level of danger was low enough to be ignored so long as one took sensible precautions. This complacency changed abruptly when three swimmers were killed by sharks in separate incidents within the first two weeks of June 1995 at popular beach areas in Sai Kung. Since I was responsible for sports I was also responsible for recreation and recreational swimming and things that might kill recreational swimmers.

One of the very good things about being in the government is that people will normally come and talk to you if you explain nicely that you want to try and take advantage of their knowledge and wisdom. It was not at all necessary to try and become a shark expert but rather to learn quickly and effectively from those in the Agriculture and Fisheries Department, the Biology and Zoology Departments of the local universities and so on and to draw conclusions that would yield the best possible solution to the problems that we were facing.

An early lesson was that there are still big gaps in the existing understanding of sharks and shark behaviour. It could not be easily established whether it was one shark or more that was responsible for this spate of attacks or what type it was although a consensus emerged in favour of it being a single tiger shark. There was equal uncertainty about what might have caused this sudden spate of attacks although there was an interesting theory that the dredging works for the big 'Rose Garden' project of the new airport at Chek Lap Kok might have disrupted the sharks' normal migration routes and feeding grounds and diverted them into our swimming beaches and once they had discovered prey they would return there again and again.

Our assembled experts could not offer us a definite answer to the problem either. They did agree, however, that an enthusiastically advocated solution of going out and hunting down the rogue shark was unworkable as there would be little likelihood of finding the shark responsible and dispatching it. We also consulted the South African authorities whose visiting team told us about shark nets not only in their own country but also in Australia. It seemed that once sharks found it impossible to enter beach areas with netting they would eventually avoid those areas altogether. They described the different types of net that were used and highlighted the importance of not inadvertently killing other sealife that might get trapped in badly designed nets. The Leisure and Cultural Services Department let tenders to have installed on all Hong Kong's gazetted beaches shark nets that are designed in such a way that they will exclude sharks but will not kill them and will pose negligible damage to marine life. There have subsequently been shark sightings in Hong Kong but, happily, no attacks.

One of the variety of things that came with my new post was a seat on the board of Ocean Park. This had been another of the gifts of the Jockey Club to Hong Kong, opened in 1977 as an oceanarium and then developed with amusement rides and as a theme park. The government had given the land for it on the south side of Hong Kong Island and the Jockey Club had funded its construction and in 1987 given it a trust fund before it became a non-profit-making entity operating under its own ordinance. To go there for meetings was more fun than being in some regular office building although the subjects we discussed were often the same as in any similar organisation. Almost all had problems with the pension arrangements for their staff. There was normally a provident fund system which relied on stock market investments and these were only slowly recovering from the great crash of 1987. However, I had one experience connected with Ocean Park which was not at all like anything else to do with any other organisation. It was in fact a day that unrolled rather like a film script.

It was a Sunday in August 1995 and I was at home with the family when there was a phone call from my boss, James So, the secretary for recreation and culture. He had got a message that there was some kind of problem at Ocean Park and he asked me to go and find out what was going on there. At the time, Ocean Park had no chief executive. One had just left and a replacement was being recruited; in the interim things were being looked after by the chief financial officer, Matthias Li, a conscientious and hardworking man. I had seen quite a bit of Matthias in discussions of the accounts and so on; these were definitely his specialty rather than the management of the park itself.

I had no inkling of what might be troubling the park and in those days before mobile phones, texts and e-mails there was no easy way to contact anyone to find out, so actually going there seemed to be the only practical option. Hong Kong distances are short and normally it would not have taken more than about half an hour to get there from our home. There was not a typhoon although following a storm the day before it was raining and the rain seemed to be getting heavier. Considering the weather, Michael wasn't keen to take our car out so I phoned up for an office car. Like most government departments we were blessed with a team of reliable drivers. Ah Ho was on duty and we proved to need all his resourcefulness. There was a dramatic difference between the northern and southern halves of Hong Kong Island. The former was simply experiencing a particularly rainy day while there had been severe landslides in the latter and we kept finding our way blocked, having to turn around and try another route. It took much longer than I had anticipated to reach the gates of Ocean Park where their offices were located. I still had no idea what to expect but impulsively decided to take with me the bulky *Government Telephone Directory* from the seat pocket in front of me.

The scene in the conference room was like something from a disaster movie. The park's key staff, including Matthias, the acting CEO and Stephen Leatherwood, the chief veterinary officer, wore an air of the deepest possible concern. They had obviously been there a while as the table was strewn with the debris of snacks and coffee cups. The whiteboard was covered in marker pen details of the park's stock of fish and marine birds and animals such as seals and penguins.

A landslide in Aberdeen, quite nearby, had cut off the park's electricity supply and the backup generator had failed. The entire stock of fish and marine animals were dependent on water whose temperature was perfectly controlled to meet their specific needs and that in turn required electricity. There was a small reserve capacity within the system but that could not last long. A suitable replacement generator had been located and the power company could get it to the park but there had also been landslides blocking the park's internal road system so the new generator could not be moved into the right position to connect with the electrical system. The only solution that presented itself was to transport the generator above the broken roads slung under a heavy-duty helicopter but where was such a thing to be found?

We knew each other through the Ocean Park board. I was the government and they looked at me hopefully. All I had in my armoury was the seven hundred pages of the *Government Telephone Directory* and I began flipping through it, not exactly at random but not with a well worked out plan either. I came across the entry for James Blake, the secretary for works. James was always friendly and he was in the right sort of post to be able to help. I called his home number and his wife, Caroline, answered. 'Oh sorry,' she said. 'He's not here. They've gone to the Emergency Control Centre which was opened up a little while ago. You probably don't realise but although the weather doesn't seem too bad there are some trouble spots, apparently: on the south side of the island and some other places.'

Caroline gave me the number at which I could contact him and I made another call and explained the problem to James. He passed me on to John Climas, an engineer who was on duty in the control centre. He would do what he could but he warned me that the helicopter fleet was committed to many urgent calls and that our case was complicated because we could not make use of just any helicopter. Only a Black Hawk could lift and carry the heavy generator.

The afternoon wore on. The nearest helipad was at the Police Training School in Aberdeen, thankfully unaffected by the weather, and so the generator was driven there to be ready. The data on the whiteboard was updated and we spoke to John from time to time to remind him that we were still here and waiting and hoping. There was nothing else we could do as there did not seem to be any possible Plan B.

As we were really beginning to think that we were not going to be lucky at all the phone rang. There was a Black Hawk on its way to the helipad. CP Chiu, the park's chief engineer, and I drove there to meet it. The winds were strong and the down draught from the approaching helicopter worsened the gusts. We pressed ourselves against the hedge but even so we could hardly stand.

The days of the Royal Hong Kong Auxiliary Air Force with its part-time pilots were gone. The recently established Government Flying Service was making the transition to become fully local before the transfer of sovereignty in 1997 but there were still a few remaining pilots with backgrounds in the British military. Out of the helicopter that had hovered to a halt a magnificent specimen of this disappearing species emerged. He was slightly bald but offsetting this was a superb white handlebar moustache and a bearing that would have perfectly fitted him for a role in a classic World War II story of derring-do.

'There's only room for one passenger. Who's the engineer?' My own part in the drama slipped into the background as CP got ready to get on board. The pilot looked at the sky darkening as twilight was setting in. 'This is absolutely on the margin. I can make one more flight today and one only. I'm sorry but if you don't succeed the first time with what it is that you want to do, there won't be a second chance.'

I went back to the group in Ocean Park and gave them the news. Our period of waiting was surprisingly short. Everything had worked. The replacement generator had been lifted and carried above the road block and lowered into the right position. It had been connected and the electricity supply had been restored. Ocean Park was safe.

For a couple of months the park had to operate on a rather reduced scale as roads were repaired and so on. When it was restored to full operations there was a wonderful party one evening. In those days the park had an attraction called the Middle Kingdom which was an area which set out to replicate a traditional Chinese town and staged shows with acrobats and clowns. It could be hired for private functions and this is what the management had done. The newly appointed CEO, who had arrived in time for the clearing up, all the board members, many of whom had given invaluable assistance in the days immediately following that anxious Sunday, and all of us, the Brothers and Sisters of the Whiteboard and the Conference Room, were there, together with husbands and wives.

The Middle Kingdom and its attractions was opened just for us. It was a beautiful place to be on a warm and settled autumn evening with a sea view and a slight breeze. One of the things on offer was traditional fortune telling. Intellectually, I think that this is ridiculous and, as a paid-up Anglican, even mildly morally reprehensible but emotionally I'm a complete sucker. People away on business trips indulge themselves in ways in which they would be embarrassed to do at home. Some visit strip clubs, Hong Kongers who come to Geneva would want to go across the border into France to try their luck at the casino in Divonne. I might seek out a fortune teller. Here was one on offer with no queuing and nothing to pay. I was definitely going to consult him! His cubicle was decorated with charts of faces with Chinese characters on different sections and on his desk was a small globe of the world, the kind that was sold as a child's toy. He asked me for date and time of birth and then to identify on the globe the exact place of birth. England was easy enough but it was quite difficult to pinpoint Oxford. He studied my palms rather in the Western fashion and my face in the Chinese way. Finally he pronounced, 'Your husband will be rich because of you.'

There was a convivial meal, some short speeches and a presentation ceremony. In my role as a board member, I thought it was commendable that the park's selection of corporate gifts was quite limited. As a mark of gratitude those of us involved in the generator saga were each formally given a tie bearing the Ocean Park logo. I immediately passed mine on to Michael. See, the fortune teller had been proved right already! The calculations could well have been a bit skewed because the data I had provided on place of birth was not as accurate as it could have been. Perhaps if I had managed that a bit better I might have picked up a winning lottery ticket as well.

A few weeks before this evening party I had been to another ceremony in another park. The event was to mark the completion of works at the Kowloon Walled City Park. It was held in the daytime and in the heart of Kowloon although, as it happened, the officiating guest of honour was the same James Blake who had been the link in the chain that got us the helicopter and restored the electricity supply. As a by-blow of history, in the margins of the meetings about the future governance of Hong Kong, the British and Chinese sides had found a moment or two to consider the fate of the Walled City and in 1987 had agreed that the old, dangerous and insanitary buildings should be torn down, the ancient fort (the *yamen*) preserved and a park built on the site. Implementing this agreement proved complex, mainly because of wrangles over compensation claims by the residents and property owners, but eventually it was all done.

The specialists in my Antiquities and Monuments Office had helped with certain aspects of the building of the park. Our archaeologists had been involved in the excavation of the site of the South Gate, the ancient name plaque of which they had unearthed together with one inscribed with the characters for the Walled City itself.

As we arrived and moved towards our seats I noticed an elegant middle-aged lady. Once I was sitting down she suddenly poked me in the back. I turned round and realised that my assailant was a broadly grinning Jackie Pullinger. Jackie had kept faith with Hong Kong. Journalists' accounts of the work that she had done in the Walled City had made her something of an international celebrity but she had simply continued with her own unique approach towards some of the most lost and vulnerable in our community. She moved from one set of ad hoc premises to another until the government gave her a piece of land in the hills above Sha Tin where she could build a residential centre.

The Walled City Park is, I think, one of Hong Kong's most successful pieces of municipal design and I believe that the main reason for that is that it is uncompromisingly Chinese in both inspiration and execution. The site is imbued with history and the original *yamen* forms a genuine centrepiece for the park. Beyond that though, the design demonstrates the traditions of pavilions and shaded walks which are culturally consistent and produce a pleasant, restful atmosphere that can be appreciated by anyone from any background.

A feature of the park is the use of rare and exotically shaped rocks which, to Chinese tastes, make particularly attractive additions to the landscape. In the Walled City Park this had been developed further by assigning a rock to each of certain notable personages associated with the place, with a plaque informing visitors about the connection. Jackie Pullinger had been honoured with her own rock and this was what its inscription said:

> Ms. Pullinger came from the UK to Hong Kong alone in 1966 to spread the Gospel. In the Walled City she looked after teenagers who were led astray and despite interference from the triad society, she fearlessly helped drug addicts overcome addiction through the teachings from the Gospel. Her pastoral work subsequently developed into a number of Hang Fook Camps in various parts of the territory leading many drug addicts, prostitutes and street sleepers to start their lives anew. Even some triad members have subsequently turned over a new leaf through believing in Jesus and dedicated themselves to missionary work.

That day's excursion was a happy reminder of one of the most distant parts of my Hong Kong past and also a symbol of the positive things that had been achieved. The area surrounding the park was by no means an elite enclave of the wealthy but was dominated by public housing estates. Yet it was well planned with convenient transport and facilities and services that allowed the residents to thrive and find their own destinies.

In my own life, in parallel, other decisions from the past were casting a shadow. When I had got married in 1976 I had decided to change my terms of service from the pensionable arrangement on which I had been recruited to one of employment on the basis of three-yearly contracts. I was told that this should make no difference to the progression of my career. This had for a long while been proved to be the case and I had benefited from a series of promotions and a variety of postings. My last performance appraisal had recommended that I might now be made a head of department. But this was not to be and even my existing position in the hierarchy was under threat.

Michael and I were now being swept up in the tide of changes to the administration in preparation for the transfer of sovereignty. Michael was by then secretary for financial services, occupying a post in the most senior rank which, the Basic Law made clear, would, after 1997, be open only to Hong Kong citizens holding Chinese passports. Furthermore, it was, understandably, not considered advisable to have all expatriates leaving together at the moment of the handover. Michael was therefore told that he should prepare to retire in 1995.

In addition, there was a commitment generally to speed up localisation of the civil service. It was believed (wrongly, as it turned out) that a large proportion of the expatriates in the administrative grade would want to remain in post after the transfer of sovereignty blocking promotion opportunities for local officers. It was not at all straightforward to remove those who had pensionable status and so the focus was placed on the handful of us who were employed on contract terms. It seemed that I would simply not be given another contract.

I tried exploring the possibilities back in the UK. A consultancy company who had advised us on the economics of television broadcasting referred me to their executive search division in London. I had an encouraging meeting with them. My experience should fit me for something. How much was I earning? My interviewer blanched at the answer and became much less cheerful. This was a period during which the Hong Kong economy was booming while the British economy seemed mainly to be continuing on the path of decline that, despite intermittent patches of brightness, had been its overall characteristic since the end of the

Second World War. Some ten years previously, John Bremridge, our financial secretary, had predicted that by the time of the handover Hong Kong's per capita GDP would be greater than the United Kingdom's and that proved to be more than correct. On the other hand, neither my London interviewer nor I foresaw the 1997 Asian financial crisis that would begin with the collapse of the Thai baht and would usher in years of financial stringency in Hong Kong that would include the cutting and freezing of civil service salaries.

We had two children still in education. Thinking it over, I concluded that the kind of work that I liked best was the kind of work that I was already doing. Some expatriates were not willing to remain and try to make a life under Chinese Communist rule. I did not share this view. It was conceivable that there would be an abrupt military takeover and that everything about our society would be turned upside down. It was within the bounds of imagination but it did not seem within the bounds of common sense. There was no indication that such a thing would happen and, on the contrary, every indication that it would suit China best if Hong Kong kept functioning much as before. The other possibility that some feared was an insidious takeover of all the mechanics of government, perhaps by the planting of new staff representing the new sovereign power. This, too, seemed unlikely to me. Our systems were quite intricate and could baffle any outsider who wanted to change them but had not developed the necessary years of understanding and familiarity. And, of course, I, as well as my family had passports that would allow us to go hurrying back to Britain if such proved necessary.

I asked for a meeting with Michael Sze, the secretary for the civil service and explained my dilemmas. He put a deal on the table. The emigration that had led to the leaking away of well-educated Hong Kongers and which had surged in the wake of Tiananmen had had particularly severe consequences for certain government departments such as Social Welfare and Education which had lost those who should now be in managerial positions. He could find me a place in one of those but there was a snag. It would be at the level of assistant director, a rank which I had passed through some six years before.

Having steadily climbed the ladder, I would now be sliding down the snake. Because of the stipulations in the government rulebook, I would lose salary but more than that too. We were living in a government-provided flat that was consistent with Michael's position. We would have to move to somewhere in keeping with my new status and, on a more trivial level, I would lose the use of an official car for my daily commute and I could no longer expect to be assigned a spacious corner office with an expansive harbour view.

Weighing it all up, I decided to accept Michael Sze's offer. We would be able to meet our financial needs and I believed that I would still be given something interesting to do. I was told that I would become an assistant director in the Social Welfare Department, responsible for social security. I would go from my senior post with its small team of staff and no money to speak of under my direct control to a junior post with a budget of billions and more than a thousand personnel spread through forty offices.

My father had died some eight years before but my mother was sanguine about my plan, which was rather surprising in view of her analysis of Hong Kong's likely future. 'What a pity there won't be any more Boy Scouts or Girl Guides there.' 'Why do you think that's going to happen, Mum?' 'Well, that was one of the first things Hitler did in Germany, got rid of the Scouts and Guides.'

Before my move, I would get a closer view of China than ever before and soon after that the whole of Hong Kong would be reintegrated with the Motherland.

CHAPTER ELEVEN

China Bound

IN THE DAYS WHEN THERE WAS less public scrutiny of the activities of the Hong Kong government the bowels of the Secretariat were, in some senses, reminiscent of the Bastille as described in Dickens' *Tale of Two Cities*. Patrolling the corridors one would discover names on office doors of people that one had not heard of for years, had indeed forgotten about altogether. The titles of their positions would be there too and usually included some combination of 'special', 'general' and 'duties'. These were the ranks of the 'posting problems', carrying out invented tasks because no one knew what to do with them. I was now to have a temporary sojourn in limbo, working out the last little bit of my senior level contract. Still entitled to the official car I was driven in every day. I had my occupation like Dr Manette in the novel; I was not shoemaking but had been given a project on civil service training to write up. I had plenty of time on my hands and since it was winter, I also signed and addressed all our Christmas cards.

I was quite soon released and, indeed, given a treat that I had been promised when the demotion deal was hammered out. I was to join a specially arranged Cantonese training course for expatriate civil servants. Our class consisted of five administrators and four police officers. The theory seemed to be that those of us reckless enough to consider a continuing career after the change of sovereignty should at least have our language skills polished up. In fact, the erosion of use of English in the government was slow. A decision was taken that work on files would continue to be in English although increasing amounts of Chinese correspondence did creep in. Civil servants who had been speaking and writing English since schooldays were hardly going to un-learn their skills overnight although they perhaps became a little rusty and awkward as the requirement to speak to native-English speakers diminished. The simultaneous interpreters in the Legislative Council, who must be among the best in the world, continued to ply their trade.

Anyway, the course was something to be eagerly looked forward to, mainly because of its format. We would spend a month at the University of Science and Technology in Hong Kong and two weeks at Zhongshan University near Guangzhou.

Opened in 1991, the University of Science and Technology (HKUST) had been another of those gifts of the Jockey Club to the people of Hong Kong. It occupies what, by Hong Kong standards, is a most spacious campus in Sai Kung with sweeping sea views, and well planned with student accommodation on site so that it feels like a real learning community. The subjects studied there are as its name suggests but it also has a school of humanities and social sciences whose staff at the time happened to include a couple of academics with a particular interest in teaching Cantonese, something quite rare even in Hong Kong. The government no longer had a systematic Cantonese training programme since the days of routine recruitment of expatriates were also firmly in the past.

Studying Cantonese seems to have a narcotic, trippy effect and although the members of our group were in their mid-thirties and above, an adolescent air began to pervade the classrooms and I noticed a sort of edginess in our teachers who seemed a little uncertain as to whether they could go on controlling this class or whether it would descend into helpless laughter and practical jokes.

We undoubtedly learnt something at HKUST but it was the experience of Zhongshan University that proved really memorable. It was an outstanding programme that combined language study, visits, briefings and informal interaction with the university people. If the course had taken place earlier I would have been the delegation leader but post-demotion I had to cede that position to Gordon Jones, who was now senior to me. Gordon was charmingly embarrassed by this reversal of fortune but I didn't mind at all. Apart from anything else, Gordon's language skills were greater than mine so he was much better equipped to deliver all the necessary speeches of thanks and so on.

We took the train to Guangzhou as a group and were met, which was a blessing as the station was chaotic. I suppose that must be true of many railway stations all over the world but Guangzhou, with the endless comings and goings of migrant workers from other provinces seeking to escape rural poverty in the ever-expanding manufacturing industry of Southern China, seemed to be a flood of people that could only be navigated with a knowledgeable guide. We were being lodged in the Canton Plaza Hotel which was perfectly adequate, although not as luxurious as the famous White Swan. From our rooms we could look down into the courtyard of the municipal hospital across the way. The decrepit buildings and the disorganised milling around of people made us resolve to do all in our power to avoid illness and accident so as to stay away from that uninviting place.

Every day we were taken in a minibus to and from the campus of Zhongshan University, which enabled us to get an insight into Guangzhou's horrendous traffic. One day we saw a motorcycle policeman bump into a civilian motorcyclist. It was entirely the policeman's fault but he dealt with the matter by dismounting, administering a swift uppercut to his victim and riding off again.

The university was a different kind of place and very likeable. Zhongshan is a rendering of the name of Sun Yat-sen, revered as the father of modern China, leader of the movements that over-threw the Qing dynasty and ended the thousands of years of Chinese imperial rule, who was born nearby and founded the university in 1924. It was a very pleasant place, criss-crossed with paths shaded by fine trees and dotted with impressive statues and buildings in a Chinese style. At the university we were given VIP treatment. Lunch was served to us in the staff restaurant and afterwards the next item on the programme would be a short siesta in a room with blinds drawn and heavy armchairs in which to take a nap. Our classroom course was cleverly devised, consisting of lectures on China's government, economy and so on delivered in Cantonese, but with English translations provided so that we gained some general knowledge as well as language learning.

Not all the excursions in our programme were riveting and what we dubbed the Great Armchairs of the People could be as soporific as those provided in the university and we would find ourselves drifting off to sleep during briefings in various offices of the Guangdong provincial government. These were the times that I was glad to be tucked away in a corner of a great room and that it was Gordon who had the group leader's responsibility of sitting next to the top official and looking alert throughout.

We were near not only Sun Yat-sen's birthplace but also the birthplace of Hong Kong, in that here had taken place the events that led up to the First Opium War as well as the actual fighting itself. We were brought to one of the old imperial forts and given a frank briefing on the corruption and ineptitude that had left imperial troops completely vulnerable to nineteenth-century British firepower while the Chinese military relied on elite soldiers dressed as tigers to frighten the enemy.

We visited the Opium War Museum in Humen which is at the site of one of the most significant actions of the period: Commissioner Lin's destruction of the foreign traders' stocks of opium. Lin was not corrupt nor corruptible. He was on the contrary a civil servant who was determined to end the opium trade that was undermining the health of the Chinese nation and making it prey to foreign powers. He had the emperor's backing and confronted the Canton traders and their local go-betweens, forcing them to hand over substantial stocks which were dissolved to nothingness in deep water-filled trenches near the beach at Humen. Lin was ultimately unsuccessful in the face of the determination of the traders, led by William Jardine, to ensure that their ends were achieved by the deployment of Britain's irresistible military might.

Lin is nevertheless considered a great national hero. At the museum 'An Exhibition on the History of Lin Zexu's Crusade against Opium and the Opium War' exposes the crimes of the colonialists who invaded China, demonstrating the heroic deeds of the Chinese people who were against foreign invasion and the opium trade, singing the praises of the lofty national integrity of the Chinese people and their strong spirit of patriotism.

Before we toured the displays inside the museum we were taken to a reception room and along with the normal fare of green tea and fresh fruit were given a speech by the museum's director which made it clear that he regarded us as, at most, one remove from being war criminals ourselves. I found this quite disconcerting. The Opium Wars had merited no more than a sentence or two in my school history textbooks and did not register as a major episode in British history. Since having come to live in Hong Kong I understood more about what had happened and thought of it as something pretty squalid and disgraceful, a dressing up of commercial aims to justify an armed intervention. Yet these events had taken place long ago and seemed to me to be entirely overtaken by our day-to-day efforts to do our best for Hong Kong, which received an endorsement from the generally friendly relationship with the Chinese people among whom we lived and worked.

History can be almost as much about the historians as it is about what took place. Certainly, the Opium Wars occupy a fundamental place in the Chinese national narrative of weakness, subjugation by alien powers, a long struggle to adopt some useful Western techniques culminating in the 1949 Communist Revolution and Mao's declaration in Tiananmen Square that 'the Chinese people have stood up'.

Some years later, I found a poem by Margaret Atwood that for me cast some light on the situation. It is titled 'Nobody Cares Who Wins' and the last lines read:

It's never in the past, defeat.
It soaks into the present.
It stains even the morning sun
The colour of burnt earth.

Our hosts kept us occupied in the evenings as well as during the day. We went to dinners with them in the private rooms of restaurants and where the chief entertainment was karaoke. The Zhongshan group demonstrated a tremendous gusto for socialising that was in contrast with similar functions in Hong Kong which would have been participated in with enjoyment but with a little more inhibition, a sort of mental looking over the shoulder to be sure that one was doing the correct thing.

The stock of karaoke discs that our group could sing along to was soon exhausted. Fortunately, Gordon and another of our number, Gavin Ure, had Scottish blood and had fine voices as well as a comprehensive knowledge of the works of Sir Harry Lauder. Consequently, we were able to treat our friends to *a capella* performances of gems like *A Wee Deoch and Doris*. It was probably only a small proportion of the party who were able to say 'It's a braw bricht moonlicht nicht' but we were 'a'richt, ye ken'.

Over the years, Hong Kong cuisine had lost its more exotic edges but that was not true in Guangdong Province. There was more space than in Hong Kong and so there were some low-rise restaurants set in fairly extensive grounds. One day, we were on our way to lunch in such an establishment when I noticed an unfortunate kookaburra in a cage by the kitchen door doubtless destined for the pot although not on our menu. Nor were we the recipients of the lavish gesture made to some of the first Hong Kong visitors to be received when things began to normalise after the Cultural Revolution for whom a lion from the Guangzhou Zoo was slaughtered and served up. We were however offered snake wine, draughts from great jars of alcohol in which a snake had been pickled and which still lay there, preserved. Peter Mann, an administrative officer, was very taken with this refreshment and at one lunch with some civic dignitaries managed to put away fourteen tots of this beverage, thus claiming victory for Hong Kong in a drinking competition with the mayor of Shun Tak. Peter also liked the whole black water beetles fried to a crunchy crisp and I must agree that these made a very good pre-dinner snack.

Given our schedule, we did not have opportunities to talk to students at the university but this lack was offset by the many chances we had for informal exchanges with the academics there. They were diverse in their views. Some were intensely patriotic, some less so and some quite critical of aspects of the Chinese system. Some envied the Hong Kong way of life and some fiercely attacked its shortcomings. In absolute terms, none was wealthy but they seemed to have comfortable, sociable lives, enjoying close relationships within their extended families.

For many years, southern China had been the most outward facing and cosmopolitan region of the People's Republic and in 1980 the special economic zones to experiment with more market oriented policies had first been set up there. The children of some of the older academics were at college in the US, thanks to scholarships and the relatively benign climate of the US-China relationship. Overall, they were generally optimistic, positive people with an enthusiasm for life and a thirst for new experiences.

We never discussed Tiananmen Square. During a short official visit to Beijing some four years before I had tried raising the topic but was always met with extreme hostility whether expressed in verbal aggression or in shocked silence and refusal to engage. In Zhongshan, there was an unspoken consensus that we would not raise this sensitive subject.

On the other hand, there was a willingness to recall the ten years of the Cultural Revolution, which had ended in 1977, and seemed to have left no one in the entire nation untouched. The effects varied according to where one happened to be in one's life course when this enormous upheaval struck and we had access to the accounts of a cross-section.

Those who had already been established in careers as scholars and teachers became caught up in the feverish cycle of denunciation and persecution of the unfortunates who had fallen foul of the ever-changing official line of what was and was not an approved belief. One of the professors who was shrewd and perceptive remarked with a wry smile that almost twenty years later everyone somehow portrayed him or herself as a victim or martyr and yet, as he pointed out, that could not have been the case. He knew quite well the details of who had betrayed and denounced whom but thought it better to keep his counsel.

To have been aged around fifteen or eighteen when the Cultural Revolution began seemed to have been a particularly hard fate. Students who had worked hard, who loved to learn and had foreseen only a bright future absorbed in their specialisms were whisked away from their families and sent to labour in distant rural communities with no intimation that the remainder of their lives would consist of anything else. Even though they were rehabilitated they had lost the golden years of their twenties and felt that however much effort they made they would now never be able to fulfil all their intellectual potential. In the circumstances, it was hard to avoid some feelings of bitterness.

Small children were comparatively better protected but they were not unaffected. At first, it was fun to have normal lessons suspended so as to perfect the performance of new songs praising Chairman Mao but soon they were terrified by the sight of hanged bodies suspended from the lamp posts. It was safest then to be kept at home quietly until this terrible storm blew over and life could resume.

In the same geographical region as Hong Kong, everything could be made worse by torrential rain. On our way to some soggy sightseeing I was stuck on a two-person seat next to a rather elderly chap whom we had nicknamed Tremolo Ted on account of his fondness for the use of plenty of *vibrato* when karaoke singing. He was one of the keenest proponents of the position that Hong Kong was going to enjoy great good fortune in getting out of the grasp of the evil British and being reunited with the Motherland. This bus trip had given him the perfect chance to expound on this to me and there was no sign of his tedious speechifying coming to a halt. When I could insert a couple of words into this one-sided conversation, I irritably said, 'How can you be so sure of all this? How can you be sure that there won't be another Cultural Revolution here?' He fell silent and then, to my utter mortification, tears rolled down his cheeks. 'You don't understand,' he said. 'It was so terrible. We will never let that happen again.'

Our last day came and there was an exchange of gifts. We were given impressive certificates of our academic achievements mounted in smart red satin folders embossed in gold. For each of us there was as well a traditional seal engraved with our Chinese names. Gordon had a supply of items for presentation brought from Hong Kong but we had also taken up a little collection among ourselves so that we could give a bouquet and a necklace to Miss Yung, who had been assigned as our liaison person and had brightened the Zhongshan experience with her uncomplaining cheerfulness.

We parted in an atmosphere of great goodwill and cordiality. Despite the differences in culture and background, we had discovered that we were not so alien after all.

On the wall of my new office in the Social Welfare Department I stuck up as a talisman the group photograph that we had had taken on the university steps. Next to it I hung an embroidery my daughter had done as a birthday present for me. It showed a group of rabbits picked out in careful tent stitch and above the punning text 'Who's afraid of a few grey hares?' Well, I certainly was. I had glumly told Sir Roger Lobo that I was pulling out an average of one white hair each month although he, ever rational and doubtless in the course of his life having come across a few worse things than the normal signs of natural ageing, pointed out that that would only make a total of twelve each year. Anyway, the pulling out technique had to be abandoned once things had got to the point where baldness seemed to be the greater risk.

I was now the department's assistant director in charge of social security, sitting on top of literally thousands of staff and dozens of offices scattered around the territory. These staff were not generalists but had been recruited from university or, more usually, school to work in the department and had normally spent their entire career administering some aspect of the social security schemes. Those with the longest experience could recall the days of some thirty years before when their jobs had consisted of simply handing out food to the needy. Since then, partly on the advice of experts from the British government the system had been developed into one based on means-tested cash payments. In essence, it was much like the UK's Supplementary Benefits Scheme and it was useful for us that we could look to the UK as well as countries like Canada, Australia and New Zealand where comparable policies could serve as reference points.

I visited all the corners of this new kingdom of social security together with the people from headquarters. They frankly pointed out all the shortcomings but to me it seemed to be a machine that was working, albeit with some definite weaknesses. Unlike some of my previous posts, I had the luxury of being able to get acquainted with what was going on in a reasonably relaxed way. When Americans talk about 'social security' they mean what we think of as a pension system, while what we use the term for they thought of as welfare payments. Once the terminology was cleared up, there were plenty of interesting academic studies to read from all around the world. It took me back to my Oxford days of politics and sociology but now the impact of the conclusions drawn was on the real world rather than mere theories to be tossed around and argued over.

One rather unusual new responsibility was disaster relief. The classic types of Hong Kong disasters had been the fires and typhoons that swept through squatter areas and rendered thousands homeless. The original core business of social security had been providing food, whether cooked up in the giant woks at our Kowloon kitchen or in bags of rice and cans of staples. It was what was required after a disaster too and so it made sense for us to undertake that function. This had continued even though the need for this traditional type of assistance had been declining and Hong Kong and its citizens were changing. This was brought home to me very clearly during our involvement in one of the most dramatic events of 1996: the fire at Garley Building.

Garley Building was a sixteen-storey commercial block in the west of central Kowloon. Built in the 1970s, its installations for fire detection and fighting were inadequate. Renovation work going on in the building resulted in sparks from welding setting fire to flammable material within a lift shaft which created a chimney effect, fast spreading a ferocious blaze throughout the entire structure. All this became apparent later on in the course of the commission of enquiry into what turned out to be Hong Kong's worst peacetime fire as far as casualties were concerned, with a final toll of forty-one deaths and eighty injuries.

None of this was known in the late afternoon of 20 November when word of what has happening began to reach us. I went home to change into casual clothes and then set off for Kowloon with

Cheng Chok-Man, the chief social security officer whose schedule included disaster relief.

It was less than twenty-five years since I had arrived in Hong Kong, to be regaled with stories of the corruption that plagued the Fire Brigade and vitiated the service that they were supposed to be providing. There had been a complete change within this relatively short space of time and now the courage and integrity of the Fire Services were undoubted. They had set up a tender at the site as a mobile command centre and we went there for a briefing almost as soon as we arrived. We had heard that one of their men had already been killed that evening while searching for victims within the building. I wondered if that was correct as their most senior officer began his report in a completely cool and disciplined manner. It was true, though, and as he came to the point where he had to report that tragic death he did not stumble, his professionalism keeping his emotions in check.

The nature of the fire and the deficiencies in the building made it exceptionally difficult to deal with and it would take twenty hours altogether before it was put out. Many of those who had been in offices there when the fire broke out could not escape because of swirling flames and smoke and the intense heat. A helicopter was brought in with the aim of taking people off the roof but this risky manoeuvre proved counter-productive since the draught from the rotor blades actually worsened the fire.

We had followed our usual protocol for disasters and had mobilised the local team according to the standard rota. If this had been the kind of fire that we were accustomed to they would have been liaising with other departments to find a community hall or similar where those who were now homeless could be lodged as well as arranging to supply them with food, toiletries and so on. It was obvious that there would be no such requirement that night and so we stood them down and sent them home.

CM Cheng and I did not want to leave, however, and offered to stay and help in any way that we could. The police referred to us a man who was looking for his wife who had been at work in the building. As it happened, he was an off-duty detective himself, he and his wife both less than thirty and not long married. He was in civilian clothes, very smartly dressed, and I could not help imagining the cheerful mood in which he had probably left his home that morning. Casualties were being taken to two different hospitals: the Queen Elizabeth and the Kwong Wah and we stayed with him as he ping-ponged desperately in a hopeless quest for news. Much later, some weeks after the fire, we heard that his wife's body had finally been identified.

I could not help noticing that conditions at the hospitals were chaotic. This was not in terms of the treatment being provided as the medical staff worked with ferocious efficiency. However, there was a dearth of information and increasing numbers of relatives of those who had been in Garley Building were arriving, hoping for news of the missing. The medical social workers were on duty but there was not much they could do in the circumstances.

At Queen Elizabeth Hospital I was shocked to see someone I had known in a very different context. In the days when I was commissioner for Recreation and Culture Vincent Chow had been chairman of the Arts Development Council. He held this position as voluntary public service although it reflected his own genuine interest in the arts. In his professional life he ran the family business, Chow Sang Sang Jewellers. Now this sophisticated and cultivated man was one of those who was desperately waiting. We embraced and he told me some of his horrifying story. His company had been thinking of setting up a mail order business and they had picked out some of their brightest young talents to work on this project under the leadership of Vincent's wife, Josephine. They had been clustered together in premises in Garley Building.

As it turned out, Josephine and those who had been in the same room as her survived, although injured, because they took the bold decision to leap from the window onto a roof below after they found that the door knob was so hot that they could not even turn it. Chow Sang Sang suffered grievously, though, perhaps more than any other group. Twenty-two of their employees died on the fifteenth floor of Garley Building.

After this, it was hard to believe that we would see two more serious fires with loss of life within the next two months. They took place at the Mei Foo Sun Chuen private residential estate and the

Top One Karaoke Lounge. The same sad scenes were repeated and again, the tragedies more poignant because of the youth of the victims. It was even more extraordinary that all three of these disasters took place within our West Kowloon region. June Sherry, the district social welfare officer, was given a punning office nick-name, which roughly translated as the 'inflammable' or 'fiery' one and usually applied to ladies who aroused heated passions.

June gave evidence to Mr Justice Woo's Commission of Enquiry on the Garley Building fire, including the points about making better information available during and after disasters and this was covered in the recommendations in his report. It can happen that worthy recommendations are welcomed when publicised but then they are not, or only partially, implemented. I resolved to do everything I could from my corner to see action taken on these, as the smallest recognition to be offered to those who had suffered so much. An inter-departmental help desk to be set up at receiving hospitals or at the scene is now a standard part of the government's protocol for dealing with disasters. In addition, Helios Lau, the Social Welfare Department's chief clinical psychologist, worked out new ways of incorporating elements of psychological assistance and counselling into our response to such events, drawing on what we had learnt from the aftermath of those disastrous fires.

We were now just a couple of months away from 1 July 1997 and the transfer of sovereignty to China. The time for any talking on substantive issues was long past and the focus was now on organising things, an activity that Hong Kong felt more at home with anyway.

As far as I could tell, the happiest people in Hong Kong were the Commissioner of Police and the Commander British Forces. They had cheerful personalities anyway and they were engrossed in the detail of what they had to do. The incoming head of the People's Liberation Army was apparently of a similarly practical turn of mind and the complex negotiations of what would be handed over and when were comparatively smooth. Events on the day itself and the period surrounding it required all sorts of considerations from the assembling of sufficient numbers of bagpipers to the exercise by which at midnight exactly on 30 June all uniformed officers of the Royal Hong Kong Police would swap their cap badges for their new Hong Kong Police insignia.

Stephen Lam, a mid-career administrative officer, who went on to become chief secretary in 2011, was put in charge of the running of the ceremonies. It was perhaps a lapse of judgment that a significant part of the event was scheduled to take place outdoors given that at the end of June in Hong Kong there was a high risk of heavy rain. There was also some criticism of the innovative police tactic of drowning out anti-Beijing protesters at midnight on 30 June by the playing of Beethoven's Fifth Symphony. Overall, though, the efficiency and sensitivity of the operation was judged to be up to the high standard set by Hong Kong's past.

One of the most taxing aspects of the planning was coping with what seemed like the world's entire press corps descending upon Hong Kong. I had always been, and indeed still am, something of a news junkie. On most days I read several newspapers either in the old-fashioned paper mode or online. Mouth slightly agape, I breathlessly follow the development of the latest news, the insights and the inside stories. This is despite the fact that what I witnessed at the time of the handover shook my faith in the omniscience of the international media and, indeed, in their ability to render a balanced or objective analysis of what was going on.

To be fair, the situation was doubtless worse than it might otherwise have been because so many reporters were being drafted in that any specialists in Hong Kong and Chinese affairs were seriously outnumbered. All the same, it did seem to me that the journalists were mainly deciding what to write on the basis of talking to each other rather than anybody else and their touchstone was the ease with which the material could be accessed and written up.

It seemed as if all had simultaneously decided that the aspects of current Hong Kong life in which their audiences would be most interested would be 'cage homes' and the 'King of Kowloon'.

The cage homes were a kind of private-sector housing occupied by some of Hong Kong's poorest, usually located in some of the older and more traditional areas. Essentially, these were tenements rather like hostels in that the tenants each had only a large sleeping space set in tiers like bunk beds. The 'cage' aspect came in because each bed would be surrounded by a lockable grille so that the residents had some secure place in which to keep their meagre possessions. Five years previously, Jacob Cheung had made an award-winning film called *Cageman* which while it clearly showed the poverty and deprivation also concocted a complex and touching story about a group of men living in one of these places.

The government was making some headway in getting the cage homes cleared and, in the way of business, I went to visit a building whose elderly residents were soon to move to public housing at the eastern end of Hong Kong Island, in Chai Wan. The affluent shoppers in Central and the workers in the financial district always rushing to get somewhere or other might have been shocked if they had realised how close they were to those cramped and squalid homes with no indoor lavatories. All the same, the move was a mixed blessing as far as these old people were concerned. They were mostly quite illiterate and navigated their neighbourhood by familiarity rather than reading and so the possibility of being marooned in a new place where they did not know where the buses were going was deeply worrying. 'They're so tired,' confided the social worker who was showing me around, 'and then all these foreigners turn up wanting to take their photographs and ask them questions.'

The 'King of Kowloon' was the other favourite quarry of the media looking for local colour. This gentleman was decidedly eccentric and in furtherance of his belief that he had some sort of claim to the whole territory of Kowloon engaged in an unremitting graffiti campaign. His outsize Chinese characters fiercely etched in black and crammed together on walls, pillars, water meters, essentially any surface he could find, had a power of their own and could legitimately be considered some kind of 'outsider art'. The King died in 2007 at the age of eighty-six but at the time of the handover he was very active, scrawling out his protests all day long and all over the place, and much appreciated by the photographers who needed something interesting to send back to their editors.

It is perhaps a sad commentary on what has happened subsequently in Hong Kong that in 2013 almost none of the King's works survive, while the number of those living in cage homes has actually grown although the term has now been extended so that it also covers the rundown flats sub-divided into very small living spaces whose occupants are often recent arrivals from the Mainland waiting to be allocated in the public housing which in recent years has not been built on the large scale of former years.

Another journalistic approach to the 'handover story' was to describe at length some of the 'colonial' aspects of Hong Kong and then to send a shiver down the spine of the reader by rhetorically posing the unlikelihood of such things surviving the 'communist takeover'. A popular subject for this approach was the question of street names. Hong Kong had a plethora of road names derived from major and minor British royalty, government officials and military officers. The writer could also throw in Rednaxela Terrace, assumed to have been intended to be Alexander Terrace but transposed by a signwriter who did not understand English and the Duke of Windsor Social Service Building, alleged to be the only place anywhere in the Commonwealth named in honour of the abdicated monarch.

Frankly, the alarmist tone of such articles was a bit unconvincing as far as I was concerned. Street names were not decided on a whim but were the work of a committee. I had never been to any of its meetings but I knew roughly who was on it. It somehow seemed unlikely that these stolid highways engineers and technicians were bent on an ideologically motivated name changing mission.

Government departments that had been the 'Royal' this or that dropped the adjective, as did the formerly Royal Hong Kong Jockey Club, but the Royal Hong Kong Yacht Club retained theirs and suffered no consequent disadvantage. A regal name which was, understandably, lost was that of the British Forces' headquarters, the Prince of Wales Building, taken over by the People's Liberation Army to be used for the same purpose. The old name remained visible for many months, however; we heard that the letters were proving exceptionally difficult to remove and even after that had been accomplished for a considerable period the words could be easily made out from the lighter coloured patches that had been left on the walls.

After the transfer of sovereignty there was, as far as I am aware, only one significant attempt at name changing and that related to Government House, the name used in Hong Kong as in all British colonies for the residence of the governor, the head of the administration and representative of the monarch. Mr CH Tung, first chief executive of the Special Administrative Region of Hong Kong in the People's Republic of China, declined to live there, preferring to stay in his flat in a modern and luxurious block in the Mid-Levels.

It was decided that Government House would be used as an official guest house and reception facility. A special working party was set up to decide on its new name. It took them an inordinately long time to reach a conclusion and there were leaks to the effect that some of its members were pressing for really racy new terminology like 'Monument to the expunging of the sins of the colonial era'. The final decision was something instantly forgettable, on the lines of 'Central Administration Hall', a simple rendering of its changed function. I had never become proficient in reading Chinese and so if I wanted to add to my vocabulary I had to ask someone and then try to remember what I was told. Consequently, one day, stuck in a taxi in a traffic jam on Upper Albert Road I said to the driver, 'What's the new name for that building please?'

'What do you mean?'

'The Gong Duk Foo,' I replied, using the Chinese name for Government House that we had always used in the past. 'I know that it's got a new name but I don't know how to say it in Cantonese.'

'New name, eh? Well, I don't know anything about that. We all just call it Gong Duk Foo,' he shrugged. And that was that.

As the moment of the transfer of sovereignty drew ever closer the media continued in their crusade to whip up international anxiety on our behalf. A television reporter stood in the stock exchange. 'This bell has just rung to signal the start of the last trading day on the Hong Kong Stock Exchange under British rule. Who knows if it will ever ring again?' Presumably, all the investors who had left their money there must have had a pretty good guess, not to mention Tony Neoh, my boss at the city district office,

Kowloon City in 1973, and in 1997 chairman of the Securities and Futures Commission.

The stock exchange would, it was true, be taking a fairly long break as indeed would many other workplaces. One of the details of the transition process was the need to bring the public holidays into line with the new order of things. The Queen's Birthday would no longer be celebrated, but China's National Day would, while the Christian and traditional Chinese festivals remained unchanged. By a rather inspired sleight of hand, the shuffling around of the holidays was being done in such a way that, in a one-off arrangement, there would be five successive days of public holidays. This was pleasing, even if the weather forecast was not encouraging.

On the morning of 30 June, our friend Shelley Lee, who had also become an administrative officer in 1972, held a grand and extended celebration of her birthday which happened to take place then. Her guest list included many old friends who had settled overseas but were returning for these historic few days. It was an informal brunch in the light-filled rooms of the Furama Hotel, just across the road from the Legislative Council, whose members regarded it as their canteen and in whose restaurants plots were hatched and agreements hammered out. It had a short lifetime though, as the property developers who altered the face of Hong Kong more or less at will decided that it would more profitably be replaced by an office block.

In the early evening, Michael and I set out for the first part of the official ceremonies to be held outside at Tamar, the large open area beside the Prince of Wales Building. Charles, Prince of Wales was there in person as the representative of his mother, Queen Elizabeth II, to preside over the proceedings. Chief among the other dignitaries were Tony Blair, the recently elected British Prime Minister and Chris Patten, the last governor of Hong Kong. This part of the programme was the 'Farewell' for Britain and Hong Kong and did not involve the Chinese Government.

All the guests as they arrived were given an umbrella. The government with its typical unsentimental, roguish practicality had persuaded a business corporation to sponsor them. These stylish green, gold and turquoise brollies had on one panel the English letters and Chinese characters for Hong Kong together with the figures 1997. On another panel was the sponsoring company's logo: a circle made up of the letters AIA and the words 'American International Assurance' with inside the circle an impressionistic sketch of a mountain range and the word 'EVERLASTING'. This was a puzzle. What was meant to last for ever: the mountains or the American International Assurance Company? One could make out a case for the impermanence of both and, indeed, less than fifteen years later the crisis of 2008 that gripped the banking and insurance sectors would shake to its foundations AIA's parent company back in the USA.

Putting these metaphysical musings on one side, we were glad that we had been provided with something so strongly made. It was absolutely essential as the rain was pouring down and, apart from a tiny number of the most exalted personages, we were all sitting on metal benches that had been temporarily erected with no shelter whatsoever. Despite the dreadful weather, the British military bands whose performance was a key feature of the show marched and played undaunted.

Rather to my surprise, I found myself gripped by emotions so strong that I was not sure whether it was rain or tears that I could feel on my face. The first was an unexpected rush of fear. I wanted these bands and these soldiers not to leave us on our own to face whatever threats there might be to our way of life. The second emotion was, I think, provoked by the stoicism of those marching bands. Normally, I barely gave the nationality of my birth a thought but I was suddenly struck by a consciousness of my British identity, by a certain pride in the crazy genius, the flair, the self-discipline and the self-belief that had led my forebears to plant their culture all over the world, including in this prosperous and paradoxical corner of China and by a wistfulness at its disappearance.

The rest of the night's programme would encompass the hand-over itself, to take place in the nearby Convention Centre. Michael could go on to this but I was excluded. My new lower-rank determined not only the quantity and quality of my office carpeting but also which bits of the transfer of sovereignty I could witness.

I had given careful thought to what I would wear that evening. My shoes were flat and my dress was black with a small white pattern but this was not a sign of mourning. Among the slightly more formal outfits that I possessed this one had the widest skirt and I had, correctly, estimated that transport after the end of the farewell ceremony would be difficult to get and it would be more realistic to expect to walk. I squelched back towards Central and up Wyndham Street where, 150 years earlier, William Pedder, harbourmaster and former first lieutenant of HMS *Nemesis*, had his base from which he could survey the expanse of the sea and the strange new territory that he and his comrades in the Royal Navy had won for Queen Victoria. I was making my way to the Fringe Arts Club where Benny Chia and Catherine Lau were holding a party.

The insurance company's umbrella was doing its best but the onslaught of rainwater was overwhelming. As I got close to the Fringe, I realised that my calculations about my clothing had not allowed for the possibility that the weather would be wet enough to render my dress dripping and clinging and partially transparent. Fortunately, however, a seriously bedraggled appearance is not too much of a hindrance when in the company of old friends.

All the things that I did not see with my own eyes were faithfully relayed by those armies of the press. There was the picture of the stage at the Convention Centre where, unposed, Anson Chan formed a natural focus, chief secretary both before and after the transfer of sovereignty and in her bright scarlet *cheongsam* standing out in the centre of the ranks of dark suits. There was the swearing in of the new government by President Jiang Zemin while knowledgeable commentators made pointed remarks about the way in which the Hong Kongers struggled with Putonghua, the language of Beijing. The Royal Yacht *Britannia*, on its last voyage before being decommissioned, set off in the early hours of 1 July with the Prince of Wales and Chris Patten and his family on board. They travelled in this grand manner as far as Manila and then disembarked and took an aeroplane back to London. Finally, as day was breaking, the photographers got their 'money shot' and filmed the Chinese army's trucks and soldiers as they came through the New

Territories and into Hong Kong. Since it was hardly light it looked impressively sinister but the fact of the matter was that the troops went into their barracks and have pretty much stayed there ever since, usually emerging only for well-choreographed open days, showing off their guns and their singing skills.

We were all rather glum in the days following the handover. The continuing and unceasing rain ruined our, once only ever in history, bloc of public holidays. The weather had been so bad that it would be quite a relief to go back and huddle in an air-conditioned office and watch the water drip down the outside of the windows.

I was one of the seven assistant directors of the Social Welfare Department. In a standard bureaucratic pattern, we occupied similar adjoining rooms on one side of a long passageway at either end of which sat the deputy directors and the director himself. By 9:00 a.m. on our first day back we were all behind our individual doors. At approximately 9:03 a.m. one door after another was opened and one head after another poked out. It was as if we were in a play and had been told what to do by the director. My next door neighbour broke the silence. 'We're all just the same. Nothing has changed.' He seemed to be right. We closed our doors, went back to our desks, re-opened our files and began to work on them in the way that we had always done.

CHAPTER TWELVE

Welfare and Work

THE MOST SIGNIFICANT SOCIAL SECURITY SCHEME that we administered was the CSSA, Comprehensive Social Security Assistance. It was aptly named because it really seemed able to cover every kind of needy person. Applicants would be placed in a category according to their case type: elderly, disabled, ill health, unemployed, single parent, low earnings and other. At the beginning, I sometimes used to wonder who could possibly be left to go into the 'other' category: in fact, this small number of cases seemed to be mainly made up of children who, for some reason, needed financial support but did not belong to a household of social security recipients, as well as cases that were temporarily stuck in some transition phase between one category or another.

One of the questions that was, understandably, most often asked by outsiders was: 'How much can people get under this scheme?' There was no simple answer as the amount payable depended on the circumstances of each case. Although we could say that the average monthly payment to a family of four would be just over HK$10,000. Needs would be assessed, taking into account whether any members of the household had, for example, disabilities or required help with school-related expenses. The application process could only begin if the applicant was below the asset limit, which meant that he or she did not possess any substantial savings, investments or valuables that could be easily liquidated. Once that hurdle had been crossed, the front-line staff in the Social Security field unit would look at the income side of the equation. Income would be deducted from the needs side, although if it came from employment some would be disregarded so that there would be an incentive to work, as well as some allowance for costs like transport and eating out incurred in undertaking employment. The sum that remained at the end of this calculation would be remitted each month into the bank account of a successful applicant. This somewhat simplified description does not go into the many details of administration, the lists of exceptions, discretionary powers and so on. It is perhaps not to be wondered at that we operated off a gigantic *Manual of Procedures* and that social workers would come and visit us begging for an explanation of the 'disregarded earnings' rule and other such mysteries of our craft.

There were firm beliefs within the department, and generally, about the make-up of our caseload. Despite the different categories, CSSA was thought of as, most importantly, a financial safety net for the elderly whose families did not, or could not, conform to Chinese tradition and support them and did not have sufficient savings of their own, pensions being rather rare. Even though the elderly made up by far the greatest proportion of CSSA recipients there were, we were aware, many who needed that level of assistance but refused to apply for it, being too proud or seeing being 'on the dole' as some kind of social stigma. They would try to survive on the Old Age Allowance, colloquially known as 'fruit money' which had originally been intended to provide a little pocket money and hence a measure of dignity and independence for old people living with their families and fully looked after by them.

Within the category of 'single parent' I enquired about the number of 'never married mothers' and the answer was that it was too small to be reliably measured, which would surely have been a shock to my counterparts in Western countries, accustomed to dealing with pregnant schoolgirls or those who had children by a succession of men and then turned to the state to provide. Our single parents were mainly older women who had been married but were now bringing up children on their own, following separation or divorce. We also encountered the phenomenon specific to Hong Kong of a high proportion of single fathers, generally as a result of a cross-border marriage in which the wife had not yet been allowed to emigrate from Mainland China to Hong Kong, although the children were already here. It was not uncommon for the Hong

Kong father to be considerably older than his wife and these men would often struggle with the discipline problems of trying to bring up children on their own.

When it came to the 'unemployed', I was firmly told that the reality of the composition of this category was that it was made up of drug addicts and other misfits. Other Chinese people, following long-established cultural norms, would always want to work and be self-reliant and, hence, would not apply for social security unless it was absolutely necessary, perhaps as a result of ill health. As in the old British system on which ours was modelled and which had long been superseded in the UK, our unemployed were simply required to register with the Labour Department once each month as seeking employment, but no effort was made to find out whether they were actually doing so. With the general feeling that, despite the healthy state of the government's finances, the public sector demonstrated insufficient compassion towards the vulnerable in our thrusting competitive society, and feeling confident that those who did not need social security would not apply for it, it was decided at the highest levels that there should be a significant real increase in all the social security rates. The decisions were made in 1995 and implemented in 1996.

In early 1997, I went off to New Zealand to an international conference where the main focus was on the increasingly widely discussed concepts of 'welfare to work', the basic intention being to induce the unemployed to search for work and leave the welfare caseload. I was to give a presentation myself on some of the more technical aspects of our system. Afterwards, a couple of the delegates from Australia and Canada came up to talk to me. 'We were really amused by that,' they said. 'We were both laughing like mad.' Perhaps years of dealing with social security led to an odd sense of humour, since I had not included any jokes at all, as far as I knew. 'It was that slide you put up, showing the unemployed caseload going up while the unemployment rate was stable or going down. We fell about at that one because several years back there was exactly the same situation in our countries and no one thought it was important or did anything about it and now we're having to introduce all sorts of programmes to combat welfare dependency and get long-term recipients off the caseload. Just thought we'd let you know what will be coming Hong Kong's way.' And still chuckling a bit, they strode off.

Back in Hong Kong, I shared with my trusted lieutenants, the veterans of the social security service, the insights I had gleaned from my new friends. 'It seems that we're showing the same sort of patterns as many other places and people are coming on to our unemployment caseload and staying there even though there are plenty of jobs available in the market that don't require very much in the way of skills and qualifications and where the pay and conditions are quite reasonable. That shouldn't be happening if it's correct that Chinese people always want to work and not be dependent on government handouts.' There was a bit of thought and a new hypothesis was advanced: 'Well, Chinese people are very smart so if you have a system that allows them to benefit, they will work out how to take advantage of it.'

Almost as soon as the transfer of sovereignty had taken place, a financial crisis, originating in the collapse of the Thai baht, had rolled through the region including Hong Kong. All the same, our fundamentals were so strong and our reserves so extensive that we did not see the same degree of misfortune as suffered by our Asian neighbours. We were still able to consider new policies carefully and plan thoroughly. I was able to spend three weeks with the Alberta provincial government in Canada looking at the way in which they tackled similar problems and, in the fine Hong Kong tradition of copying anything that looks useful, I brought home plenty of their forms and brochures to use as inspiration. We assembled our ideas into a document that we called 'Support for Self-reliance', put it out for public consultation and implemented it with effect from 1 June 1999.

We drew a broad distinction between the able-bodied and the vulnerable, leaving the latter untouched and, indeed, we had put up the rates for the elderly since a survey conducted for us by Hong Kong University had shown that they were short of money for socialising and for buying small gifts for friends and family. On the other hand, we cut back the grants available for the able-bodied, trying to restrict what we gave to the most basic requirements, although we were careful not to cut those for school-related expenses.

The part that was most complicated to implement was our more proactive approach to getting people back to work. Instead of 'signing on' once a month, the unemployed would have to undergo interviews every two weeks to discuss what they were actually doing to find work and to produce proof of job applications made. We were still in a period when new government initiatives would be matched by making some new staff available but, sadly, the trades unions representing our front-line staff refused to accept that this was a proper sort of thing to be engaged in and so they lost the chance of new posts and we had to make new hires on a contract basis.

The community work component was the trickiest of all. The concept was that once an unemployed person had been on CSSA for six months he or she would be required to do one day a week of community work. We knew that we could be open to accusations of exploitation and so we took it as a principle that we must not displace any paid employment and that the community work conditions would be reasonable with transport by coach to the workplace, breaks, drinking water provided and so on. We had set ourselves so many constraints that we realised that we were not actually going to have any community work to offer to anybody on our scheduled implementation date. What to do? We knew that the kind of work that we had in mind would be, say, tidying up in country parks and so we commissioned Friends of the Earth to make a demonstration video for us. They threw themselves into this and their short film exuded joyfulness and positivity. They made clear how enjoyable it was to be out in the fresh air while at the same time providing a valuable public service and helping in nature conservation.

On the day we launched our 'Support for Self-reliance Scheme' we waited anxiously in headquarters to hear from the thirty-three field units scattered throughout the territory as to how it was being received. I went down one floor to the section that had done the detailed planning and waited while phone calls were made to find out what was happening at the front line. Almost immediately, reports began coming in that applicants were just going away as soon as the new arrangements were explained to them. The community work video was apparently particularly effective. Our clientele were not of one mind with Friends of the Earth. On the contrary, they would watch with horror the cheerful scenes of litter picking, clearing of branches and simple repainting of planters and benches and scuttle off as quickly as possible, saying that in preference they would go and look for an ordinary job. We laughed so much that we slid down the walls.

When I was growing up my parents would never allow the *News of the World* Sunday paper into our house, considering the content shockingly improper. This ban naturally made the newspaper seem particularly alluring and I was drawn to the posters advertising it that were plastered around town. A black and white photograph showed a queue of rather serious looking people. 'All Human Life is There', the caption read. I doubt that was really true of the *News of the World*, which seemed mostly to be interested in the sexual activities of the famous and the almost famous. It seemed to me that a more plausible case could be made for all human life being found within the caseload of the Social Security Branch of the Hong Kong Social Welfare Department.

Our front-line staff were not academics and a few of them could be unsympathetic but many had a sensitive understanding of the recipients of social security that derived from a real familiarity rather than book learning. They would advance their theory that those on the unemployed caseload could be divided roughly into three. One third sincerely wanted to work and could get into the job market again quite quickly with a modicum of the right sort of help, one third were pretty dubious characters of one sort or another and had to be vigorously deterred from lingering on the caseload while one third were ill equipped to function in the mundane world and would probably have to stay with us for ever.

For those who fell into the third category, community work could be a surprisingly positive experience. Once we had the system well established, I went out to visit one of the country parks where real people were busy with the sort of chores that Friends of the Earth had depicted in their video. Among these was a lady who, unlike most Chinese women of middle age, did not dye her hair. Instead it was a wild grey pompadour like a flying saucer that had landed on her head while her choice of clothes was equally bizarre: layers of skirts and tops of clashing patterns and colours. The worker in charge told me that she lived in a probably illegal structure on a rooftop with her nine dogs and, previously, her only outings had been to the market to buy food. When she had first turned up for the work programme she had smelt bad too but some sort of long hidden coquettishness had made her start taking regular showers now that she was spending her day with a group largely comprised of men. I was in the lift going up to our Mong Kok field unit a couple of weeks later when she stepped in so I said hullo. 'Why,' she said in amazement, 'you recognise me!' I refrained from telling her that her appearance was so startling that it would be more or less impossible not to.

We saw more of this when we began working with an NGO partner, Crossroads. We had never wanted to link up with profit-making businesses as we did not want to be accused of providing them with cheap labour to be exploited, and the NGOs were not keen to become involved, fearing the kind of reprobates that we might send in their direction, but Crossroads was an exception. This was a fairly recently set up charity the aim of which was to collect unwanted goods from all over Hong Kong, repair and refurbish as necessary and then distribute to the needy locally and all over the world. When we first started working with them they were in the former British Military Hospital, no longer required as the British presence was scaled down in the run up to the transfer of sovereignty. They then moved to the former Kai Tak Airport site, and are now in the former Perowne Barracks, right next door to where we used to live in 'Dunrose'.

Malcolm and Sally Begbie who had founded Crossroads and the volunteers who had worked with them were so kind to us. What we had dreaded most happened and some clothing meant to be packed for dispatch was stolen by our workers but we weren't shown the door. There were false injury claims and a lady who tried to bring a court case on the grounds of the offence that she had felt at seeing a male volunteer who had removed his shirt to work in the heat. The Begbies put up with these nuisances with great patience and fortitude. By the time that they moved into the spacious premises in the old barracks Crossroads was well loved by our CSSA recipients and one of the most favoured community work assignments. We found ourselves having to say firmly that, however pleasant, a life on benefits spiced up with regular stints in the Crossroads kitchen was not an acceptable long-term option as far as we were concerned.

As time went by, we added new elements to our programme including commissioning NGOs to provide 'intensive employment assistance' through coaching, counselling and placement assistance. One of these was Jackie Pullinger's St Stephen's Society and Carrie Lam, then director of social welfare, wondered whether we could not find a method to get other NGOs to replicate St Stephen's good success rates. Other NGOs, I explained, were not likely to be willing to adopt Jackie's preferred strategies of living in total poverty together with the clients and relying entirely on prayer when in any tight spot. Sadly, too, St Stephen's connection with us was relatively short lived. When the programme's funding source switched from General Revenue to the Lotteries Fund Jackie and Margaret Kendall, who worked with her, came to see me and explained that it would be against their principles to accept money derived from gambling, even if indirectly.

We wanted to be sure that we weren't wasting money ourselves. There would be no point in carrying out a project that sounded impressive but did not in fact yield useful results. The department had a great team of statisticians and they were able to make the calculations for us. We found we were 'making a profit' in that the reductions in the social security bill that we were achieving were greater than the amount it cost to run the scheme. In fact, for the first eighteen months that we ran it there were substantial drops in the total caseload numbers. This trend did not continue as economic conditions worsened and the caseload began creeping up again. Also, our unemployed were often just migrating to the 'low earnings' category so they were at work but still needing a top up every month in order to cover their basic bills. Others would cycle back onto our caseload after a while. The truth was that these were mainly middle-aged men with low skill and educational levels and they were not so competitive in the Hong Kong economy which had become more or less entirely service oriented from the 1990s onwards. It would have been nice to have had the resources to try some other approaches such as longer and more individualised training even if it were to mean that we might have seen immediate cost effectiveness reduced.

Not all our stories were happy ones. A long-time recipient of CSSA gained confidence through the Community Work Programme to the extent that we took him on as one of our supervisors. His wife told us later that he had been completely transformed in personality and self-esteem at this change in his fortunes. However, in the course of his duties he suffered an attack from one of the group that he was supervising who, irritated over some trivial event, hit the supervisor over the head with a spade when his back was turned. He recovered from his injuries but not sufficiently to be fit to resume work.

Violence was a constant risk. Most of those who came into our offices were decent and reasonable and since the majority were elderly the biggest challenge was sometimes one of mutual misunderstanding, especially given the essentially bureaucratic nature of our operation. I was in our Sai Kung office one day when a staff member was trying to explain to an elderly gentleman and his wife that while he was entitled to a special grant to cover the cost of his false teeth it was necessary to go to the right sort of dental clinic in Hong Kong and show up with the receipt in proper order and that we had no way to process a bit of paper from some random dentist in Guangdong Province. To make things worse, the enquiring couple had rural accents so thick that their Cantonese was barely comprehensible. Our staff were sometimes criticised, sometimes quite rightly, as being brusque, hurried and uncaring but at moments like these I could understand their side of the story too.

The CSSA caseload would normally be running at more than 200,000 and inevitably among such a large number there were some with psychological problems and others lacking in ability or inclination to keep their emotions in check. There could be trouble in any of our field units or in the ancillary units like those of the Traffic Accident Victims Assistance Scheme but we generally reckoned that there was most pressure in the offices in the New Territories, particularly those in the northwest. These were areas with big concentrations of public housing estates but few nearby employment opportunities and high transport costs for those who wanted to travel into places with more opportunities. Meanwhile social welfare facilities and NGO activities tended to be clustered in the traditional locations of Hong Kong Island and central Kowloon where needs were comparatively less. This was particularly true of Tin Shui Wai, a new town developed in Yuen Long district but quite remote from the market town of Yuen Long itself. Our office there was normally a trouble hotspot and was the location of a particularly horrific incident.

A married couple were sitting on the other side of the counter from our staff member completing application procedures when entirely without warning the man removed a big melon knife from the bag he was holding and attacked his wife fiercely. She slid forward across the counter bleeding from her wounds and her life was probably saved by the very young contract worker who came forward with blankets from the office stock kept for distribution in cold weather and wrapped her tightly. Meanwhile her husband raced out of the office and to the top of an adjoining tower block where almost before it was realised what was happening he had thrown himself off. I travelled out to the office later on and from the hero of the hour received the standard Hong Kong response: 'It was just my duty.' Not long after, we felt compelled to redesign our offices so as to put a thick glass barrier between staff and customers and so the timing of that tragic event had, in a sense, been quite fortuitous; a short time later and the injured woman might not have been so lucky.

As part of a generally more rigorous attitude we took a fresh look at the detection of social security fraud. This had always been a crime of course but the department had become rather reluctant to take cases to court; there had been an occasion when our performance had been criticised by the magistrate and that had proved a big deterrent. However, we now instigated discussions with the Prosecutions Section of the Department of Justice and agreed guidelines as to which cases should go forward. We set up a fraud investigation team, a data matching team and a committee to meet each month to look at potential cases.

Because of the ID card system we were not vulnerable to the large scale frauds that could affect systems like the UK's; in Hong Kong it was not possible to claim under multiple identities. The frauds that we came across were mainly claimants with jobs that they hadn't told us about or rent receipts that had been forged to claim bigger sums. Sometimes people concealed assets that they held and although we could do things like cross checking with the civil service pension records it was quite hard to track down such cases unless we were tipped off.

I received a letter from a solicitor settling an estate of some HK$186 million blandly advising that there might be a sum owing to the Social Welfare Department as the deceased had been claiming CSSA all along. I got out the file, concerned that we had made some error that had allowed such a miscarriage. No, it had all been properly handled by one of our most reliable officers who had followed all the procedures and paid a home visit before approving the application. This multi-millionaire had chosen to live in a tiny lodging in a run-down tenement and to manifest poverty in every possible way. Still, the lawyer was very helpful and we got all our money back.

The fraud cases often concealed the saddest stories and it was good that we had discretion as to whether they would end up in court or not. There was a woman who had an undeclared job as a waitress because her husband was a gambling addict who spent all the social security money and she had to find some way to feed their children. The man was also a wife beater, so in this case the social workers did not expend any effort to keep the family together but advised her to get a divorce straight away. There was another woman who was determinedly accumulating savings beyond the amounts allowed for in our rule book because she hoped that one day a 'cure' would be found for her mentally handicapped daughter and she wanted to be able to pay for it when the day came. Even when the situation was not so extreme the family often seemed to be struggling. The father might be a crook and the mother feckless but there were often hapless children dragged along in the wake and, more often than not, an embattled grandmother trying to hold things together.

About some of the frauds, there was less ambivalence and there could be some satisfaction in passing these on for action. There was the security guard spotted in his uniform on an MTR train by the staff member who processed his regular claim that he had no employment at all. There was the couple saved from the dreadful tsunami in Thailand who then milked the situation by giving endless interviews stressing their devotion to each other until the lady was recognised back in Hong Kong as someone who had been claiming for years citing separation from this very man.

Then there was the case that didn't fit any of those categories. It was blandly put before our committee as 'undeclared earnings' but the earnings came from prostitution so it didn't seem that that it could be right to treat it just as if the money came from waitressing or something. From the case file it also seemed that the welfare of a child was involved. An investigation was carried out and the results reported back. Since the lady concerned was operating on her own no crime was being committed. It was true that previously the little boy had been making his own supper but her mother had now arrived from the Mainland to look after him so that was no longer a problem. The putative fraudster was herself of Mainland origin; her one ambition was to send her son to an overseas university and the profession she was following was the only way she could think of to achieve this. Now she understood the rules about applying for social security she would pay back the money she had already obtained, withdraw from the scheme and never trouble us again. So she did and so it seemed that we had no reason to trouble her either.

We did our best with the policies we drew up but not everyone liked them, and pressure groups would regularly organise large-scale demonstrations in the lobby of the building in Wan Chai in which we rented office space. Sometimes, too, what had been billed as an exchange of views in our conference room degenerated into something more menacing so that we would wonder whether we were going to be able to leave at all. The local police were really helpful, however, and would turn up whenever we asked and would come prepared with useful strategies for defusing the situation.

The demonstrations could be quite imaginative and we would be presented with, say, rice cookers drilled with holes to symbolise the inadequacy of what we were handing out. Some of the protestors we would see over and over again, especially from the groups representing the elderly and if we happened to bump into each other 'off duty' we would greet each other like old friends. We and the press would be presented with details of terrible hardship cases but more often than not when we investigated we would find a more complex story often including some really irrational behaviour by vulnerable people who were taking what seemed to them the best and indeed, only possible, course of action but actually only added to their troubles. These were frequently women obsessively devoted to their children but burdening them with their own troubles and depriving them of a childhood.

Usually, the attacks would be quite general and against the government or the department in general but it happened one Sunday that I was on Battery Path which leads up to the Government Secretariat and discovered a small group of women were engrossed in the traditional form of objection, using their shoes to whack a piece of heavy paper laid out on the path. I crept up behind them and looked over their shoulders. Heavens, they were hitting a portrait of me, presumably in complaint about the rather controversial scheme we had recently introduced to impose work search requirements on single parents on social security. It was in fact a very flattering head and shoulders on quite a large scale with profuse deployment of orange crayon for my hair. Should I interrupt them and ask if I might have the picture? That seemed though not to be taking their intentions very seriously and might lead to a difficult conversation and so I took the easy way out and slipped away unnoticed.

We also had individuals with grievances turning up. There was always one social worker on a rota to see these complainants and try to soothe them. It was not a popular posting since these aggrieved parties could be hard to convince. We had one success with a man who came up over and over again with a complex query about a rent deposit which, he claimed, should have been refunded to him many years before. A member of the social security staff, who was not a professional social worker but had a high degree of empathy managed to discover that the real problem was the ghost that haunted his home telephone which then led to being able to get his schizophrenia treated.

The possibility of suicide was a worry. During my early days in the department I became aware of a linguistic subtlety which was new to me. Some of the staff rather casually reported that an old lady had committed suicide because she was dissatisfied with the level of payments she was getting from us. 'Now she says she'll ask a Legislative Councillor for help,' was the mystifying remark. I could not make any sense of this until it was explained to me that the Cantonese term for 'committed suicide' actually meant 'attempted suicide' and it needed one more character added to the end in order to mean 'successfully committed suicide'. This lady had only inflicted some rather superficial damage on her wrists with a not very sharp knife.

I was going home one evening after working late when I noticed a giant mattress being inflated in the side road that ran up beside our office. 'That can't be anything to do with me,' I thought but I had forgotten about the office of the Traffic Accident Victims Assistance Scheme, which was a small part of the social security empire. Someone had got up on the roof, discontented that his claim for a further payment under the scheme had been turned down. He was a Mainlander and the compensation he had received had been a life-transforming sum, but he needed more despite the fact that the Hong Kong doctors said that he was fully recovered from his injuries. The potential crisis was quickly ended when one of the police team up on the roof with him offered him a bottle of water and the others used the distraction to grab him.

There was another unsuccessful suicide attempt at our Social Security Appeal Board. On that occasion I got the news first of all that someone had set fire to himself and yet he seemed to have only minor burns on his legs. The unfortunate gentleman had retired with a moderate lump sum of provident fund contributions but had fallen victim to pathological gambling and lost the lot in short order. He decided to end it all and jumped into the harbour where, amazingly enough, he simply floated around for a couple of hours until picked up by a police boat and taken to hospital. While he was there, the social workers arranged for him to be signed up for social security but sadly some inefficiency or glitch in the system had led to delays in the payment coming through. He despaired again but decided he would die in a grand gesture and so settled down outside the Appeal Board with a protest banner and his lighter. What he didn't realise though, was that he had chosen a spot immediately below the sprinkler system which was activated as soon as the smoke from his burning trousers began to drift upwards.

This mighty public service required a mighty engine to keep it going. Just before I arrived in the department an Information Systems Strategy Study had been finished and one of its major recommendations was the complete computerisation of the social security service. Libby Wong, the secretary for health and welfare at the time, had also stipulated that we needed some sort of machine where you could press a few buttons and answers to any question one wanted to ask would instantly be spewed out.

I had limited enthusiasm for computers. About fifteen years earlier I had had a brief stint working for the science adviser, who had been brought in from outside to do what the title of his post suggests. The science adviser had been keen to get a computer but I did not do much to advance this ambition. Office computers were not standard equipment in the early 1980s and, anyway, the science adviser's database could all be fitted into one small filing cabinet drawer so it seemed like an unnecessary extravagance. Not long afterwards, the government, rightly or wrongly, decided that it could manage without advice on science or at least without a science adviser. My thinking had not advanced very much over the intervening period and, despite knowing almost nothing about the subject, I felt that Libby's vision of the machine that could make answers available was not realistic.

My attitude was changed substantially by a couple of things. The first of these was a visit to our Aberdeen field unit, which was not un-typical of many others. Aberdeen was one of those areas on Hong Kong Island that was, comparatively, de-populating. It had been the centre of the fishing industry, a thriving area, even though one in which there was a great deal of poverty. The economic focus had shifted towards the Central Business District with its teeming hordes of bankers dressed, male and female alike in black and grey while demographic analysis now saw the New Territories and, in particular, its western side as the new growth area for population. At that time, the Aberdeen office was housed in a shabby old rental building. Water dripped through a leak in the ceiling and, even though there was a semi-computerised payment system, staff were essentially carving out the paperwork for the largely elderly clientele with government-issue black ballpoint pens. I realise that Bob Cratchit did not use a Biro but the atmosphere was broadly Dickensian. If there was any possible alternative to this, it seemed worth pursuing. The second mind-changing experience came when we asked for expressions of interest in supplying our new system and the presentation by IBM showed columns of data somer-saulting over each other and rearranging themselves, probably exactly as Libby had imagined.

The project to install our Computerised Social Security System proved very enjoyable. The team of people that we had committed to it in the Social Security Branch were essentially civil servants who knew all about the social security system and had also developed an interest in information technology. Wu Shu Wing, the team leader, was close to retirement and no one involved was going to profit enormously in terms of career advancement. They worked long hours and wrestled with challenging implementation problems simply because they wanted to do a good job and not let down their colleagues who would rely on the outcome. I have no problem either with giving a pat on the back to IBM, our chosen contractor. They were very receptive to all our requests and suggestions, which made a big difference to the smooth progress of the project. Right at the beginning, we told them that their team looked too foreign and we feared there might be cultural and language difficulties ahead. They were sensible enough to recruit Judy Wong, recently retired from the Immigration Department. She had the same sort of experience as our staff: a non-specialist who had learnt a lot about information technology through working on departmental projects. She was good at explaining IBM and the government to each other.

Our system went live in October 2000, on budget, on schedule and doing what it was supposed to do, which was to allow all calculations of social security payments to be carried out automatically rather than by people with pens. For this to happen, we had to feed into the machine all the salient parts of our *Manual of Procedures,* which could now also be read online, if anyone cared to do that as well as all the data related to the hundreds of thousands of recipients of assistance under our different schemes. Almost as soon as it went into operation, the grumbles began that the new system needed to be even bigger and faster, but it was, all the same, acknowledged as a great improvement and, indeed, indispensable if we were to go on coping with what we were called upon to do every day.

Many of our field units were not big enough to accommodate the new system and so we had to find new premises for them. Even those that did not have to move all had to be extensively refurbished. Into our progress meetings we brought the Architectural Services Department which would design the new offices and the Government Property Agency which would find locations for them, which had to be conveniently located for the customers in the area that they served.

The final contribution I could make was to ensure that the team had enough time for the 'user acceptance testing' that ensured that the system would actually work reliably after it went live. From reading about other projects, I knew that very often there would be pressure to get the system running, to skimp on the testing and hope for the best with consequences that could be disastrous on opening day. Although we had a contingency plan if there was failure when we went live, obviously it would be much better if everything worked well straight away. There had been a breakdown years before when the existing system was introduced and for a few days more or less everyone in the department had been mobilised to make cash payments. Now with a total caseload of about 800,000 households receiving benefits under our major schemes such a stratagem would not be feasible. We had to build into our planning time for sufficient testing and stand firm against any suggestions that we should move faster than we were comfortable with.

We did this and towards the end the experts were really busy. I went down to see how they were getting on. They were all tapping away at their keyboards, incomprehensibly as far as I was concerned. 'How are things going?' I asked.

'Oh great. As at present, we only have . . .' consulting a list, 'two thousand and four outstanding errors to be corrected.'

'Gosh, that seems rather a lot.'

'Oh no,' airily. 'Many of them are quite minor.'

Anyway, whatever it was that had to be done was done and our new system operated smoothly from the very first day. One would think that that would not be much of an achievement since it basically involves drawing up a plan and then carrying out the plan but it seems that in the majority of cases of big government computer projects anywhere in the world something goes rather seriously wrong at the beginning.

A fundamental part of the development of the Computerised Social Security System had been a self-contained contract for staff training that proceeded in parallel to the system development. Initially, we had to be quite bossy and insist that staff come in and learn how it was going to be operated but as they realised that there was no escape and the new system really was going to be there they concentrated hard on mastering it, whatever their original doubts about whether they were too old, did not have the right sort of aptitude and so on. The process was a two-way street as IBM scattered models of the new desktop throughout our network of offices, got our staff to try them out, listened to their views on what was good and what wasn't and made adjustments accordingly.

We tried to expand the training of social security staff in other ways. They called themselves the 'little brothers' because, with their comparatively lower educational qualifications, they could easily feel themselves to be a tad inferior to the professional social workers.

In conjunction with Hong Kong University's extra-mural department we linked up with Middlesex University in the UK to offer their degree courses to our staff. The approach was rather novel because it involved a coursework project related to the student's job. This meant that they could find an outlet to shape and express their feelings about the stress they suffered at work or could use their interviewing skills to explore in depth some of the concerns and motivations of social security recipients. Since this was at undergraduate degree level their findings had to be analysed by reference to scholarly literature. This was challenging for those whose academic study had previously ended at the level of School Certificate, especially considering that studying had to be fitted into limited spare time.

It would be wrong to imply that the front-line staff were all happy and contented. We heard often that they felt pressured by the heavy workload and they wanted us to recruit more staff. We in turn were limited by the resource allocation that we could obtain from the centre. Since about 1999 there had been a cool climate regarding such requests. It was understandable because the external financial circumstances had changed for the worse. I did feel, however, that this attitude was taken to excess and the efforts to make us 'do more with less' ended up in damaging morale. We did not realise it as 2002 ended, but all of us and all our staff would shortly be tested in a way that we could not have expected.

CHAPTER THIRTEEN

The End of Days

T HE YEAR 2003 WAS TO BE REMEMBERED as one in which disease turned normal life completely upside down. This was Severe Acute Respiratory Syndrome, known by its acronym, SARS. We had little warning of what was to come and we did not recognise the warnings for what they were.

Around the beginning of the year stories were circulating of some strange illness affecting residents of Guangdong. Across the border from Hong Kong vinegar was apparently running short since for some reason it was believed to be a remedy. Mainland authorities were not good at disseminating information but Hong Kong was quite skilled at piecing together snippets and estimating whether there was some real cause for concern. We were told that this was atypical pneumonia and that it was quite usual for there to be some cases every year. We had confidence in the ability of our medical services, yet the informal Hong Kong radar was registering some signs of disquiet, given the persistent suspicion that Beijing was prone to covering up any news that might not be to its credit.

Our daughter was studying Chinese at Oxford University. Her year group was about to leave for Beijing for four months of language study at Peking University. I e-mailed her tutor telling what I knew with the sub-text that it might be worth reconsidering the planned trip. Apparently, however, the British Foreign Office had been consulted and had advised that there was no cause for concern and so the students set off as planned.

From 10 March onwards, events in Hong Kong snowballed with a frightening rapidity. In the Prince of Wales Hospital, the major hospital for the New Territories and the teaching hospital for the

Chinese University, medical personnel were suddenly falling ill in great numbers with a pneumonic illness. Later, when the history of the pattern of cases in Vietnam, China and Hong Kong was drawn up, the 'index case', the guest in the Metropole Hotel in Kowloon who had been unwittingly responsible for infecting hundreds was found, the virus that caused the disease was identified and a link made with the too close contact between humans and animals in Guangdong markets, with civet cats being the likely culprits. At that time, though, we seemed just to be witnessing a mystifying progression of events that had moved quickly from an unknown illness affecting an unknown number of patients in the Mainland and possibly Vietnam, to a plague that was decimating our doctors and nurses. It was terrible to think that they were seemingly being put at risk by their vocation to care for others.

The government was now mobilising all its resources to deal with the situation. It is very common that some disproportionate attention can be paid to a minor aspect of a crisis. In Hong Kong, there was some resistance to the proposed name of SARS because it was felt to suggest 'special administrative region', which was what Hong Kong had been since the transfer of sovereignty. For a short time we were bombarded with e-mails reminding us of the preferred term 'atypical pneumonia' until defeat was accepted and SARS was what it was called, in Hong Kong and everywhere else. In parallel, though, a great deal of more focused action was being taken.

Within the Social Welfare Department responsibility for our response to SARS was initially given to Ophelia Chan, the assistant director whose normal duties included supervision of the medical social work service, presumably because of the way in which the illness seemed to be one which principally affected staff working in hospitals. Although Ophelia remained our coordinator, more and more of us were drawn in as it swiftly became clear that the illness was a community-wide one, and, it seemed, any Hong Kong resident was potentially at risk of this serious disease which was fatal in about seventeen per cent of cases.

A structure of new internal government committees was quickly set up to deal with all the different aspects of the problem. Because the Social Security Branch handled disaster relief I was asked to join

Ophelia to represent the Social Welfare Department on the working level inter-departmental coordinating committee. We met at 8 a.m. every day in Murray Building, across the road from the Government Secretariat. We sat around a big table in a large conference room and there were many of us, representing many different parts of the public service. A dense city state like Hong Kong had some advantages in executing a strategy that required such a variety of expertise in that reporting lines were straightforward and many in the group had worked with others there on other projects. To an outsider, some of those included might have seemed surprising choices yet all had a role. The lawyers would often be working flat out drafting necessary legal orders, the Housing Department had to find accommodation for possible quarantine camps as well as for hospital doctors who did not want to go home and risk infecting their families while the Food and Environmental Hygiene Department had to consider the provision of adequate facilities to dispose of clinical waste and, later on, sewage systems in evacuation camps.

The mood around the table was deeply sombre. We had seen disasters and crises before but in those, however desperate, it was much more feasible to work out a plan of action. This time we were confronted by a disease that was new not just to us but to the entire world. This time there was no contingency plan, textbook or manual of procedures to take off the shelf to consult. We did not know what caused SARS, how it spread or how it was to be treated. Hence, we could not feel energised, primed and ready to go but, on the other hand, running away was not on anyone's agenda. We believed that we would stay at our posts until the end, whatever that end might be, and we knew that we could rely on each other. Our cohesiveness was a comfort but it could not dispel the thoughts about the seriousness of what we faced.

By now, the entire community was galvanised. All educational institutions had been closed down so as to reduce the possibility of infection. Hong Kong was soaking up the world's supply of medical masks and it was considered a social faux pas not to wear one in public while anyone with a cough of any sort was regarded with deep suspicion. Economic activity was slowing down sharply as

Hong Kong became a sort of international pariah, shunned by all travellers. I was in touch with our daughter in Beijing. The Hong Kong Government Office there was helpful but there was a general dearth of information and plenty of rumours circulating about SARS cases in Beijing's university district.

There was no set seating arrangement for our morning meetings but, as is usually the way of such things, once we'd picked out where to sit on the first occasion, we would always return to the same seat. I was between Steve Chandler from the police and Dr Cindy Lai from the Department of Health. I had never seen anyone under as much work pressure as Cindy was during SARS. I once shared a car with her going out to Tin Shui Wai and during the whole of that long drive she was bombarded by phone calls which were making requests or asking questions and none of the questions were straightforward, each one a judgment in a field where nobody had answers that she could refer to. She seemed to me like a piece of tissue paper that was being pulled and stretched but she never broke.

The hypothesis had been that SARS was spread only by close contact, but around the end of March doubt began to be cast on this because of a clustering of cases in Amoy Gardens, a private residential estate in Kowloon. This raised the spectre of an uncontrolled wave of infection rolling through the territory. As we were waiting for the morning meeting to begin I turned to Cindy and gave her my own difficult question: 'What will we do if SARS turns out to be airborne, Cindy?'

'We don't know,' she whispered. 'We don't know what we'd do.'

We were all at the working level and saw almost nothing of the ministers, who under the new system of government introduced in 2002 headed the policy bureaux, nor of the chief executive, but the effects of their debates and decisions percolated down to us for action. Throughout SARS I never saw any evidence of anything being done from anything but honourable motives. It simply was sometimes very difficult to decide on the best course of action. This was true of the question of quarantine, which was increasingly being suggested as the best way of limiting the risk of infection. Medical professionals like Dr SH Lee, the former director of medical and health services, recalled the cholera camps that the government had set up during a devastating outbreak in 1961. There was much hesitation, however, about putting this into practice, mainly because of the concern that fear of being quarantined would deter the sick from coming forward for diagnosis and treatment so that in the end things would have been made worse.

Finally, the decision was taken that the residents of the most badly affected block in Amoy Gardens would be evacuated to camps which were normally recreational facilities for youth groups and so on. This responded to the possibility that there was something within the buildings that was causing the outbreak there. The accommodation and facilities that would be provided for the evacuees were in basic but adequate buildings, set in spacious grounds which would ensure isolation. Panic was now gripping Hong Kong. I did not mention to anyone at the private members' club where I went to eat lunch that I was planning to go to Amoy Gardens because I knew that if I did so I might be politely asked to stay away for a while.

My social security section was involved because part of our remit was to provide food and other necessities for those in emergency situations. I went back to Social Welfare Department headquarters to talk to Ng Yiu-hing, who was in charge of this section. Yiu-hing had started his working life as a prisons officer and generally preferred being out and about to being deskbound with files and his present position was a good fit for him. I hoped that we would find a driver willing to take us. Up to that point, Mr Au and I had had a rather mutually unhappy relationship. I would always hang on in the office doing 'one last thing' which forced him to drive faster than he wanted to while I was frustrated because unlike some of the other drivers he didn't seem to know any sneaky shortcuts to make up for my tardiness. He turned up trumps that day, though. He was waiting for us in the office car park calmly ready to set off. I thought I should be fair to him. 'Do you know where we're going, Mr Au? Is it all right with you?' He pulled his face mask down below his chin, contrary to all the advice on how you were meant to wear these, turned round to look at us in the back seat and grinned as broadly as a Jack o'lantern. 'Yes, I know. It's Amoy Gardens. No problem.'

In fact, we went first to one of our field units. I made a little impromptu speech to the staff about testing times for public servants but no one seemed very impressed or, indeed, very ready to spring into action. I had a quiet chat with Ng Yiu-hing about the best way to manage our part in the evacuation exercise. We decided to draw up a list of likely volunteers in order to get it started and to demonstrate to those who were reluctant that what they were being asked to do was not so impossible after all. Yiu-hing began making phone calls and we were soon ready to go.

Amoy Gardens was a private residential estate, home to the middle-class types who were the backbone of the new Hong Kong. They worked hard to buy their flats, to make homes of them, to bring up their families and to enjoy the things and the activities that their modest, carefully husbanded wealth could buy. Now they were being marshalled into coaches to be taken off for what would, at best, be a period of discomfort, anxiety and uncertainty. Meanwhile staff from the Agriculture and Fisheries Department carried away cages containing immaculately groomed pet dogs to be cared for in anticipation of being reunited with their owners but also as a precaution in case they might have some clue to offer about this mysterious outbreak of the disease.

The same sort of pooling of Hong Kong's scientific resources and urgent dedication that had identified the virus had, about a fortnight after the evacuation, come up with the explanation that a design flaw of Amoy Gardens had allowed infection from the excretions of one very sick SARS patient who had stayed there to be transmitted into the bathrooms of other flats. Sarah Liao, the environment minister, had gone back to her roots as an environmental engineer, donned a protective suit and joined the investigation. Across the entire public sector, there was a level of cooperation and mobilisation which I had never seen before.

A comprehensive quarantine system was devised and put into place. While SARS patients were nursed in isolation wards their family members or other close contacts were required to remain within their homes with supplies being brought to them by Social

Welfare Department staff, with daily health checks from visiting nurses while the police ensured that they were abiding by the quarantine rules. These duties were carried out, day after day, by junior staff who had no reason not to believe that by doing so they were putting their own lives at risk. There was activity going on of which the public were unaware. There were, for example, children both of whose parents had SARS and who had no family able to look after them. The government stock of accommodation was scoured and suitable places found where they were cared for by shifts of staff from our department. Those who had responsibility for homes for the elderly were on high alert because the SARS mortality rate was particularly high among the elderly, as high as for Ebola Fever, some said, and the symptoms were masked in the early stages. The great fear was an outbreak rolling through one of the residential care facilities. Fortunately, this did not take place, perhaps at least partly thanks to the draconian cleaning régimes that were imposed.

The ventilation system at the Queen Elizabeth Hospital needed modification to cope with the new demands; no contractor was willing to do the work and so staff of the Electrical and Mechanical Services Department took it on themselves and, indeed, one of the workers did contract SARS. Our police representatives at our daily 8 a.m. meetings came from the Police Public Relations Bureau but one day they brought along colleagues from their Information Technology Section who 'thought they might be able to help'. They held up a diagram that they had put together of patient locations in Amoy Gardens and explained how they believed that it might be possible to adapt a programme that they had for tracing criminal suspects to trace the contacts of SARS patients. Their confidence was justified and it became an invaluable corollary of the quarantine strategy.

As we worked, we were always conscious of those who were in the greatest danger, the hospital staff and the desperate battle that was going on in the isolation wards. Dr Fung Hong, the chief executive of the Prince of Wales Hospital, and Dr William Ho, chief executive of the entire Hospital Authority, were old friends whom we knew from policy discussions and seminars but now both were SARS patients themselves.

The first couple of days of April 2003 were perhaps the worst of all. On April Fool's Day a teenager doubtless bored at home after an enforced absence from school created a fake website mimicking that of the *Ming Pao* newspaper and planted a false story that Hong Kong had been declared a quarantine port, which would affect our ability to import goods, including basic foodstuffs. The rumour burnt through the community. During SARS the government had been making use of the relatively new communications mode of text messages and with the help of the telecommunications companies they now sent out messages to mobile phone subscribers informing them that this was a hoax.

On the evening of 1 April, Leslie Cheung jumped to his death from the Mandarin Hotel in Central. The shy young man whom I had met briefly some twenty years before as the brother of my colleague Ophelia Cheung had become an international star, notably in the award-winning film *Farewell My Concubine,* while his singing and his spectacular stage shows were deeply enmeshed in the popular culture of Hong Kong. Sadly, Leslie had been suffering from clinical depression for several years but the timing of his suicide at the height of the anxiety about SARS added an extra sharpness to the mourning of the millions of fans who had idolised him.

It was a shell-shocked group that met for the regular morning meeting in Murray Building on 2 April but we tried to address the agenda in as businesslike a manner as possible. A question came up about the administration of the evacuation camps and the morale of those who had been rehoused there. 'Let's send a doctor to do some extra visits,' came the suggestion. 'We don't have any more doctors to send anywhere,' said Cindy Lai in a small, tired voice. 'And,' Steve Chandler added grimly, 'if we have many more days like yesterday we won't have any police to send anywhere either. We had officers out all over the territory stopping fights in supermarkets between customers who were trying to grab what was left off the shelves because they believed this silly quarantine port story. And meanwhile our hostage negotiating team was trying to coax out a man with SARS symptoms who had barricaded himself in his flat because he didn't want to be admitted to hospital.'

In parallel with all this, Hong Kong was suffering from the world's fear of having anything to do with it. On 2 April the World Health Organisation issued a notice advising travellers to avoid Hong Kong and Guangdong. Our economy was reeling. Michael had been in Switzerland when the epidemic began and flew back on Cathay Pacific, our flag carrier, on a jumbo jet that was almost entirely empty. Our social security staff were not only playing a full part in carrying out the quarantine arrangements for SARS contacts but were also trying to keep up with their normal work, with increases that were running at an unprecedented rate. The numbers claiming Comprehensive Social Security Assistance because of unemployment were climbing by ten per cent per month. An early morning visitor to any field unit, even those that we normally considered relatively low pressure, would be greeted by the sight of a long queue of new applicants filling up the normal waiting area and spilling out into the corridors and lobbies, even in some cases outside the building.

Relative to its population, Hong Kong had more SARS cases than anywhere else in the world but it was not the only place that was affected: there were significant numbers of cases in Mainland China, Vietnam, Singapore, Taiwan and Canada. Our daughter, Caroline, and her fellow students from Oxford University were still in Beijing. I was telephoning her as often as I could and passing on any information that I had since they were hearing nothing reliable locally. After just a few weeks their situation seemed untenable especially since the British Embassy could not give a firm under-taking that they would be able to be evacuated if necessary. The group took a collective decision to leave and after a brief stop in Hong Kong Caroline was back in the UK. The compass needle had swung completely from the atmosphere in which they had blithely set out and on their return they were asked to stay in and away from their colleges and the university facilities. This made no particular sense as none of them had any SARS symptoms nor had been in contact with any known SARS patient and as well the logic of this quasi quarantine seemed to be that they could move around the city as much as they liked, presumably despite the danger of infecting customers in the supermarkets they would visit, their flatmates and so on. Fortunately, the decision was soon reversed and their life resumed even to the point where the following year they were able to come back to Beijing and enjoy the course that they had missed out on.

Back in Hong Kong, we had reached the lowest point, although we did not immediately understand that that was the case. The strategy of isolating patients and quarantining contacts was as effective as we could have hoped for. SARS, as it turned out, was not as infectious as it might have been. It was at its most dangerous at times when the symptoms were most obvious and at their worst which was why medical personnel were so vulnerable and Amoy Gardens remained a special situation, with such a concentration of cases not replicated elsewhere. We began to see a decline in the number of new cases.

The last new case was reported on 2 June and on 23 June Hong Kong was removed from the World Health Organisation's list of SARS-infected areas on the grounds that there had now been an interval equal to twice the incubation period for the disease. By 26 June the WHO was saying that: 'The global public health emergency caused by the sudden appearance and rapid spread of SARS is coming to an end'. The entire crisis period had lasted less than four months. In Hong Kong there had been 1755 cases of SARS infections, of which 299 resulted in deaths.

I was fifty-three years old with a lifetime of varied experiences behind me and yet I could not find a way to analyse this one. Only some thirteen weeks before I had been part of a group which believed that we might be looking at a long period of sacrifice and tragedy and suddenly it was all over with an outcome much better than we might have expected and yet it was hard to feel a sense of victory or triumph. We had not shirked or absconded and yet the end of SARS seemed arbitrary rather than the direct result of our efforts.

In 1588, the mighty King Philip II of Spain had launched his invading Armada of ships against the much weaker England and the English Navy. The Armada was a spectacular failure and a major factor in that failure were fierce winds and storms that were unfavourable to the Spanish. The English afterwards had no doubt about what had happened and why: 'God blew with his winds and they were scattered', said the commemorative medals. The defeat of the Spanish was a sign of divine favour, that the English had chosen the right side in the contemporary conflicts between the Catholic and Protestant brands of Christianity. What had happened in Hong Kong seemed as arbitrary as the rising up and dying away of a great wind yet for us, more sceptical in the twenty-first century, it was hard to interpret events as in any way purposive.

In the wider community, there were different emotions in which bitterness, anger and resentment played a bigger part. The deaths from SARS were a tragedy for the bereaved, those who had been ill faced a protracted and uncertain period of recovery and many would suffer financially for a long time to come. It was understandable that there should be some degree of negativity and yet, frankly, it seemed disproportionate and not in keeping with the spirit of resilience that had characterised Hong Kong over the previous fifty years or so.

I believe that the government suffered from two failures of understanding and that these stood in the way of a healing process. First, we did not appreciate that we who were so stretched, strained and at risk were in some ways the lucky ones. We were constantly occupied in meaningful work, however difficult it was and we were part of a large and mutually supportive team. The situation for the general public was almost exactly the opposite, with normal activity in decline and primal fear the emotion that gripped them. It was small wonder that the reaction was a cry of anguish. The second failure of understanding was the failure to recognise the importance of a narrative and of rituals and ceremonies. Although I had always valued fairness and truthfulness in our relations with the media I had previously not had much time for trying to 'spin' events to create a specific effect. In the case of SARS, however, I believe that it would have made all the difference in the world if there had been an opportunity for the community to come together, to mourn what had been lost and to celebrate the courage that had been shown.

Instead, the focus seemed to be all on simply getting back to 'business as usual'. Harbourfest was mounted, a series of musical performances which were a mixture of pop, easy listening and light classical. The Rolling Stones presented a couple of concerts on the waterfront site where some six years before the Prince of Wales had stood in the rain to take the salute at the ending of British rule in Hong Kong. This did not prove sufficiently cathartic and Harbourfest itself became bogged down in complaints of maladministration.

Since 1998, the Social Welfare Department had introduced a policy emphasis on volunteerism, and the wife of the SAR's chief executive took on the honorary title of volunteer-in-chief. There was an annual ceremony to acknowledge the undeniably worthy folk and companies who had given up many hours of their time for youth work, the helping out of the elderly and so on. Since this was considered an important event, all senior staff were expected to attend whether or not volunteer services formed part of their schedule of duties and so I was there with all the others at the first such occasion to be held after the epidemic.

A middle-aged man with a kindly smile and an air of modesty walked onto the stage to collect the award for 'Volunteer of the Year'.

'What did he do?' I asked my neighbour.

'He's a paediatrician in private practice,' she replied. 'When SARS broke out he shut down his practice and worked as a volunteer in the public hospitals caring for children with the disease. You know, the children were particularly difficult patients because they couldn't understand why they had to be in isolation and they kept trying to pull their face masks off and so on. That's why he's volunteer of the year.'

A panel of international medical experts was commissioned to examine what had been done during the SARS period, how things could be improved and so on. Their report was ready by the end of 2003. They concluded:

> Overall, the epidemic in Hong Kong was handled well, although there were clearly significant shortcomings of system performance during the early phase when little was known about the

disease or its cause. The Committee has not found any individual deemed to be culpable of negligence, lack of diligence or maladministration. In reaching this judgement, full account was taken of the hazards of retrospective judgement, and efforts were made in each instance to examine the subject matter in the context of what was known, and what could have been done, at the time.

In April 2004, less than one year after the SARS epidemic, the Hong Kong government set up the Centre for Health Protection (CHP) to deal specifically with the prevention and control of infectious diseases and give priority to improving various areas of public health.

In June 2004, my mother died, just short of her ninetieth birthday, and Michael and I travelled to England for her funeral. My sister, Alicia, and I asked Joyce Bennett if she would deliver the eulogy. Age was taking its toll on her too and she hesitated at the thought of the long journey to Portsmouth but her generosity of spirit prevailed and she agreed. It was a perfect summer's day as we gathered at the chapel in the cemetery where the burial was to take place. There was, however, no sign of Joyce who was to have been driven down by her goddaughter, Mary. Eventually, the priest who was to conduct the service told us that we would have to begin regardless as there were other funerals scheduled to follow. Rather reluctantly, I offered to say a few words myself.

We were just coming to the end of the first prayer when there was a mighty knocking on the closed chapel doors. They burst open and Joyce, garbed in full priestly robes, almost fell in. 'So sorry,' she gasped, 'terrible traffic.' Fortunately, she was quite all right by the time she was to speak. She did not give a religious message nor try to sum up my mother's life but reminisced about the time when they had been young girls some seventy years before. We were a small congregation and our singing was faltering but there was one of us, the husband of Alicia's best friend from her schooldays, who had a glorious voice and it began to soar, encouraging all of us to join in more confidently:

Swift to its close ebbs out life's little day;
Earth's joys grow dim, its glories pass away;
Change and decay in all around I see;
O thou who changest not, abide with me.

Our mother's grave was in the plot next to our father's, reserved immediately after his death some fifteen years before, but there was one on the other side which was obviously recent as the flowers on it were still fresh, including a cleverly devised wreath the shape and size of a football and made up of blue and white flowers, the colours of our local team. This rather uninteresting part of town was looking at its very best, with the sun glinting on the railway line and the slate roofs of the streets of little houses. I was walking with my sister's friend, the wife of the inspiring singer. 'Do you ever think of coming back here permanently?' she asked. 'No, to be honest, I don't,' I told her. And we made our way to the nearby pub where my sister had arranged the wake, and the sandwiches and sausage rolls, the whisky and beer which are traditional components of the last act of a British life.

Back in Hong Kong, there was still no sense that peace had been made with the events of the year before. Since 1987, the Legislative Council had become more and more politicised and many of its members saw an important part of their role as finding out, and drawing attention to, any shortcomings in the government's performance. The council had set up a 'Select Committee to inquire into the handling of the Severe Acute Respiratory Syndrome outbreak by the government and the Hospital Authority' and it reported in July 2004. There were some areas of similarity with the issues that the Panel of International Experts had studied but LegCo concentrated more on matters related to governance and administration rather than specialist medical questions. The tone of their comments was much more hostile than the expert panel's and they singled out a few senior people in the government for criticism. Once it came out, the committee's report dominated the news media as did follow up commentary including on all the popular radio phone-in shows.

At the time, I belonged to a hiking group and sometimes we used to go out for short evening walks. This was feasible thanks to Hong Kong's superb network of country parks and we particularly liked to do this during the hot summer months. On the evening of 8 July 2004 I changed into a casual outfit that I had brought to the office with me and joined my friends to walk up the steep Wan Chai Gap Road and into the Aberdeen Country Park. We had torches but in one stretch our path was illuminated by a spectacular display of fireflies. Thoroughly refreshed, I was back at the office by about 9 p.m. to pick up the things I had left there earlier. From the outside lobby I could see threads of light under the door but this was no reason to be alarmed as it happened very regularly that someone would still be working there at that time.

I made a bit of noise as I went in and one of the internal doors opened quite abruptly. It was Ophelia Chan, a fellow assistant director in the Social Welfare Department, who had been the major coordinator of all our SARS efforts. She had tears in her eyes and couldn't wait to share what she had been hearing on the radio news bulletin. 'EK has resigned,' she blurted out. It was not an enormous surprise but it was a terrible blow.

Many of us knew Dr EK Yeoh from long ago days when he had been a consultant surgeon at Queen Elizabeth Hospital in Kowloon and also on the council of the Government Doctors' Association advocating improvements in hospital conditions to benefit patients. He had transferred to a post in the Hospital Authority, becoming its chief executive before being appointed secretary for health and welfare, the minister with overall responsibility for policy in these two areas. Now, after unremitting attacks by members of LegCo and in the media, he and Dr Leong Che-hung, chairman of the Hospital Authority, had both stepped down.

The next day when we were all together we shared our feelings of shock and sorrow. We held EK in high esteem. He had paid due attention to our area of his portfolio as well as the more familiar concerns of medical and health issues. He was open minded and conscientious, constantly looking for ways to improve life for the whole community. He was not status conscious or snobbish but treated everyone equally. I remembered, for example, how on a day of stormy weather he had come out to one of our distant field units to talk to one of our most junior staff members who had been assaulted by a violent and unstable customer. During SARS he had been our leader and we were all aware that he was working as hard as, and harder than, any of us to combat this previously unknown disease. He was now the victim but it felt like an attack on every one of us. We wondered briefly if there was any useful action we could take in response but swiftly concluded that there was none. We felt that what had happened was grossly unjust but it seemed we must simply suffer it and go on.

It took years to get over all the effects of SARS. In 2001 the total CSSA caseload was 228,000 and by 2004 it was 291,000. We got no extra staff to cope with this increase and I found the situation a literal nightmare as I would jerk awake in the middle of the night full of foreboding that we could not continue and the entire system would break down. Somehow, though, the breakdown never occurred and we never hit the psychologically important mark of 300,000 cases although we got within a couple of thousand of it.

My very last contract with the Hong Kong government came to an end at the beginning of 2006. If this was a novel there would have been some accompanying drama or at least some strange coincidence or twist. This was, however, real life and nothing very particular occurred. My colleagues clubbed together and took me to various meals and gave me various things. When they asked what I would like I would suggest a nice pen. Perhaps in the UK I might have been presented with a clock but that is a complete taboo in a Chinese society since the expression for 'giving a clock as a present' sounds far too similar to 'watching at a deathbed'. I recalled with a little inward laugh how, when I had been in the Recreation and Culture Branch we had to come up with a suitable civic gift in connection with a Hong Kong Festival to be held in Canada. However hard I tried not to say the word 'clock' it was almost irresistible as it seemed such a suitable thing to give; in the end, though, we handed over a dragon boat which I hope they found very useful.

I cleared out my office, dividing the things in it into three different piles. Some things belonged to the government and I left them there for the next incumbent of the post. Some things belonged to me and I those took home. Some things were of no use to anyone and those I threw away.

Afterwards, I took up the kind of occupations that were not uncommon among retired civil servants: a bit of consultancy, an active interest in public affairs that sometimes spilled over into protests against the government and some volunteering with NGOs. I had many friends made during my civil service days, including some still working there. I travelled more outside Hong Kong but less within it. When I had been in the Social Welfare Department I could not understand why middle-class citizens seemed to be unfamiliar with the relatively more deprived parts of the SAR, which I was constantly visiting. However, I now found that my life was busy and fulfilled even if mainly spent within the small compass of Hong Kong Island.

One day in June 2010 I went to the Catholic Cathedral of the Immaculate Conception, which was close to my home although not close enough to walk when the weather was so humid and also threatening rain. My reason for going there was a sad one: it was to attend the memorial service for Archie Chan, Anson's husband. Archie was a wonderful person and such a great support to Anson as she climbed the ladder to become Hong Kong's first Chinese and first female chief secretary. He was always jaunty and cheerful and it was a bonus to get to some formal occasion and see that Archie was there as he never took things too seriously. He had been an executive with the Caltex Oil Company but his passion was for the Auxiliary Police which he headed for nine years; at the service a police bagpiper played *Amazing Grace*.

The cathedral was completely full and those present included powerful figures from Hong Kong's past, present and future. My friend and former colleague, Shelley Lee, was assisting Sir SY Chung who could no longer walk so easily. I had first met Sir SY many years earlier and before that meeting I was told that it was thanks to research that he had undertaken as a young man at Sheffield University that we were able to have ridged stainless steel draining boards. When he returned to Hong Kong he had set up Sonca Industries, manufacturing torches and similar products and providing jobs for thousands. He had had long periods of service on the Executive and Legislative Councils, where he earned respect for his total integrity and disinterestedness. I saw a wreath with a message from Sir Run Run Shaw and his wife Mona Fong who had created a film and television industry and had given millions upon millions to good causes. I caught glimpses of Sir Roger Lobo, who had been the senior member of LegCo during the crucial period of the Sino-British negotiations over the future of Hong Kong and of Helmut Sohmen who had taken over the enormous international shipping interests of his late father-in-law, Sir YK Pao.

Tsang Yok Sing, president of LegCo since 2008 and widely admired for his rigorous intellect and rationality was there. Interviewed in 1996 about his attitude to the 1967 riots in Hong Kong he had said, 'I was already a committed Marxist and was in total sympathy with the workers who were only protecting themselves against the oppressive colonial government of the time.' He had gone on to lead the Democratic Alliance for the Betterment of Hong Kong, a political party seen as pro-China. Another person present who was considered sympathetic with the Mainland was CY Leung. In 1985, the Chinese side had appointed him secretary-general of the Basic Law Consultative Committee and since 1997 he had been convenor of ExCo. Despite these distinguished positions, I think that most of those there that day would have been surprised if the curtain concealing future events could have been lifted and shown them that in 2012 CY would be elected chief executive of the Hong Kong SAR to succeed Donald Tsang.

From the other end of the political spectrum came the leading barristers Ronny Tong and Audrey Eu who were founding members of the Civic Party, regarded as strongly pro-democratic and intent on protecting Hong Kong against what they perceived as undue influence from China. Anson herself, although a political independent, had demonstrated some support for the Civic Party and its way of looking at things.

In other circumstances, there might have been a lively political discussion particularly as there was a concurrent debate taking place in the community on proposals that Beijing had recently and quite unexpectedly agreed with the Democratic Party on changes to the electoral arrangements for LegCo which might or might not, according to differing viewpoints, take Hong Kong closer to true democracy. This, though, was an occasion of quite another kind, a day not for arguments but for respect and solemnity and a recognition of the more basic concerns that unite human beings.

Martin Lee, retired from LegCo for some two years but still thought of as the founding father of Hong Kong's democratic movement, a lawyer and like Anson, a devout Roman Catholic, went to the lectern to give a reading from Ecclesiastes, which ended with the words:

> That which hath been is now; and that which is to be hath already been; and God requireth that which is past.
> For that which befalleth the sons of men befalleth beasts; even one thing befalleth them; as the one dieth, so dieth the other; yea, they have all one breath; so that a man hath no preeminence above a beast: for all is vanity.
> All go unto one place; all are of the dust, and all turn to dust again.
> This is the word of the Lord.

'Thanks be to God' we all responded following the formula. The liturgy rolled on but I pondered the sobering, even bleak, thoughts that had been laid before us and couldn't help wondering how grateful for them I really was. One could hardly start arguing with these age-old sentiments . . . and yet, and yet. It seemed not so bad at all to spend that short time between dust and dust in a place as fascinating as Hong Kong and among its people, so vivid and various, so courageous and amusing. I could, I thought, be full of thanks that chance had been so kind to me and the journey that had started long ago in England had turned out so well.

CHAPTER FOURTEEN

Afterlife

IN FEBRUARY 2012 AN ARTICLE APPEARED in the *Asian Wall Street Journal* under the heading 'Hong Kong Was Better Under the British'. The text was rather more nuanced than that stark sentence suggests but its message, nonetheless, was one of contrasting the strengths of the régime before 1997 with weaknesses that had developed subsequently. It created a small stir, not least because it brought out into the open a sentiment that was to be heard from time to time, even if expressed in a rather shamefaced, almost embarrassed, manner.

One of the points made in the article was that 'for many decades [Hong Kong] boasted a higher standard of governance than the mother country'. I think that we can proudly say that Hong Kong was ruled well and if there has been a falling off it has not, perhaps, been so great, partly because of the underpinning virtues of the social and cultural values of Hong Kong. There are still many things that I would rather do in Hong Kong than in almost any country in the world. These include:

- tangling with the police and the judiciary and ending up in gaol;
- falling gravely ill when out alone and having to rely on passers-by, the emergency services and public-sector medical care;
- participating in a peaceful protest against the government;
- walking alone in any part of the city late at night;
- having no access to a private car and being entirely dependent on public transport; and

- conducting all the small interactions with banks, postal services and so on that are necessary for the smooth functioning of daily life.

Furthermore, the government after 1997 had to face many problems that were not the lot of the previous administration or the effects of which were not felt so severely.

From 1985 onwards, more and more elements of elected democracy were introduced into the Legislative Council, Hong Kong's equivalent of a parliament. To indirectly elected members representing specific professional and economic sectors in the so-called functional constituencies were added some representing geographical constituencies in which every registered resident over the age of eighteen could vote. Since 1998, LegCo elections in geographical constituencies have adopted a list proportional representation voting system. The intention is to secure a close match between the percentage of votes that a group of candidates obtains in an election and the number of seats they fill. Under this system, parties winning a small percentage of the votes may be able to secure seats which they would not be able to achieve under a first-past-the-post voting system, which increases the likelihood of mavericks being able to obtain seats in LegCo.

In the 1970s the governor had a discreet 'cutting' gesture (an up and down movement of the first and second fingers) that he would use if one of the members of LegCo was in his view speaking at excessive length. The members of the council were all appointed and, although respected figures in the community and treated as such, would take heed of this signal and quickly terminate. By 1995, when I was acting secretary for recreation and culture, quite different conventions held sway. LegCo's time-table was organised so all necessary business could be conducted but members expected, and received, greater opportunities to speak and so we would find ourselves yawning through the early hours of the morning for a motion debate, even though the motion if passed would not bind the government or anyone else actually to do anything. In 2012, for the first time in Hong Kong, a full-scale filibuster was mounted to delay LegCo discussion of controversial proposed legislation on arrangements for by-elections. Equally controversially, the president of LegCo, a position filled by election among members, ended the filibuster, by reference to rules of procedure.

The Legislative Council could function in a more straightforward manner if it followed more closely the models of parliamentary government which it superficially resembles. Instead, the twists and turns since the mid-1980s coupled with the provisions of the Basic Law produced a bizarre situation in which Hong Kong was run by civil servants faced by an opposition comprising potentially all members of the legislature. Members from the Democratic Alliance for the Betterment and Progress of Hong Kong, considered to be the most pro-China and pro-establishment of the political parties, together with the pro-business Liberal Party and similarly inclined individuals from the functional constituencies were likely, but not certain, to support the government which, in the final analysis, could exert no disciplinary power over any member of LegCo but could only rely on lobbying, which sometimes required substantial efforts. Therefore, the government 'side' felt constantly frustrated by the slow and painful progress of its proposals through the legislative processes but the members of LegCo felt equally frustrated because they had almost no powers to initiate proposals themselves and those who were not aligned with the establishment parties believed that they were not listened to and that, in the end, government proposals would be 'steamrollered' through.

Matters were made more complicated in 2002 by the introduction of the 'ministerial system'. This was intended to provide a remedy for the situation in which, it was thought, it was too difficult to take adequate action against the civil servants who ran the policy bureaux if there were serious failings in their work performance. The concept was that ministers employed on contracts rather than with pensionable tenure could more easily be dismissed if the chief executive judged that they were not satisfactorily fulfilling their roles. As so often occurs with reorganisations of any kind, a first obvious effect was the introduction of bigger salaries: ministers would be paid more for doing what seemed to be the same jobs that civil servants had been doing. In fact, the great majority of the new ministers appointed had been civil servants and, in many cases, handling the same portfolio of responsibilities as previously. Things were made more complicated in 2006 with the introduction of posts for deputy ministers and assistants to ministers, who would also be outside the traditional civil service structure and in these cases the appointees were mainly younger people with no previous civil service experience.

In parallel, the mood of the population of Hong Kong was changing. Traditionally, Hong Kongers saw themselves as individuals and families who were working out their own destiny by means that used the structure provided by a government in which they themselves were little invested. This philosophy seemed almost to be going into reverse. There were much higher expectations that the government's function was to address many of the concerns felt by the mass of citizens while at the same time there was more doubt and criticism about proposed solutions being put forward by the government. This was a change that may have predated the transfer of sovereignty but certainly seemed to be strengthened by it. Perhaps the people of Hong Kong who had at one time tended to see the place as a transit stop now recognised it as a long-term home and also recognised its rulers as like themselves rather than colonialist outsiders bringing in peculiar ideas and customs from overseas, which had to be tolerated rather than understood.

Nonetheless, despite the good performance that Hong Kong continued to turn in by comparison with other administrations and other communities and despite the mitigating factors that could be prayed in aid there was no doubt about the volume of those whispers that 'things used to be better' and analysis suggested that there were some good reasons for those whispers.

Hong Kong's economy was still strong and indeed finding new areas of activity to explore as it became, for example, a major hub in the international wine and art markets as the swift growth of the wealth of Mainland China businesspeople to almost unimaginable levels provided extraordinary opportunities. There have been frequent predictions that Hong Kong would be eclipsed by Shanghai but this has yet to eventuate as the advantages like our well-established legal system preserved a distinctive niche for us. On the other hand, and somewhat surprisingly, Singapore, a nearby city state and also a former British colony, now seemed to some to be racing away and winning in many different aspects: in providing a balanced lifestyle for its citizens as well as producing economic growth. Although our social services outshone what was available in many other parts of Asia, there was increasing concern about poverty levels in Hong Kong, the gap between rich and poor as well as a feeling that the opportunities for social mobility were not as good as in the heady days of the 1970s and '80s. There was even a nickname, 'the post '80s generation' for the young people born since 1980 who were discontented and ready to protest.

The 'post '80s' dissatisfaction was mainly with the government although they also attacked big business, particularly the property tycoons. They saw an implicit alliance, bent on preserving entrenched special interests at the expense of the greater good of the community. The government seemed to have lost its ability to identify problems and come up with practical solutions which take account of dissenting views and which were reasonably briskly implemented. Within 2012, too, came a couple of shocks which seemed to justify the cynicism of the post '80s and deeply disturbed those of us who were working in the government in the 1980s rather than celebrating our first birthdays. The chief executive, Donald Tsang, was accused of taking inappropriate benefits from business-men in terms of hotel stays, trips on private jets and a low-rent flat in Shenzhen, just across the border. Rafael Hui, a former chief secretary, was taken in by the Independent Commission Against Corruption, and later charged with 'misconduct in a public office', allegations arising from advantages accepted from the Kwok brothers who ran Sun Hung Kai Properties, one of the biggest companies in Hong Kong.

At the time of writing, there is not yet a conclusion to the various investigations and enquiries and it would, of course, be wrong to presume what the outcome will be but it felt bad enough that there was so much of a taint and suspicion. Those of my generation looked back to Rafael and Donald as friends of old, young men at the beginning of their careers, hardworking and intelligent, part of our team who with the rest of us wrestled with the search for the best solution to the policy and practical issues that we confronted. As well as that, what had happened was an undermining of the entire ethos of the administrative grade which we had believed that we all shared and which to some extent justified the special status that we held within the community. When we discussed what had happened, 'heartbreaking' was the word that seemed to arise most spontaneously.

At the beginning of my career, I had often heard the same briefing in more or less the same words; I think that it was, in fact, written down somewhere. It began: 'As an administrative officer, you will never get rich ...' pause to achieve the appropriate dramatic effect, 'but you will be adequately remunerated and you will have an interesting and fulfilling career.' And that was what we signed up for and subscribed to. Amid the corruption that prevailed until the mid-1970s some administrative officers were ridiculously naïve or complacent, but I do not believe that members of the grade were themselves corrupt. Similarly, there might from time to time be a scandal or a court case in which an AO was implicated but the perpetrators were viewed as exceptional 'bad apples' rather than representative of the service as a whole.

During the course of a long career it was more likely than not that there would be periods when an administrative officer would be mixing with contacts who were spectacularly wealthy. They might be businesspeople who wanted something out of the government or whom we wanted to regulate, members of advisory boards or committees, or philanthropists. Since our work was not intended to be strictly nine-to-five and business entertaining was a legitimate part of the package we might end up in expensive restaurants which would not have been a normal choice if we had been paying for ourselves. Many of those that we came across in this way were immensely clever and enterprising and had made their fortunes in that way and there was no reason not to admire them for it, especially as living standards in Hong Kong rose on their coat-tails. Nonetheless, it was perfectly possible to take a fascinated peep at this way of life without being sucked into it. We had our own role to play and our own philosophy and even if we were not as clever as these plutocrats we could make our own contribution to keeping things going on the right lines simply by always looking for the fairest course of action in any given situation. And, as those briefings had promised, if our income was not lavish, we had enough for a decent middle-class way of life and we knew that many outside the government envied us the 'iron rice bowl' of stable employment in the bureaucracy.

It was not surprising that morale of those still within the administrative grade took a tremendous knock and it had, anyway, been on a downward incline since somewhere round about the beginning of the twenty-first century. During the best days of the Administrative Service, one of the joys of working in it had been the latitude given to you, regardless of youth. There was so much to be done that there was no alternative to handing over responsibility for a project or a problem and relying on the inventiveness and good judgment of the officer charged to take it forward. This happy condition deteriorated somewhat over the years as Hong Kong became richer. It seemed like the mark of a proper grown-up government to take on more staff, to set up more departments and grander commissions and quangos. Some of this was inevitable and as our society became more complex it was better to take on more professionals and experts instead of relying too heavily on the philosophy of the 'inspired amateur'.

In this process, though, there was also a loss of some of the sense of fun that had previously cast a glow on what might otherwise have been tedious toil. And, as time went by, a new mood of anxiety began to grip the government. Instead of being sent out into the city streets and the rural New Territories to find out what was troubling their fellow citizens and to dream up ways to make things better, the brightest young people were confined in the Secretariat where their task was the polishing of enormous briefs for some senior to tuck under his or her arm and take into LegCo in the hope that the information therein might turn out to be a magical talisman to ward off the evil of the question that could not be answered and subsequent humiliation on the evening newscasts.

We may not have immediately recognised it but I believe that there was a watershed in 2001, when Anson Chan stepped down from the office of chief secretary. She had been expected to retire shortly anyway, but there were worrying indications that she had been forced out because she was seen as too much affected by the old ideas, too Westernised, too keen on democracy and democratic values in the eyes of certain powerful forces in the Mainland, who got their information from a restricted section of the Hong Kong community. The circumstances of her departure were troubling enough but what was more damaging was the loss of the qualities that she brought to her post.

It is not easy to perform well as chief secretary whether before or after 1997. Governors or chief executives may involve themselves more or less, but however active they are it is impossible that they can do everything and much must devolve upon the chief secretary. This was particularly true before the introduction of the ministerial system in 2002. Before there were politically appointed ministers the chief secretary had a clear coordinating role, settling issues that cut across different policy bureaux as well as driving forward whatever items were seen as most crucial to achieving the government's current agenda. To be a good chief secretary requires a continual balancing and rebalancing between chairmanship and leadership. In order to understand thoroughly all the salient aspects of a subject it is necessary to listen carefully and to ask good questions, but if things go no further than that then the result will be a damaging inertia. So, having patiently heard all the arguments the chief secretary must make the decisions, firmly announce them and see that they are carried out. Anson did these things in an exemplary fashion and it was particularly notable that she did not cut short contrary views even if they came from quite junior people. Before she left on her retirement, she gave a final briefing to the administrative grade and reminded us that a core component of what we should do was to 'speak truth to power'. Her words struck home because we knew that this was what she truly believed, not something that she thought that she ought to say.

The motivating factors underlying the Sino-British Joint Declaration on the future of Hong Kong and the Basic Law that put flesh on its bones were not entirely clear. It seemed that one of the fundamental lines of thinking was that Hong Kong in, say, 1980 was doing just fine and the aim should be to ensure that it largely continued in much the same sort of way. The slogan 'Hong Kong people ruling Hong Kong' and the promise of 'a high degree of autonomy' were consistent with that.

There had been a handover but no 'take over'. Some of the more lurid speculation that seemed to envisage a cadre in a corner of every government office with a duty to ensure that the Hong Kong compatriots kept to the Communist Party's line proved to have no basis in the post-1997 reality. Since the end of 1995 I sat in a department doing medium-level work with no political overtones but all that I saw and heard suggested that the Hong Kong government was indeed mostly being left to run Hong Kong in the way it thought best.

There were, perhaps, two unfortunate and inter-connected phenomena within Hong Kong itself. The first was a little too much modesty about the virtues of Hong Kong and its way of doing things. There was an influential school of thought that claimed that 'Hong Kong is a business city' and which could point to the proven successful philosophies of the colonial era of laissez-faire and positive non-interventionism. This might, however, lead to the conclusion, without qualification or mitigation, that what was good for the businessman was good for Hong Kong, a case which the businessmen themselves were, understandably, keen to advance. As time went by, it became more clear that Hong Kong's greatest strength in fact lay in its adherence to the rule of law and that it was this which ensured that it had a unique niche which no other city in China has yet been able to match. The second phenomenon was the greater prominence of some Hong Kongers who identified themselves as Beijing loyalists and who had felt themselves sidelined during the colonial era. They may have been disappointed to find that Hong Kong was by and large being run in the same old way by the same old civil servants. There were some mutterings that the civil service was disloyal, obstructive and too inclined to hark back to the old régime. This was a minor but noticeable source of tension during the early days after the change of sovereignty. I believe it is true that the civil service with its established way of doing things did instinctively feel that many of its practices were worth defending because they were inextricably linked with important principles of freedom, fairness and integrity. I believe that there was something different, which had elements of the sad and the comical to it, in the charge of obstructiveness, with an implication of disloyalty. Some of the critics had no experience of, say, serving on government boards and committees because they had not been favoured by the British. Consequently, they did not understand the extent to which inertia and buck passing can be the default positions of even the best civil services, as Hong Kong's was reputed to be! If they had had that acquaintance they would have appreciated that the difficulties inherent in the task of a governor of colonial Hong Kong were not that different to those of a chief executive of the special administrative region. The problems, hedges and precautions that civil servants have a tendency to emphasise must be taken seriously but the moment arrives at which there must be a metaphorical kick and an instruction to get on with things with no more excuses to be offered!

In 1999, the Hong Kong government sought an interpretation of the Basic Law from the Standing Committee of the National People's Congress as allowed for under Article 158(1) of the Basic Law. The reason for doing this arose out of a particular judgment in Hong Kong's Court of Final Appeal on a case related to the right to settle in Hong Kong and the fear that the consequences of that judgment could be an influx of enormous numbers from the Mainland newly entitled to residence. The constitutional and legal arguments about this course of action were complex and technical but, in broader terms, there was a perception in some in the community that this was another manifestation of weakness on the part of the Hong Kong government which seemed to be over-dependent on the new sovereign power. There were whispers circulating that the Beijing government was perplexed and fed up by this attitude, having anticipated that they were taking over a sophisticated, modern city state which could look after itself while they got on with the more challenging problems of managing the development of a vast, diverse country with an economy that was swiftly growing but with a serious imbalance between urban and rural areas.

In the political relationship between the People's Republic and its special administrative region, the inflection point came in the momentous year of 2003. That was the year of SARS but in the context of that political upheaval the epidemic was a minor issue as well as contributing to the emotional atmosphere that was the backdrop. What came to the forefront was the implementation of Article 23 of the Basic Law, which states that:

> The Hong Kong Special Administrative Region shall enact laws on its own to prohibit any act of treason, secession, sedition, sub-version against the Central People's Government, or theft of state secrets, to prohibit foreign political organisations or bodies from conducting political activities in the Region, and to prohibit political organisations or bodies of the Region from establishing ties with foreign political organisations or bodies.

In 2002, the Hong Kong government met Beijing's wish and began the process of preparing laws that would put into practice what had been envisaged by Article 23. This was, however, a cause of concern to individuals and groups such as churches, journalists and lawyers as they thought that what was being proposed could prove repressive once enshrined in legislation and implemented. Anson Chan, who was taking a citizen's active interest in local affairs now that she was no longer a civil servant, as well as distinguished democrat lawyers like Audrey Eu suggested that the answer was to issue a 'White Bill' which would set out in draft form precisely what was intended to be included in the legislation. This would be the best means to spot ambiguities and possible pitfalls and to ensure that the finally approved legislation would not pose a danger to the essential rights and freedoms that were otherwise guaranteed by the Sino-British Joint Declaration. However, the Hong Kong government was not willing to adopt this approach, preferring to continue to push through its own version of the legislation.

Ever since 1997 there had been a public holiday on 1 July and it had become a custom for more radical political groups to hold protest marches on that day. The six months or so leading up to 1 July 2003 had been marked by the hardships imposed by SARS, a scandal arising from the financial secretary having bought himself a new car in the period immediately preceding a budget in which first registration tax was raised and increasing dismay about the proposed Article 23 legislation. As a result, that year the 1 July demonstration was enormous. The best estimate was that there were 500,000 participants, at a time when Hong Kong's total population was under seven million; they were patient and disciplined but absolutely determined. Like most civil servants, I did not participate in the march myself but I was very struck by the wide range within my acquaintance who did. It was not only the activists, not only the lawyers, not only the young people. It was those who sat right in the middle of the socioeconomic pecking order, it was those who would normally consider themselves too busy or not interested enough for any such exercise. It was not only the adults but entire families who marched or in the cases where the parents judged their children to be too young to take along they would all the same make an effort to explain why they were going and why they considered it important. With typical anxiety over their offsprings' polished performance, the manager of a restaurant where we frequently ate had his young son practising in the days beforehand, marching round his sitting room with a homemade placard denouncing the car-buying behaviour of the financial secretary.

The great march had dramatic effects. Before the end of the month, Regina Ip, secretary for security and thus responsible for the Article 23 legislation, and Antony Leung, the financial secretary, had both resigned, as well as James Tien, a pro-establishment figure, who left the Executive Council, signalling his doubts about the course of action that the government had been pursuing. The Article 23 legislation was shelved and has not subsequently been revived. The Beijing government was spooked. There had been no question of a heavy-handed intervention against half a million people whose fate was being watched by the world but the Chinese authorities certainly did not want such large demonstrations to become a regular occurrence. The Hong Kong government became more timid and, generally, dithered more over every issue as they did not want to provoke large numbers of Hong Kong's citizens onto the streets again and annoy Beijing. The Hong Kongers themselves were rather surprised by what they had achieved: surprised but delighted. It was not only a matter of the immediate victory of the withdrawal of the Article 23 legislation. There was also pride in the united and yet peaceful front that had been shown together with an understanding that here, potentially at least, was a powerful weapon that could be used against any rebarbative government action. Every 1 July since a major demonstration has been held, highlighting some topical political issues but up until the time of writing there had been not been another manifestation of public opinion on such a major scale.

All these issues were essentially affairs of state between Hong Kong and its new sovereign power but there were also human relationships between the Mainlanders and those who had come to think of themselves as having the distinctively separate identity of being Hong Kong Chinese.

During the period of approximately 1966 to 1976 while the Cultural Revolution raged through China there was almost no direct contact between the two places. Hong Kongers were left to endure years of anxiety about what had become of relatives in China and although there might eventually be joyful reunions these were scarred by the sufferings of those who had undergone so much fear and persecution. There was at the same time a constant inflow of illegal immigrants from China and until the Hong Kong government abolished the 'touch base' policy in 1980 they were able to obtain residency rights in Hong Kong. Many of these were young men from Guangdong Province of whom a few became prosperous but most did not and eked out a living providing the muscle power for Hong Kong's manufacturing and construction industries, never making up the education that they had not been able to obtain in the Mainland. They were often compelled to remain unmarried, not being considered attractive catches by the picky Hong Kong girls.

The opening up of the Mainland's economy and the ability to come and go more normally between Hong Kong and the Mainland gradually opened up different opportunities for Hong Kongers to find a spouse, an opportunity taken, for the most part, by men seeking wives. An income that was quite low by Hong Kong standards, even a monthly social security payment, could seem like wealth across the border, sufficient to marry and bring up children. These families would after a few years be able to join their Hong Kong husbands where they would encounter a wall of prejudice. Every possible social ill was blamed on these 'new arrivals' even though they were of the same ethnicity as Hong Kongers and normally also spoke Cantonese. The Hong Kong population, like a reflex action, lay responsibility for increases in the social security bill entirely at the feet of the new arrivals, even though this accusation did not stand up to analysis. I could not understand why people were so dismissive towards others who, to an outsider, seemed essentially similar until an American academic friend pointed out the analogous antipathy that existed between East and West Berliners.

After the reversion to China, there took place fundamental shifts in the attitude of Hong Kongers towards the Mainlanders, principally as a direct or indirect result of the explosive growth in China's wealth and hence of the resources available to some of its citizens. There were those mothers who took advantage of the legal judgment in 2001 that conferred residency rights on any baby born in Hong Kong of Chinese parents whether or not the parents themselves were entitled to live in Hong Kong; by 2010 more than a third of babies born in Hong Kong fell into that category. Hong Kongers resented the consequent squeeze on obstetric facilities and feared the consequences on welfare, educational and medical services if large numbers eventually returned to live here. In April 2012, CY Leung, the newly elected chief executive, announced that his administration would seek to ensure that children of Mainland mothers without a Hong Kong spouse would no longer enjoy permanent residency status, a move that was widely welcomed.

Hong Kongers also felt the impact of Chinese wealth through the large numbers of tourists and investors. While these made significant contributions to Hong Kong's economy, locals' gratitude for this prosperity was tinged with scorn and dislike for what were perceived as the Mainlanders' rudeness and uncouth attitudes. There was such a demand for milk powder for babies from Mainland parents anxious to benefit from the guaranteed quality in Hong Kong shops that local parents reported that there was not enough left for them. Small businesses that for years had supplied daily needs were being squeezed out to make way for emporia selling luxury goods that local families did not need and could not afford.

This friction was not the whole story. Most cross-border marriages were happy. Within Hong Kong there was a less visible but influential elite of the Mainland-born who had studied and worked overseas and, with subtle and multi-faceted thinking made immense contributions in business, the professions and academic life. The SAR also played an important role for some of its visitors from the Mainland in allowing them access to books and information about what was going on in their own home and which they could never normally access.

The Beijing government maintains a large Liaison Office in Hong Kong with officials posted to serve a tour of duty here. After the handover, I would quite often meet staff of the Liaison Office at various work-related social functions. They were always charming, friendly and courteous. Yet I could not in all honesty say that I felt very confident that they really grasped the nature of Hong Kong in all its sophistication. From time to time, too, there would be chilling accounts in the press reporting the views of some senior person associated with the central government to the effect that, say, there was really no need for an independent judiciary in Hong Kong.

It is discouraging if there is not a good understanding of the complexities of Hong Kong within the Chinese organs of government. It seems that the only way in which Hong Kong governance can truly advance out of its present hogtied condition is if it adopts full democracy. The Basic Law is somewhat ambiguous about what is actually promised as regards democratic development. There have been subsequent statements from the Standing Committee of the National People's Congress, which is a legislative body, to the effect that the election of Hong Kong's chief executive in 2017 may be on the basis of universal suffrage and that afterwards universal suffrage may also be used as the basis for election of LegCo. It is, however, not clear how this would be put into practice. And if the new situation is to prove really workable there are a myriad important aspects to be settled, including possible links between the chief executive and his or her government and political parties. If all these obstacles can be overcome and a secure, functional democracy is in place in 2017 that will not be soon enough. Hong Kong can hardly continue tolerating the administrative drift that, sadly, seems to have become a defining characteristic. A conclusion that I drew from my time in the government is that individuals really can make a decisive difference, whether for good or ill. There is no rational argument for supposing that 'the British' were the deciding factor in Hong Kong's previous success. Some Britons, and many Hong Kong Chinese, contributed as did ideas about how to run bureaucracies and legal systems which the British had worked out through the years of their own long and sometimes painful history.

The world likes simple stories and prefers them, if possible, to be limned in lurid colours. The story of post-handover Hong Kong was meant to be a tale of a communist juggernaut rolling into a capitalist enclave or, alternatively, of a brilliantly successful international agreement that allowed an anomalous little place to go on just as before. The reality proved more confusing and more complex with an outcome that was satisfactory but could have been better, with the blame for the failings more to be laid at Hong Kong's own door rather than that of its new sovereign power. This does not mean that the people of Hong Kong are not intensely interested in the well-being of mainland China, both for its own sake and for theirs too. There is a balance between hope and fear: hope born of China's economic and technological progress and the relative stability of its governmental infrastructure, fear born of the continued gross deficiencies in rule of law and human rights.

At social functions, there is one conversation that I have had more times than I can count. 'How long have you been in Hong Kong? You arrived in 1972? So then it must be your home now?' I vaguely murmur an affirmative for the sake of politeness and yet neither the question nor the answer is correct. What I fancy I have done is to assimilate some of Hong Kong's traditional ways of thinking. Our roots are strong but they are not deep. We will strive to create a Hong Kong that is as good as it can be but we are not sentimental and if one day we calculate that the odds against us are now too high we will, as the people of Hong Kong have always done, move somewhere else and it will be only in our memories and our dreams that there will still be an existence for the unique city state that perched on the edge of the South China Sea.

BIBLIOGRAPHY

When I was an earnest young schoolgirl, I used to believe that the meaning of 'bibliography' was 'suggestions for further reading'. This misapprehension used to prove quite troublesome when, say, I thought that I would not have really understood the book that I was reading about the First World War unless I had also read source documents that were impossible for me to get hold of. For these memoirs, I cannot compile a bibliography in the proper meaning of a list of references that provide the origins of what I have written. I thought that as an alternative I might produce the kind of bibliography that I had always wished for: some ideas on more reading and similar.

Two books that particularly resonated with me as I was growing up were *Jerusalem the Golden* by Margaret Drabble, which is a novel, and *A Cab At the Door* by VS Pritchett, which is a memoir.

There are plenty of nice picture books about Oxford, and I also like *This Secret Garden* by Justin Cartwright. A quick visit to Oxford to see the central area including the Bridge of Sighs and the Sheldonian Theatre as well as the recently reorganised Ashmolean Museum is enjoyable. More than that and the city may begin to seem crowded and expensive while an outsider often feels like an interloper in the colleges. The best solution would be to go and study at the University, whether a full degree or a short course.

My favourite among the histories of the British Empire is James Morris' *Pax Britannica* trilogy which I find to be comprehensive and reasonably neutral, something that seems hard to achieve. The British Empire spanned so much in place and particularly in time that it is hard to make a fair summing up. For me, the complexity of the power that it wielded is best summed up by the novelist

Michael Ondaatje in *The English Patient.* On the specialised topic of colonial administrators, Anthony Kirk-Greene's *On Crown Service* is a good account.

The first book that I read about the founding of Hong Kong was *Foreign Mud* by Maurice Collis, published just after the Second World War and showing its age in its heedless stereotyping of characters according to race and inescapable assumptions that the West would continue to be the centre of the world, rather than China, that had for so long thought of itself as the Middle Kingdom. Nonetheless, it is full of amusing touches and, indeed, this is a story that benefits from a fictional treatment, most notably in *An Insular Possession* by Timothy Mo, which contains some clever pastiche and is, I believe, the first novel to feature the painter, George Chinnery, as a character. More recently we have been able to obtain, through *The Opium War* by Julia Lovell, a really clear account of a sometimes confusing series of events and, equally importantly, a description of their effect on the Chinese psyche right down to the present day.

The book that I always turn to is Steve Tsang's *A Modern History of Hong Kong,* which covers the territory's history from the Opium War up to 1997, and also takes a small speculative peep into the future. It is really easy to read and yet every word is underpinned by solid research. I agree with all the judgments that the author makes and whenever he writes about something with which I am acquainted I can vouch for its truthfulness.

There are other books which I enjoyed a lot but may be of more value once some knowledge base has already been laid down. They include *Governing Hong Kong* by Steve Tsang, *Feeling the Stones* by David Akers-Jones, *This God Business* by Joyce Bennett, *Hong Kong Remembers* edited by Ian Wotherspoon and Sally Blyth, *Times of Change* by Eric Ho and *Metamorphosis* by Denis Bray. *Chasing the Dragon* by Jackie Pullinger gives an accurate portrait of the Kowloon Walled City in its 'bad old days'. These are all memoirs or histories but of course Hong Kong has also been a setting for stories. One of the best known is *The World of Suzie Wong* by Richard Mason: its plot is wildly improbable but it clips along at an entertaining pace and it created a vision of Hong Kong that became a widely accepted version of reality as far as Western audiences are concerned.

Generally, a good way to understand contemporary Hong Kong is to watch its own films, which have been one of its greatest cultural achievements. It would be a worthwhile activity to become an expert, researching the different genres and the popular stars. Hong Kong's crime and martial arts films have been hugely influential but I must admit that I prefer the slightly sentimental that focus on the lives of a few characters. Ann Hui's *Summer Snow* features familiar Hong Kong types, whose gritty humour and pragmatism are the qualities that made this place successful. *Echoes of the Rainbow* is set in Hong Kong in the late 1960s, before I arrived, but I can recognise the society it depicts, even if a short sequence set in Mainland China seems quite unrealistic and out of place, while *Cageman* deals with the poor of more recent days.

Some visitors to Hong Kong may find it too crowded and expensive. Others will fall so hard in love with it that they will want to come back and live here for a while. And why not? It's the only way to begin to understand the place and the economy is usually in good enough shape to offer some sort of employment for anyone who is adventurous and adaptable.

The Swiss system of government repays study; its direct democracy through referenda could surely be profitably copied elsewhere. Unfortunately, there seem to be no easy to read books in English but it would be a good topic for an Internet search one idle afternoon. Graham Greene's novel *Dr Fischer of Geneva* captures the odd and sinister side of the place. Johanna Spyri's *Heidi* offers a refreshing, and equally valid, contrast and it matters little that this is a children's book written in the nineteenth century since it captures the beauty and freedom of life in the mountains, as it still exists today. Switzerland is, deservedly, considered a dream holiday destination. I reckon that if one had the right aptitudes a job in one of the comfy little Swiss restaurants that abound in the villages and small towns would be a wonderful way of life long term.

Writing books about China is proceeding nowadays on an industrial scale. It is quite hard to know which are any good, especially among those which are making grandiose predictions about China's sparkling future, or lack of it. A bestseller, but none the worse for that, is *Wild Swans* by Jung Chang, presenting China's recent history in an accessible manner through the stories of the women in the author's family. One of the strangest events of modern times was the 1972 meeting between two of the most peculiar men in the world, American President Richard Nixon and Chairman Mao of the People's Republic of China. Margaret MacMillan takes this meeting as the theme of her book *Seize the Hour* and buttresses it with much related information so that the reader ends up learning a lot. When it comes to the Tiananmen Square massacre I would recommend *The Fat Years,* a novel by Chan Koonchung, which is not explicitly about Tiananmen. It is, however, a compelling parable about the continuing Chinese refusal to face facts, which has become the most prominent aspect of the massacre as it exists, or rather does not exist, in modern Chinese consciousness.

There are good films depicting modern Chinese history such as *Raise the Red Lantern* and *To Live,* both of which we were privileged to see in the salubrious setting of Sir Run Run Shaw's private cinema. We were ordinary filmgoers for Ang Lee's *Lust, Caution,* catching a morning show with an audience of Mainland tourists who were waiting anxiously for the sex scenes, cut in the Mainland version, and which are quite startling in their intensity. They are, however, integral to the narrative, which is based on a novella by Eileen Chang, one of the most celebrated Hong Kong writers of fiction. A personal bonus was that some of the key scenes had been shot in a three-storey house, located behind the block of flats in which we live that was favoured by many local filmmakers because it was unoccupied and interestingly historic, able to fit comfortably into the 1930s setting of *Lust, Caution.* The film was released in 2007 but that house has already suffered the demolition that is the normal fate of any Hong Kong building that is fit for re-development and not fortunate enough to secure statutory protection.

Hong Kong and China are rich places in that their cultures and histories offer the possibility of a lifetime of productive study in any of a number of fields. Even little Hong Kong is so multi-layered that anyone who begins to look at it in an open-minded manner will realise that there is enough of interest here alone to fill up a lifetime and to banish boredom for ever.

EXPLORE ASIA WITH BLACKSMITH BOOKS

From retailers around the world or from *www.blacksmithbooks.com*

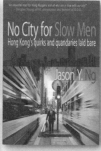

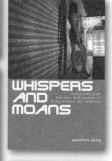